The Samoyed

ANNA KATHERINE NICHOLAS

Title page photo: Ch. Keh-Tee's Honkin Hogan of Sulu by Ch. Sulu's Karbon Kopi O'Baerstone ex Tsartar's Somewhere My Lara, at age five months. Grew up to become a Best in Show winner and a Multiple Group winner. Bred by the Hoehns, owned by Dick and Becky Mahley.

Dedication

To each and every Samoyed mentioned and pictured in this book; and to all of the members of this beautiful, joyful, smiling breed who bring such warmth and happiness to their owners.

Distributed in the UNITED STATES by T.F.H. Publications, Inc., One T.F.H. Plaza, Neptune City, NJ 07753; in CANADA to the Pet Trade by H & L Pet Supplies Inc., 27 Kingston Crescent, Kitchener, Ontario N2B 2T6; Rolf C. Hagen Ltd., 3225 Sartelon Street, Montreal 382 Quebec; in CANADA to the Book Trade by Macmillan of Canada (A Division of Canada Publishing Corporation), 164 Commander Boulevard, Agincourt, Ontario M1S 3C7; in ENGLAND by T.F.H. Publications Limited, Cliveden House/Priors Way/Bray, Maidenhead, Berkshire SL6 2HP, England; in AUSTRALIA AND THE SOUTH PACIFIC by T.F.H. (Australia) Pty. Ltd., Box 149, Brookvale 2100 N.S.W., Australia; in NEW ZEALAND by Ross Haines & Son, Ltd., 82 D Elizabeth Knox Place, Panmure, Auckland, New Zealand; in the PHILIPPINES by Bio-Research, 5 Lippay Street, San Lorenzo Village, Makati Rizal; in SOUTH AFRICA by Multipet Pty. Ltd., Box 235 New Germany, South Africa 3620. Published by T.F.H. Publications, Inc. Manufactured in the United States of America by T.F.H. Publications, Inc.

Contents

About the Author

Since early childhood, Anna Katherine Nicholas has been involved with dogs. Her first pets were a Boston Terrier, an Airedale, and a German Shepherd Dog. Then, in 1925, came the first of the Pekingese, a gift from a friend who raised them. Now her home is shared with two Miniature Poodles and numerous Beagles.

Miss Nicholas is best known throughout the Dog Fancy as a writer and as a judge. Her first magazine article, published in *Dog News* magazine around 1930, was about Pekingese, and this was followed by a widely acclaimed breed column, "Peeking at the Pekingese," which appeared for at least two decades, originally in *Dogdom*, then, following the demise of that publication, in *Popular Dogs*. During the 1940s she was a Boxer columnist for *Pure-Bred Dogs/American Kennel Gazette* and for *Boxer Briefs*. More recently many of her articles, geared to interest fanciers of every breed, have appeared in *Popular Dogs, Pure-Bred Dogs/American Kennel Gazette, Show Dogs, Dog Fancy, The World of the Working Dog*, and for both the Canadian publications, *The Dog Fancier* and *Dogs in Canada*. Her *Dog World* column, "Here, There and Everywhere," was the Dog Writers' Association of America winner of the Best Series in a Dog Magazine Award for 1979. Another feature article of hers, "Faster Is Not Better," published in *Canine Chronicle*, received Honorable Mention on another occasion.

In 1970 Miss Nicholas won the Dog Writers' Association Award for the Best Technical Book of the Year with her *Nicholas Guide to Dog Judging*. In 1979 the revision of this book again won this award, the first time ever that a revision has been so honored by this organization. Other important dog writer awards which Miss Nicholas has gained over the years have been the Gaines "Fido" and the *Kennel Review* "Winkies," these both on two occasions and each in the Dog Writer of the Year category.

It was during the 1930s that Miss Nicholas's first book, *The Pekingese*, appeared in print, published by the Judy Publishing Company. This book, and its second edition, sold out quickly and is now a collector's item, as is *The Skye Terrier Book* which was published during the 1960s by the Skye Terrier Club of America.

During recent years, Miss Nicholas has been writing books consistently for T.F.H. These include *Successful Dog Show Exhibiting, The Book of the Rottweiler, The Book of the Poodle, The Book of the Labrador Retriever, The Book of the English Springer Spaniel, The Book of the Golden Retriever, The Book of the German Shepherd Dog, The Book of the Shetland Sheepdog, The Book of the Miniature Schnauzer, The World of Doberman Pinschers,* and *The World of Rottweilers.* Plus, in the newest T.F.H. series, *The Maltese, The Keeshond, The Chow Chow, The Poodle, The Boxer, The Beagle, The Basset Hound, The Dachshund* (the latter three co-authored with Marcia A. Foy), *The German Pointer, The Collie, The Weimaraner, The Great Dane, The Dalmatian,* and numerous other titles. In the KW series she has done *Rottweilers, Weimaraners,* and *Norwegian Elkhounds.* And she has written American chapters for two popular English books purchased and published in the United States by T.F.H., *The Staffordshire Bull Terrier* and *The Jack Russell Terrier.*

Miss Nicholas's association with T.F.H. began in the early 1970s when she co-authored for them five books with Joan Brearley. These are *The Wonderful World of Beagles and Beagling* (also honored by the Dog Writers Association), *This is the Bichon Frise, The Book of the Pekingese, The Book of the Boxer,* and *This is the Skye Terrier.*

Since 1934 Miss Nicholas has been a popular dog show judge, officiating at prestigious events throughout the United States and Canada. She is presently approved for all Hounds, all Terriers, all Toys and all Non-Sporting; plus all Pointers, English and Gordon Setters, Vizslas, Weimaraners, and Wirehaired Pointing Griffons in the Sporting Group and Boxers and Dobermans in Working. In 1970 she became only the third woman ever to have judged Best in Show at the famous Westminster Kennel Club event at Madison Square Garden in New York City, where she has officiated as well on some sixteen other occasions over the years. She has also officiated at such events as Santa Barbara, Chicago International, Morris and Essex, Trenton, Westchester, etc., in the United States; the Sportsman's and the Metropolitan among numerous others in Canada; and Specialty shows in several dozen breeds in both countries. She has judged in almost every one of the United States and in four of the Canadian Provinces. Her dislike of air travel has caused her to refrain from acceptance of the constant invitations to officiate in other parts of the world.

Chapter 1

Origin of the Samoyed

The Samoyed as a breed of dog takes his name from the Samoyede, the Siberian tribe by which he was owned. The dogs were originally used for herding reindeer and other purposes by this nomadic tribe of Finnish origin, which inhabited the Yamal or Samoyede Peninsula—a vast stretch of tundra which extends along the shores of the Arctic Ocean from the White Sea to the Yenisei River in West Siberia.

To accommodate the reindeer in their eating habits, it is necessary for the Samoyede people to be quite regularly on the move, seeking new feeding grounds to provide the specific kind of lichen, or moss, which is plentiful in the vast wide spaces of this area. As each area's natural fodder is depleted, the Samoyede people take their tents and move on, thus satisfying the needs and appetite of the herd. It was at such times that the dogs were of particular importance, performing the herding duties necessary for getting the reindeer about unharmed.

The Samoyed dogs performed duties in excess of these, however. They distinguished themselves as sledge dogs; they were also affectionate dogs, combining utility with beauty, strength, intelligence; basically they were a strong and healthy breed.

The attributes of these dogs were discovered, and admired, by the explorers who became acquainted with them and aware of all they had to offer. Thus they participated in numerous expeditions, through which they were first called to the attention of the world.

Dr. Fridtjof Nansen is believed to have been the first to use Samoyed dogs on a North Pole expedition, which he did most satisfactorily. His sledge dog pack was made up of 28 Samoyeds (19 dogs and 9 bitches) who, under most stressful conditions and with the carefree abandon so characteristic of the happy temperament

7

#21 in *Dog Studies*, a series of 25 reproductions from photo etchings put out by Ardath Tobacco Co., Ltd. The description reads as follows: "This breed is a comparative newcomer to England, the first specimens being imported less than half a century ago. Hailing from the Arctic region, in its natural state the Samoyed is used as herd dog, as guard, for hunting, and sometimes for sledge work. Since the introduction into this country they have been mostly treated as companion dogs, to which purpose they are admirably adapted by disposition, or prepared for show, but it is worthy of note that they have been broken to the gun with success; they are also keen ratters. The Samoyed carries a beautiful heavy coat, weather resisting, close and standing straight away from the body. His tail is carried over the back."

of the breed, hauled one-and-a-half times their weight in supplies and performed whatever other tasks were asked of them.

Other explorers followed in the use of Samoyeds, all enthusiastic in their praise of them. A few of the dogs returned with the explorers, who were the people who helped to introduce the breed, with all its many assets, to its present world.

Color was not a matter of concern to the Samoyed people. In modern days, pure white is the color associated with the breed, accentuated by the sparkling darkness of the eyes and nose leather. The original British Standard accepted "Pure white with slight lemon markings, brown and white, black and white. The pure white dogs are from the farthest north and are the most typical of the breed." This variety of color is due to the fact that colors were mixed in some of the early dogs, although the feeling is that these dogs were interbred with other types of Arctic dogs rather than the true Samoyed. In numerous works on the breed, I have read reference to "the Samoyed dogs," or "Arctic dogs" who "breed true white"; these are always spoken of as being friendlier and more companionable to man than the dogs with mixed coloring. Pale biscuit dogs (or white dogs with biscuit markings) are, however, considered typical Samoyeds; they, too, should have the pleasant Samoyed disposition.

Left: Peter of Kobe was an example of the handsome Samoyeds bred and owned by Mrs. D. L. Perry. *Right:* (*Top*) This cigarette card from England is #18 in a series entitled *Dogs at Work*. It says of the Samoyed, "This dog takes his name from the Samoyed people of northeastern Siberia, where some 3000 years ago he hunted big game, herded reindeer, and hauled sledges. A very sturdy breed used in the explorations into the Arctic Circle, he is also much in demand as a companion or show dog." Again undated. Put out by the Molassine Co. Ltd., Greenwich, London, England. (*Bottom*) Still another cigarette card featuring the Samoyed. This one put out by Turf cigarettes, with the Samoyed #23 among *50 Famous Breeds*.

10

Chapter 2

The Samoyed in Great Britain

In preparation of this chapter, I have frequently wondered what might have been the early English history of the Samoyed had it not been for Mr. and Mrs. Ernest Kilburn-Scott! So great was their interest, involvement, and general support of the Samoyed that we can only think of them as "those to whom the Samoyed Fancy owes so much," a fact which never should be forgotten as we admire the smiling face of a dearly loved Samoyed or enjoy the pleasure of its companionship.

Mr. Kilburn-Scott, as a member of the Royal Zoological Society, made numerous trips in connection with his work during the "turn of the century" period. On one of these occasions, at the close of the 1880s, he was aboard the S.S. Sunlight on a trip to Archangel, located in the White Sea. This was a spring trip; the ship carrying him was only the second of the season (following the solid winter freeze) to get through the ice, which was just beginning to thaw. The trip was leisurely, giving Mr. Kilburn-Scott ample opportunity in which to observe the customs of the people and to become acquainted with some individuals.

Of the numerous dogs running about, one puppy in particular caught Mr. Kilburn-Scott's attention; he picked it up, commenting on its friendliness and on the fact that it seemed particularly plump. He promptly bought the puppy when informed that the guides were considering eating it as a change from reindeer meat!

Arriving home in England, the puppy attracted considerable attention and was an immediate subject of interest. Thus it seemed that a name must be selected for it and for its breed.

For the puppy, which had caught Mr. Kilburn-Scott's eye due to being the fattest one among those he saw, the name Sabarka was selected, which translates from Russian as "the fat one."

In reading an account, written many years ago by Mr. Kilburn-Scott, telling of his family's early Samoyeds, we learn that he showed his new puppy, by then a well-matured dog, at Leeds in 1893 in the Foreign Dog Class; then later on at Birmingham. It was in those days that Mr. Kilburn-Scott started to feel strongly that the appropriate name for the breed would be "Samoyed," in honor of its people. That name for the breed was officially adopted and registered with The Kennel Club in 1909.

The Kilburn-Scotts started breeding in 1896, which was the actual beginning of the now famed Farningham Kennels which were located at Vale House, Bromley, Kent. Their earliest litters were from a bitch obtained from another ship trading in the White Sea, and with dogs they had purchased from returning polar expeditions. Among them were Pearlene and Russolene, who had been part of the Jackson Harmsworth Expedition, born in Franz Joseph Land. Mr. Kilburn-Scott has written of Pearlene that she was "first champion and pure-white, with round tipped ears and a quaint polar-bearish look."

When the Kilburn-Scotts learned that the Dowager Lady Sitwell owned a splendid white dog called Musti who had come from Northern Russia, arrangements were made to breed their famous White Pechora. She was, as we have read, described as cream colored and was brought to England originally as a mate for Sabarka. From this alliance a daughter, Neva, had been acquired by and helped to spark Lady Sitwell's interest in the breed. The breeding of White Pechora to Musti took place in 1901, and with the arrival of the ensuing puppies, a whole new day in British Samoyed history was born—the beginning there of the all-white Samoyed. A memorable bitch and dog were included in this litter. Olgalene was the bitch; the important Nansen, big winner of 1903, the dog.

Neva was also bred to Musti, producing Champion Olaf Oussa.

Another stud dog who figured in the early development of the Kilburn-Scott's kennel was Jacko, a lovely Sam who had been presented to Queen Alexandra by Major Jackson. Good public relations for the breed were furthered whenever the Kilburn-Scotts had "extra" puppies in their litters, as these were presented by them to members of the aristocracy, leading to good presentation through newspaper pictures, etc.

Obviously, owing to his connection with the Royal Zoological Society, plus his interested involvement with Samoyeds, Mr. Kilburn-Scott became one of the world's most respected authorities on both subjects. Many and valued were his writings. We have read his explanation of how Samoyeds became popular for use in the polar expeditions, and much about these expeditions themselves.

He has told us that Samoyeds came into demand for the expeditions as so many Eskimo dogs had been taken from Greenland, causing the government deep concern over the safety and well-being of the Eskimo people who depended greatly on their dogs. Probably the first person to use dogs on a North Pole expedition was Nansen, followed shortly by Major F. G. Jackson in 1894. The latter had previously travelled across the Samoyede country. Another expedition was also led by the brother of the King of Italy, the Duke of Abruzzi, while the Antarctic expedition led by C. E. Borchgrevink and financed by Sir George Newnes set off in 1899.

It is interesting to read of the dog teams who were collected by Mr. Siberiakoff, some of which were shipped to Archangel for temporary kenneling in the garden of Mr. Henry Cook, British Vice-Consul. Later the Kilburn-Scotts supplied some dogs through this same source.

A further note of interest is to read of the Samoyede people themselves, in whom Mr. Cook took considerable interest. He describes them as being kindly, hospitable, cheerful and sociable, notable for generosity and high character, which makes one think a bit about these words in connection, as well, with their dogs!

The original Samoyed Club, founded in 1909, consisted of only male members—well before the days of women's lib—but I am certain that the ladies lost no time in raising their voices in protest of this injustice (and lack of appreciation of all they had contributed to the breed) in 1912, the Ladies Samoyed Association was formed.

All authorities on the breed are obviously in agreement about the fact that the great dog of the mid-1920s was Champion Kara Sea, son of Mustan of Farningham from Champion Zahrina. The impact of this dog on the breed was, to say the least, impressive. He was a superior show dog, with 21 Challenge Certificates to his credit. But it was as a stud dog that he made his true contribution. Included among his children were English Champion Kara Queen of the Arctic, English Champion Leader of the Arctic, American Champion Siberian Nansen of Farningham of Snowland, and English and American Champion Tiger Boy of Norka. His grandchildren included, among many of note, English Champion White Fang of Kobe and numerous "of the Arctic" celebrities. Kara Sea was born February 7, 1924, and was bred by Mrs. D. Edwards.

The first Specialty Show for Samoyeds in Great Britain was held in England in 1923.

Famous English Samoyeds of the post-World War I period included some of tremendous value to the breed. Another one associated with Mrs. Edwards, who was the breeder, was Champion Loga of the Arctic, like Kara Sea sired by Mustan of Farningham ex a bitch referred to as "Sara" (whom I suppose just might have been Zahrina, the dam of Kara Sea). Loga was born in 1925, and three years later started some very noteworthy winning under the banner of his new owner, Miss Keyte-Perry of "the Arctic" fame, and in 1929 he won the three Challenge Certificates, along with some other honors, giving him his title of Champion.

Miss Keyte-Perry's Arctic champions were numerous and influential. Beautiful dogs of quality breeding, they left a strong impression on the future. The same is also true of Kobe, which dogs are owned by Mrs. D. L. Perry.

ANNECY

Annecy Samoyeds are located at Clayton-Le-Woods, near Chorley, Lancashire, England. They belong to Mrs. Margaret J. Wilcock, by whom the kennel was founded in 1952.

The first Samoyed ever shown from Annecy gained title, seeming to set the tradition for the future. Since then a steady succession of English champions has followed. Mrs. Wilcock is proud to have six English Champions in residence, the only post war British Samoyed Kennel, she tells us, to have this number of champions on at one time.

Champion Sworddale Silver Minstrel of Annecy gained his title at age 18 months. Champion Northcape Simona of Annecy was the Top Winning Samoyed Bitch for 1981. She became the dam of Champion The Kingmaker of Annecy and Champion Little Extra of Annecy.

Tracing down the line, Simona became the granddam of Champion Annecy's Chrysarah. She also gained the distinction of being the only Samoyed to have qualified for the prestigious Pedigree Chum Veteran of the Year Award, which she has done twice; in 1984 at age 10½ years, and again in 1985.

Champion Annecy's Chrysarah was the Top Winning Bitch Samoyed in 1984 and again in 1985.

Champion Snowheron Serena of Sworddale and Annecy is the dam of Champion Sworddale Silver Minstrel of Annecy and of Annecy's Chase The Wind. The latter has gained two Reserve Challenge Certificates before reaching the age of nine months, and is the only Samoyed to have qualified for the Spiller's Pup of the Year Award in 1985.

Further evidence of Annecy's success as a Samoyed kennel is the fact that they held the Top Breeders Award for 1985, plus the Top Stud Dog Award for that same year—a double barreled honor extremely well deserved, from all that we have heard.

Mrs. Wilcock has a pedigree of Champion Northcape Simona which traces back to the very first Samoyeds brought into England.

NOVASKAYA

Novaskaya Samoyeds are now in the United States. But since between the years 1970 and 1981 they were a highly successful kennel located in England, we decided to categorize them as an English kennel although actually the owners have lived in several locations and Novaskaya is well known with active breed contributions in Australia and New Zealand and the United States as well as Great Britain.

The owner of Novaskaya is Mrs. Betty Moody who in 1970 returned to England with her husband for a tour of duty with the U.S. Air Force. What had been expected to be a three-year tour turned into eleven years; the Moodys did not get back to the United States until 1981. From New York they have now moved to Mountain Home, Idaho.

When the Moodys left for England in 1970, it was necessary to leave Mrs. Moody's American Eskimo dogs behind as there had been a rabies scare there which resulted in no livestock at all being permitted into the country, not even in quarantine. So the two dogs were placed in good homes with friends, and when Betty Moody was settled in England, she started looking around for another dog. She was not a lady who for long would remain without one, or a few! A Samoyed was chosen, owing to its resemblance to their earlier dogs. The first Samoyed purchased was Fairville Silver Mist who was intended solely as a pet but upon persuasion of friends was shown a bit at local events, where she did not fare too badly. But when they tried her at a Championship show, the Moodys realized immediately that she was not really show quality. So a second Sam was purchased and the Moodys were "hooked."

The first brood bitch for the Moodys was Fairville Francesca, and it was she who produced their first English Champion, Novaskaya Silva Solo. Her daughter from an earlier litter was also kept, Novaskaya Kara, and she too was a champion producer as the dam of Champion Novaskaya Silva King and Novaskaya Silva Shilokan. Both Solo and Shilokan won a Group, thus did nicely for their owner.

The second brood bitch was Champion Morgana Tisha Lafay of Novaskaya who distinguished herself by producing Champion Novaskaya Chandra Lafay, Champion Novaskaya Channa Lafay, and Canadian Champion Silva Solitaire of Ker-Lu, as well as Best in Show winning Novaskaya Chanina Lafay from her second litter.

Champion Chandra Lafay was to become the Top Winning Bitch of that year in England, and also went Best in Show at the British Samoyed Club Specialty, emulating her dam, Tisa Lafay, who went Best in Show at the British Specialty in 1977 and Best of Opposite Sex there in 1979.

Not to be outdone by the ladies, Champion Silva King was Best in Show at the Samoyed Association Specialty in a then record entry of 178.

The Moodys also owned and bred Shih Tzu and Tibetan Terriers, and have owned and bred dogs since about 1960.

16

Left: Ch. White Rover of the Arctic representing the Samoyed breed in *Champion Dogs: A Series of Real Photos* issued by John Sinclair, Ltd., Newcastle-On-Tyne, England. Owned by: Mrs. G. M. Wood, Harriseahead, Stoke-on-Trent." *Right*: Eng. Ch. Little Extra of Annecy, (England's Top Winning Bitch for Samoyeds in 1981). Daughter of Eng. Ch. Northcape Simona of Annecy. Owned by Annecy Samoyeds, Mrs. Margaret J. Wilcock, Clayton-Le Woods nr Chorley, Lancashire, England.

Eng. Ch. Novaskaya Silva King, Best in Show at Samoyed Association Championship Show 1979 in record entry of 178 dogs. The sire of Eng. Ch. Modessa Miss Terry, Best of Breed and Reserve in Working Group, Crufts 1982; Novaskaya Tsarina Lafay, New Zealand's Top Winning Samoyed in 1981 and Top Winning Puppy, all breeds, same year; and Eng. Ch. Novaskaya Imzay Lafay. Photo courtesy of Mrs. Betty Moody, Novaskaya Samoyeds.

In 1981 the Moodys returned to the United States, leaving part of the Novaskaya operation still going strong in England and in the charge of Mrs. Moody's sister.

In 1983, in the States, a litter was bred from Novaskaya Tsarina Lafay which produced Champion Novaskaya Zara Lafay, her first litter being bred in England and whelped in New Zealand. This produced four dogs and one bitch. From these five puppies came Champion Kimchatka Achilles, Top Winning Samoyed of all time in New Zealand; Champion Alexie, five times a Best in Show winner; Champion Angelique; and American Champion Anatole.

Betty Moody tells us that all of the Novaskaya Samoyeds are either bred by them or are from dogs who were bred by them. Their stud dog in England, Novaskaya Silva Starsun, has produced champions in England, America, Canada, New Zealand, and Italy.

Novaskaya bloodlines are based principally on Whitewisp and on Kobe; they have remained, most successfully, within these lines for the past ten years. The Moodys have owned or bred 20 champions in five countries, with quite a few others having points

Eng. Ch. Little Extra of Annecy and Eng. Ch. The Kingmaker of Annecy, two of the famous Samoyeds owned by Mrs. Margaret J. Wilcock, Lancashire, England.

Eng. Ch. Yanik of Airebis, by Eng. Ch. Kalman of Airebis ex Eng. Ch. Sigrid of Saratov. Breeder, Mrs. Terry Malabar. Owners, Mr. and Mrs. G. Tyler. Pictured with the Best of Breed rosette and trophy from Crufts. Photo courtesy of Mrs. Betty Moody.

towards their titles or Challenge Certificates. At the present time the Moodys have seven Sams with them, ranging in age from four months (Novaskaya Czar Lafay) through Novaskaya Snow Tansy (one year), Novaskaya Silva Snowblaze (two years), Icezones Moonlight Artemis (three years), Champion Silversams Petranov Novaskaya (four years), English and American Champion White-wise Snow Crystal (four years), and Novaskaya Tsarina Lady (seven years). All live in the house as family. With the exception of Czar Lafay and Snow Tansy, all of the Moodys' dogs are pointed or finished.

The Moodys also co-own Novaskaya Silva Sedalia and Novaskaya Anastasia Lafay, both major-pointed.

Chapter 3

Samoyeds in the United States

It was in 1906 that the first Samoyed was officially registered with the American Kennel Club and assigned Stud Book #102,896. This dog was a Russian Champion by the name of Moustan of Argenteau. A dog with a glamorous background, as in 1904 Moustan had come to America with the Princess de Montyglyon who had acquired him two years earlier as a gift from the former Grand Duke Nicholas, brother to the Czar.

The Princess was an avid dog fancier who exhibited her dogs quite frequently at the European shows. Among these was St. Petersburg, where she first made the acquaintance of Moustan. So great was her admiration for this lovely dog, who was one of those being shown by the Grand Duke, that he presented Moustan to her as a gift—one which delighted her, we are sure, and who accompanied her along with three other Samoyeds, two Collies and two Chow Chows when she immediately resumed her hobby as an exhibitor when she was settled in the States.

Moustan was registered "pedigree unknown." There had been assorted theories advanced with regard to his parentage, some of which were plausible while others rather stretched the imagination, and one's credulity. Obviously whatever forebears were re-

Facing page: *Top:* Dutch, German, International, Belgian, and VHD Ch. Nikara's Kareena, Bundessieger 1984. Junior Warrant and Winner 1983. Owned by J. A. C. *Bottom:* Ch. Karandash Byelo was handled to many successes by Jane and Bob Forsyth during the early 1970s. Pictured here in 1973 taking Best of Breed at Westminster for owners, Mr. and Mrs. F. J. Kite.

sponsible, they were dogs of quality, as Moustan's type was admirable and he, too, was a sire of quality. Without pedigree himself, he managed to make his presence strongly felt, with his own name to be found behind an imposing number of worthy Samoyeds down through the generations.

The three other Samoyeds accompanying the Princess and Moustan to America included Sora and Siberia of Argenteau, also of undefined parentage, and the pedigreed Martyska of Argenteau. Siberia completed her title of champion in 1908, a year after Champion de Witte of Argenteau, son of Moustan and Sora, made history by becoming the first Champion of Record among Samoyeds in America. Samoyeds were decidedly not just a passing fancy with the Princess. She became increasingly enthusiastic over the breed as both an exhibitor and a breeder as the association with them increased. A dog named Etah joined the Princess's Samoyeds in 1913, again a gift to her, this one from a member of the Amundsen Expedition, where it had been a lead dog. She eventually moved to La Jolla, California where her interest continued.

In addition to having sired deWitte, who had accounted for the distinction of having been America's first Samoyed champion, Moustan also had produced Czarevitch (from Martyska). This dog and Moustan's grandson, Champion Zuroff, were constantly to be found in the winners circle at the shows of their period in competition.

Another early enthusiast was Mrs. Ada Van Heusen (at that time Mrs. E. E. Lincoln) who arrived on the scene with Tamara and Volga, litter sisters, and with Katinka and Soho, daughter and son of Southern Cross, coming to the Fancy in about 1912. To her went the honor of owning the first American Champion Samoyed bitch when Tamara completed title for her.

Mrs. Van Heusen bred Champion Tamara to the Moustan son, Czarevitch, thus producing the already-mentioned Champion Zuroff. Also Czarevitch was the sire of Champion Greenacre Kieff and Evalo. Kieff made his presence felt as grandsire of Champion Fang of Yurok, Champion Kazan of Yurok, and Champion Zanoza, all names familiar to pedigree students.

Many new people joined the ranks of Sammy owners during the early decades of this century. Miss Elizabeth Hudson, later to become well known in the breed, made her initial appearance with littermates in 1908. Sisters, Mrs. Borg and Mrs. Cahn, brought over dogs from England, these from the kennels of Mrs. Cammack and Mr. Common. But the next really big development in Samoyeds was provided by a bitch named Wiemur, who was presented to a young lady named Ruth Nichols by her Dad in 1914. Although she came to Miss Nichols in 1914, Wiemur was not registered until the close of World War I in 1918. Her influence on Samoyeds was notable as she was bred to Czarevitch thus becoming the dam of Champion Malschick and Champion Shut Balackeror. These two left their mark on the breed, Shut Balackeror by becoming a successful foundation stud at Yukon Kennels for Mrs. Frank Romer, a kennel which continued to prosper into the late '30's under the Romers' ownership, then was transferred to Eddie Barbeau.

Meanwhile Ruth Nichols's Top O' The World Kennels was also flourishing, and Champion Malschick sired, from an imported Scottish bitch which had been acquired by Miss Nichols, Otiska, the latter making her presence felt through her progeny and theirs.

The Samoyeds who became Champions of Record prior to 1920 are as follows:

de Witte of Argenteau (Moustan—Sora of Argenteau)
Siberia of Argenteau (breeding unknown)
Zuroff (Czarevitch—Tamara)
Greenacres Kieff (Czarevitch—Tamara)
Malschick (Czarevitch—Wiemur)
Shut Balackeror (Czarevitch—Wiemur)

A look at this list makes it very clear that Czarevitch was *the* influential sire of the first two decades of the 20th century in the United States.

Mrs. Romer started the 1920's off in an exciting manner when she purchased Tobolsk, a widely publicized dog purchased for her abroad by Percy Roberts. As with most truly important dogs, this one had his admirers—and his detractors. The proof of the pudding was in the performance, as this son of Fang ex Vilna was used on Otiska, with whom he produced such outstanding Sams as Champion Toby of Yurok II, Nanook II, and Nanook of Donerna. With Sunny Ridge Pavlova he produced Champion Fang of Yurok and Champion Kazan of Yurok. With Champion Donerna's Barin and Champion Yukon Mit he was credited with a noticeable improvement in American Samoyed type. He had, as well, at least several other offspring who made valuable contributions to the breed.

Tobolsk's litter sister, Champion Draga, came to America at the same time he did. In litters sired by Champion Shut Balackeror and Zev of Yurok, her offspring included Champion Kritelka of Yurok, Boy Yurok and Toby of Yurok.

A kennel of long duration which I recall personally from the early days was Parke-Cliffe owned by Mrs. Mildred Sheridan Davis, which started in 1920 with an importation from Russia and was still going strong five decades later.

Obi Kennels also appeared on the scene soon after 1921, as did Norka towards the close of that decade.

One could not write of the period of the 1920's without including Barin or, to be formal, Champion Donerna's Barin, who was brought to this country by Mr. and Mrs. Alfred Seeley. A son of English Champion Kieff ex Ivanofva, he was bred by Mr. Pitchford, and was a direct descendant two generations down the line of the famed Antarctic Buck. A most interesting story of the Seeleys and their dogs appeared in the *American Kennel Gazette* in February 1925. Barin's popularity as a sire is confirmed when one considers that he was responsible for 120 registered Samoyeds.

Forty Samoyeds had been registered with the American Kennel Club prior to 1920. In the two years between 1920 and 1922 there were 42 new Stud Book entries in the breed.

The need of a Samoyed Specialty Club was becoming increasingly obvious when, during Westminster, a meeting for its formation was held in Madison Square Garden, New York on Feb. 14, 1923. The English breed Standard was adopted, except for the addition of the words "black or black spots shall disqualify," plus a paragraph of description of correct disposition.

At this period, Samoyeds were shown in the Non-Sporting Group, as were several other of the Working breeds. Interestingly, this Group included at that time, in addition to the Sams, only Boston Terriers and French Bulldogs of those still part of it, the others then having been Collies, Doberman Pinschers, Great Danes, Old English Sheepdogs and St. Bernards (which were later placed, along with the Sams, in the Working Group and some, later on, switched to the Herding Group). The remainder of Non-Sporting were Maltese, Toy Poodles and Yorkshire Terriers which are now Toys.

As the 1920's progressed, Samoyed interest started to spread across the United States, with a steady influx of new owners joining the ranks.

Throughout the 1920's the importations came, bringing with them the finest dogs and bloodlines available from England's leading kennels—Farningham, Kobe, of the Arctic, and all of the others of note. Progeny of English lines were active in establishing the background for our modern American-bred Sam, and it is to the credit of our Fancy here that these purchases were not just shown but were used advantageously in each kennel's breeding program, too.

It was the great English dog Champion Storm Cloud, imported late in the 1920's by the aforementioned Elizabeth Hudson (one of the really early Sam owners here) who provided the foundation behind the Snowland Kennels, so highly successful for Mrs. Helen Harris at Merion, Pennsylvania. Mrs. Harris had become recently involved with Samoyeds when she brought her first one back from England. The lovely bitch Taimir was bred by Mrs. Harris to Storm Cloud, leading to the birth of Vida of Snowland, foundation bitch of the Snowland Kennels which attained such prestige for this lady.

Mrs. Harris evidently visited the English kennels and dog shows frequently. Sabarka of Farningham was one she imported. But her true ambition at that period was to own Champion Kara Sea, whom she found it impossible to part from owner Mrs. Edwards. Later she determined that next best to having Kara Sea would be to have puppies of this dog, and so she purchased and brought to America the entire litter of Kara Sea and Pinky of Farningham, bringing the whole lot of them, which as it turned out consisted only of two, over here. Kara Sea was 13 years of age when all this took place.

The anticipated litter when born included a very famous dog, Siberian Nansen of Farningham of Snowland, and a bitch who unfortunately died very young. They were born in England, coming here in accordance with the agreement, when of an age to travel. Nansen earned an enviable record as a sire of champions, still doing so at age 11 years. Among the especially memorable of his progeny, Champion Starvyna of Snowland became a valuable addition to the kennels of Robert and Dolly Ward.

What Siberian Nansen accomplished for Mrs. Harris is now a

matter of history. The aforementioned Vida of Snowland was bred to him to produce the sort of litter which makes the dreams of breeders come true. Champions Nadya, Nianya, Nikita, Nim and Norna were the result; and it has been stated as a fact that the effect of these marvelous Sams on great winners, right up until the present day, is undeniable and can be proven beyond question by a survey of pedigrees.

Many words of praise have been written about the fact that, contrary to many breeders, Mrs. Harris was always willing to sell really outstanding bitches to fanciers in other parts of the country. Quite the opposite of being selfish about this, she truly enjoyed sharing her finest with fellow breeders, enjoying their pleasure in the successes of their progeny. Snowland Samoyeds were making people happy from coast to coast, producing worthy champions and themselves winning well for many years, with their descendants continuing to do so right to the present day.

Later importations brought here by Mrs. Harris included Sabarka of Farningham and Champion Ice Crystal of the Arctic. And again she had done well, as both added to the quality of her line.

As time progressed, the Pacific Coast became increasingly a hotbed of Samoyed activity with importations from the leading English kennels and outstanding dogs from the East Coast. It is a noteworthy fact that the first Samoyed Specialty to exceed 100 entries was in California, in June 1950, in conjunction with the Harbor Cities Kennel Club Dog Show at Long Beach. One hundred and ten of the breed assembled for the opinion of judge Chris Knudsen. The winner, Champion Verla's Prince Comet. This was the twelfth Samoyed Club of America Specialty event.

The first two Samoyed Specialties in the United States had been held at the prestigious Tuxedo Kennel Club event in 1929 and 1930. The first of these drew a very respectable entry of 40, to be judged by Louis Smirnow. The winner of Best of Breed was Champion Tiger Boy of Norka, owned by Mr. and Mrs. H. Reid. Strangely, there was a drop to only 12 the following year, with the same general date and same location. The judge was well-known breeder Mrs. F. Romer, and the Best of Breed winner was Champion Storm Cloud, owned by Mrs. E. Hudson.

Seven years passed before another National Specialty, at which time the fabulous Morris and Essex Dog Show was the host.

26

Again Louis Smirnow judged, but this time a smaller entry than 40 as there were only 19 of the breed. The respected Msgr. Keegan led the field at this one with a Sam named Krasan.

Morris and Essex continued to host the Samoyed Club of America through 1941. Entries ranged between 43 in 1938, for the judicial opinion of Msgr. Keegan, to 29 in 1941 for C.H. Chamberlain. In between, there were 31 in 1939 for Enno Meyer, and 20 in 1940 for Ruth Stillman. A.V.W. Foster's Champion Norka's Mogoiski was the 1938 Best of Breed; B.M. Ruick's Champion Prince Kofski top award winner in 1939; Msgr. Keegan's Champion Prince Igor II in 1940; and Champion Alastasia's Rukavitza for A.L. McBain in 1941.

Owing to World War II, there was a break in the Specialty Show schedule from 1942 until 1946, when the show moved to Chicago, becoming part of the Chicago International event. There Alva Rosenberg as judge was greeted with 46 Sams, chose as his Best of Breed J.J. Marshall's Champion Frolnik of Sammar, and another milestone was reached when this dog went on to become the first Specialty Best of Breed to continue on, at the same event, to first place in the Working Group.

The 1947 and 1948 Specialty events were both in California, at Pasadena Kennel Club and Los Angeles Kennel Club respectively. Dr. Richard Walt, from among 47 entries at Pasadena, found his Best of Breed in Champion Staryvna of Snowland, owned by Mr. and Mrs. Robert Ward (now so popular in our judging rings). Dr. William Ivens at Los Angeles did likewise in Champion Gay of White Way, owned by Agnes and Aljean Mason. There was no Specialty in 1949. In 1950, Harbor Cities had its record 110 entries. And again no Specialty for the National in 1951.

San Mateo, California, August 1952, was the second largest Specialty turnout to that time, 78, for judge John W. Cross, Jr. A repeat for Champion Verla's Prince Comet from 1950, thus giving Shirley Hill the top award at the two largest Sam Specialties up to then.

In 1953 to the East Coast again at Westchester Kennel Club. Ruth Stillman judged 40 of the breed here, the Best of Breed winner, A.V. Ruth's Champion Zor of Altai.

International Kennel Club again in 1954. Col. E. D. McQuown, judge. There were 51 Samoyeds, the winner being Champion King of Wal-Lynn, owner E. M. Smith.

The Samoyed Club of America sponsored two Specialty Shows in 1955, Westchester in September with 16 entries judged by C. H. Chamberlain; Los Angeles in November, 83 entries, judge Alf Loveridge. Bests of Breed to Champion Tazson's Snow Flicka owned by A. E. Ulfeng and to G. Klein and M. Mueller's Champion Polaris Pan.

Two shows again in 1956. Seattle Kennel Club on February 25th judged by Alfred E. Van Court; Mason and Dixon Kennel Club on September 9th, judge Mrs. Marie B. Meyer. The winners, Champion Bunky Jr. of Lucky Dee (Mr. and Mrs. B. P. Dawed) and Champion Nordly's Sammy, J. M. Doyce.

Champion Nordly's Sammy finished out the 1950's with three more Specialty Shows: in 1957 at Monmouth County (39 entries, Charles A. Swartz, judge) where he also made further history by winning First in the Working Group and Best American-bred in Show; in 1958 at Chicago International, 49 entries for W. H. Reeves; and in February 1959, at Santa Cruz, California, 71 entries for judge Major B. Godsol.

It was in 1964 that the first Separate Specialty Show was held by the Samoyed Club of America, this at Montecito, California, where 92 of the breed turned out for judge Albert E. Van Court. The winners on this memorable occasion were Champion Shondra of Draylene, owned by J. M. Dyer, Best of Breed; and Champion Noatak of Silver Moon, owned by R. J. Bowles, Best of Opposite Sex.

The first Samoyed to win a Best in Show in the United States did so in 1949 at Toledo Kennel Club in Ohio. She was Sweet Missy of Sammar, a bitch from the puppy classes, who went through to this honor, and she was handled by her breeder-owner, Mrs. Joseph J. Marshall. The judge was Mrs. Enno (Marie) Meyer.

Two years later Champion Princess Silvertips of Kobe came along to take Best in Show at Central Maine Kennel Club in 1951, then at Green Mountain Kennel Club in 1953. She was an imported bitch who came here undefeated from England with nine Challenge Certificates, and in the United States she made a record of 48 times Best of Breed from 49 times shown.

The first multiple Best in Show winner in the United States was a son of Princess Silvertips and sired by Champion Martingate Snowland Taz. He was Champion Silver Spray of Wychwood, and he accounted for no less than five all-breed Bests in Show and one Best American-bred in Show during the 1952-1954 period. Four times successively this marvelous dog was Best of Breed at Westminster, twice placing in the Group there.

Champion Silvertips Scion of Wychwood, another littermate to the above, followed right behind Silver Spray, with a Best in Show each during 1953, 1954 and 1955.

Then came English and American Champion Americ of Kobe, another famous British import who made his debut here by going from the classes to Best in Show, adding three additional such honors for a total of four Bests during his career.

Princess Silvertips, Silver Spray, Silvertips Scion, and Americ all were owned by the fabulous kennels of Mrs. Bernice Ashdown and under the management of Charles L. Rollins. And this hardly even starts to list the credits of the total Wychwood family! Literally dozens of great Samoyeds lived or were bred there, and this lady deserves the heartiest respect of everyone in the dog show world for her accomplishments. On the Best in Show front alone, how impressive it is when one considers that of the early Best in Show winners, four of them with a total of 14 such honors between 1949 and 1959 were from this kennel. We salute Mrs. Ashdown with sincerity.

We have numerous interesting kennel stories of the current Samoyed breeders, many of which have their roots back in the early period. So let us now turn our attention to them for the continuation of the history of Samoyeds in the United States. We feel that you will find them interesting and valuable sources of additional information.

AHDOOLO

Ahdoolo is a small, private Samoyed kennel owned by John E. and Marie M. Gemeinhardt at Cedar Grove, New Jersey, along with their daughter, Linda.

This family has owned Samoyeds since 1967 and has been exhibiting their many good dogs since 1971.

The first of the Ahdoolo title-holders, Champion Cinnamon Snow of Yate-Sea, completed championship in 1972.

The foundation bitch here was Cinnamon Snow's half sister, Champion North Star Mist of Yate-Sea.

Left: Ahdoolo's Cloud Climber, handsome son of Ch. Ahdoolo's Chase the Clouds ex Ahdoolo's Frosted Folly. Owned by Linda M. Gemeinhardt, Cedar Grove, New Jersey. *Right*: Ch. Aladdin's Silver Snow Shadow, foundation bitch at Aladdin Samoyeds. Owned by Joseph and Joyce Johnson, Kirkland, Washington.

Although it is unusual for the Gemeinhardts to campaign their dogs in specials, Champion North Star Mist was Best of Breed over the males on numerous occasions.

Ahdoolo Samoyeds are owner-handled, and many of them are out of their foundation bitch. It is the owners' ambition to maintain and improve her quality, at which they would seem to be succeeding handsomely.

ALADDIN

Aladdin Samoyeds are owned, at Kirkland, Washington, by Joseph and Joyce Johnson, whose first Sam was acquired in 1964 after they had seen some of them in an all-breed dog show.

Unfortunately this first one had bad hips and other problems, which caused several years' setback for these folks. However, they did get a nice female of excellent bloodlines whom they bred to Champion Chu San's Silver Folly which finally got them under way in the proper manner, as from her they got their first foundation bitch, Champion Aladdin's Silver Snow Shadow.

Shadow began her show career by taking Best of Winners at the 1970 National Specialty. She was bred three times, producing champions in each of her litters. She was recognized in 1977 as #2 Brood Bitch.

Shadow's daughter, Champion Aladdin's Lightfoot Lass, was a most imposing bitch in personality, soundness and character. She was bred to Champion Knight Nicholas, in which litter (born in 1978) she produced that very admired and memorable dog, Champion Aladdin's Dominator. This was the only litter Lass ever had, which is a pity as it was a great one. But it has been impossible for her owners to find out why she never again conceived. Nonetheless she made her contribution to the breed in the form of Note, as Dominator is called, who became the backbone of Aladdin Samoyeds, this through his daugter, Champion Aladdin's Jezebel.

Joyce Johnson, in speaking of Dominator, says, "Note is one of those special dogs who *knows* from the beginning that he *is* special. He finished his championship during the second half of 1982, then finished out the year as #3 Samoyed that year. For the next four years between #3 and #6 Samoyed with limited showing. Note has produced several champions who are spread all over the United States. We have several champion children and grandchildren of his here as well."

Unfortunately Note has had a couple of accidents that have required his early retirement from the show ring. However, there is a son of his, very special to the Johnsons, Champion Neaderlander's Dutch Treat, who is carrying on his sire's winning ways. The Johnsons consider themselves really lucky to have been able to persuade the breeder of this dog to allow them to have him at one year old. He is a big-bodied dog, the type which matures slowly, but along the way he has already taken some mighty exciting breed and Group wins and placements coast to coast.

Dutch Treat has also produced several litters, in one of which all the offspring already are either finished to the title or nearly there at less than two years. There are pups in the second litter who are nearly finished, these under a year. And the third litter as we write has not yet reached show age.

Frozen semen has been collected from Note and we are awaiting the chance of proving this method of producing Samoyeds.

The Johnsons have truly enjoyed their 22-year-period of breeding and raising Samoyeds, and hope to continue for a long time to contribute to their beautiful breed. Someday they may consider judging, which would be great, as obviously they are very knowledgeable fanciers.

AUTUMN

Autumn Samoyeds, located at Southbury, Connecticut, have grown from the first introduction of Lynda Zaraza to what has now become her favorite breed.

Lynda was no stranger to the dog show world even at that time, for as a child she was in the habit of accompanying her mother to the shows with her Collies. The hobby never lost interest for her, so in 1973 she purchased her own first show dog, who was a Samoyed.

Four years later, she took her first champion into the ring for the first time as a special. To say it was a memorable day would surely win an award for understatement, as this was the 1977 Specialty Show of the Samoyed Club of America, and before it had ended, Lynda had won the National Specialty Best of Breed with her American and Canadian Kristik's English Autumn.

This very handsome dog went on to become a Group winner and a Group placer, winning with both his owner on some occasions and with Joy Brewster handling on others. He has produced 12 champions to date. His daughter, Champion Suzuki's Final Edition, was Best of Opposite Sex at the 1979 National; and another daughter, Suzki's Miss-B-Havin, C.D.X., has won Highest Scoring Dog in Trial at the 1981 National, where his granddaughter, Champion Suzuki's Autumn Elegance, was Reserve Winners Bitch.

American and Canadian Champion Kristik's Modesty Blaze came to Lynda in 1980 as her foundation bitch, finishing her title very quickly in five shows. Modesty has produced Champion Autumn's Rainbow Connection and Canadian Champion Kristik's Blaze of Autumn.

Rainbow and half sister Champion Autumn's Fruit Loops are now carrying on for Alfie, as English Autumn is known. Fruit

Left: Ch. Devonshire's Sudden Stop taking Best of Breed at Wachusett Kennel Club in 1985. Bred by Jan Russell, owned by Pat Kirms, co-owned and handled by Lynda Zaraza, Southbury, Connecticut. *Right*: Edens Taren O'Barron, by Am. and Can. Ch. Nordika's Polar Barron, C.D., ex North Starr's Final Edition, born January 1984. Bred by Pat Erdos and owned by Nancy Little.

Loops is owned by Lynda in partnership with Pat Kirms, Suzuki Samoyeds.

The future of the Autumn Samoyeds will be carried on by Champion Devonshire's Sudden Stop, owned by Pat Kirms and co-owned and handled by Lynda. Skipper has already become a Group placer and an asset to the Autumn breeding program in the few short months that he has been with the Zarazas.

BARRON'S SAMOYEDS

Barron's Samoyeds are the result of Barbara and Dan Cole of St. Charles, Missouri, having become involved with the breed in 1975 when they purchased a pet puppy from a "backyard" breeder as a Christmas gift. They named him Barron, BAR for BARbara's name and RON from Dan's middle name, then added White Lightnin' later on. At first Barron did not live at home with them as they had an apartment from which they were in the process of moving to a house. When Barron did join the family, they realized

33

in no time flat that a five-month-old puppy could definitely use some obedience training.

The Coles attended a local dog show, where they saw Ray Diaz take High in Trial and 2nd High in Trial with his two well mannered Irish Setters. Subsequently they enrolled in his classes, liking his technique. Ray advocated no force measures, such as ear pinch, pinch collar, stringing up, etc. To this day the Coles continue to adhere to and practice his principles in their own training program.

Barron subsequently went on to become the first Obedience Trial Champion (O.T.Ch.) Samoyed in all American Kennel Club history. He had also done Tracking; was a member of the California Rescue Dog Association (CARDA); twice represented Northern California in the Utility division of the Western Regional Interstate Obedience Competition; and, to date, has been the only Samoyed to participate and qualify in a Gaines Regional Obedience Competition in the Super Dog division, which he did one month after achieving his U.D., becoming one of the youngest in any breed in that division.

Barron also has been a wheel dog on a competitive Northern California Siberian Husky Team, and is proud to be a three-time recipient of the Samoyed Club of America Top Obedience Samoyed Award in 1979, 1980 and 1983. In his retirement, he has also become a Certified Therapy Dog, and is a happy ambassador for the Obedience Samoyed.

Shortly after realizing that Barron was not conformation competition quality, Barb and Dan decided to find the best conformation pup they could. It was nearly two years later when they purchased "Kappy," who was later to become American and Canadian Champion Nordika's Polar Barron, C.D. Kappy was never campaigned heavily, only attending local shows but nevertheless finished in short order with three majors. Then at his first show as a special, which was the 1980 Samoyed Club of America National Specialty, although one of the youngest specials there, he came home with an Award of Merit in a Best of Breed class with 45 contenders—one of only five such Awards made on the occasion. At his first all-breed show in specials he took Best of Breed over six other champions which he repeated at the next show where he also went on to Group 3rd, handled, as always, by his owner.

Not long thereafter Kappy earned his C.D., co-incidentally finishing that degree on the same day that he took Best of Breed at Salinas. With limited and owner-handled showing, Kappy achieved continuous ranking in the *Samoyed Quarterly* Top 10 to 25 ratings from 1982 to 1985, garnering Best of Breed on 45 occasions, 14 Group placements included four times 1st in some of the country's toughest Samoyed competition.

Kappy also attained his Canadian championship in three days of showing during which he romped off with Winners Dog, Best of Winners and Best of Breed (over specials), plus taking a Group 4th.

During 1985, Kap also passed the ATTS Temperament Test, as well as previously having run wheel with Barron on the same racing team and also having his Therapy Dog Certificate.

The Coles had no litters of their own until 1986, and only used Kapp at stud very sparingly. However, he was fortunate in having some lovely bitches sent to him just during the past couple of years, with pups out of each litter pointed and holding obedience titles. Dan and Barb have two of his pups who made their debuts, age one-year-and-a-half, both of them already pointed. Two will be ready for the C.D. soon. They are Kappy's Grizzly Barron and Barron's Night Kap. The Coles also co-own two young Kappy daughters, one nearly a champion, the other soon to come out. They are Barron's Sparkling Chablis, C.D. and Barron's Kaptivat'n Moonshine. Two other Kappy offspring have recently finished titles at less than two years' age: Danica's Russian Gambl'r Kanduit and Champion Kazakh's Lucky Duck. So far all the pups shown have been owner-handled, which pleases Barb as she is a member of the Owner-Handlers Association of America.

Barb does stained glass, and Dan works for a major airline, the latter enabling them to travel whenever they wish, and meet new friends in dogs, which they enjoy. May they continue doing so for many years to come!

BLUE SKY

Blue Sky Samoyeds are at Pine, Colorado, where they are owned by Dr. P.J. and Elizabeth Lockman Hooyman.

Mrs. Hooyman is an American Kennel Club licensed judge and, along with her husband, has been a member of the Samoyed Club of America since 1971.

Blue Sky has bred and owned Best in Show and Best in Spe-

A group of Blue Sky Samoyeds during an informal moment. Owned by Dr. P. J. and Elizabeth Lockman Hooyman, Blue Sky Samoyeds, Pine, Colorado.

cialty Show winners over the years. Drawing on foundation stock from Snomesa, through their first bitch, Snomesa Anastasia of Blue Sky; and Sulu, where they bred to Champion Sulu's Karbon Kopi O'Baerstone and his son, Champion Sulu's Mark of Distinction, they established and produced the Blue Sky line.

The handsome Champion Blue Sky's Honey Bun tied as Top Producer, Kennel Review System, for 1978. She was the dam of Best in Show and Best in Specialty Show winning Champion Blue Sky's Pound Cake, who was also the Samoyed Club of America's Top Winning Bitch in 1979. She produced, as well, Champion Blue Sky's Smiling At Me and Champion Blue Sky's Rambling Guy, all Group 1 winning littermates. Another from the litter, Champion Blue Sky's No Options, owned by Geoff and Brenda Abbott, also did nicely.

Champion Blue Sky's Pound Cake bred to Champion Iceway's Ice Breaker produced Best in Specialty Show winning Champion

Blue Sky's Breaking Away and Champion Blue Sky's Piece of Cake, also a Specialty winner. From that litter came, as well, Champion Blue Sky's Simply Smashing, owned by Paulo, Joan and Connie Lune; and Champion Blue Sky's Bedazzled, a Specialty winning bitch.

The latest Blue Sky bitches are Champion Blue Sky's Appolonia, who finished at nine months; and Blue Sky's Sertainly Sassy, who received Winners Bitch and Best of Opposite Sex at the Northern California Samoyed Fanciers Specialty in 1986 and Winners Bitch at the Minneapolis Samoyed Association that same year.

BUBBLING OAKS

Bubbling Oaks Samoyeds are owned by Jack and Amelia Price, who are situated at Commack, Long Island, New York.

Jack Price has lived with this breed for more than 20 years, his family having bred and shown under the kennel name of Suffolk. Jack's father had bred three champions.

Jack and Amelia Price became seriously involved with Samoyeds back in the early 1970's. Bubbling Oaks was the kennel name under which they chose to breed and exhibit, and they have bred nine champions, three with C.D. degrees, one C.D.X. and one Canadian Champion. Among these are three Group winning and Group placing bitches and Best in Show bitches.

Ch. Camshaft of Bubbling Oaks, by Ch. Marcliffe's Stormy of Snow King ex Ch. Foxy Loxy of Bubbling Oaks, at Mason and Dixon K.C. in 1982. Owned by Jack and Amelia Price, Bubbling Oaks Samoyeds, Commack, New York.

American and Canadian Champion Bubbles La Rue of Oakwood is the Highest Placing Samoyed in the history of Westminster Kennel Club, having won a Group 2nd there in 1978. La Rue's major contribution to the breed was the ability to break the Best of Opposite Sex barrier in the 1970's when that was a far from easy task. She was Kennel Review's Top Bitch 1974-1978; Samoyed Club of America Top Bitch 1975-1976. She was #2 Samoyed to Ransom in 1976; #3 Samoyed in Canada and #1 Bitch in 1976. Five times she won Best of Opposite Sex and once Best of Breed at Westminster. And she is the All Time Top Winning Samoyed Bitch in Breed History.

Bubbles' niece, Champion Me Too of Bubbling Oaks, distinguished herself with an Award of Merit at the National Specialty in 1981. She was the #1 Bitch for 1983-1984; and #5 and #4 Samoyed respectively in these two years.

Champion Camshaft of Bubbling Oaks began his career by winning his class at the National Specialty in 1980 and the Potomac Valley Specialty the same year. He has made an excellent reputation for himself as a weight pulling dog, having pulled 2,000 pounds when he weighed in at 59 pounds.

Champion Bubbling Oaks U.S. Mail was Best Puppy at the Washington State Specialty in 1981 and at the National that same year, going on to Reserve Winners Dog at the latter event. During a recent trip to Canada, he won the points at every show in which he was entered, needing only one point to complete title there. Both Camshaft and U.S. Mail have competed in all of the Long Distance Races Run by Jack in 1984, '85, '86.

In 1984, Jack Price and his team of five *Show* dogs were the First Samoyed team to complete the Canadian Long Distance Championship Race, consisting of more than 76 miles, at Marmora. He repeated this race in 1985-'86.

The Prices do comparatively little showing and breeding, the former only when they have something they feel really worthwhile; the latter only when they need to replace a dog or otherwise replenish their stock. The consistency with which their dogs have won over the years at truly prestigous shows speaks for itself!

CARIBOU

Caribou Samoyeds originated in 1955 in the little town of Soda Springs, Idaho. Joe and Mable Dyer had always had a dog of one

Ch. Shondra of Drayalene, by Ch. Barceia's Shondi of Drayalene ex Silver Dede O'Snow Ridge, winning Best of Opposite Sex at the Samoyed Club of America National Specialty in 1965. One of the foundation Samoyeds from this famous kennel belonging to Joe and Mable Dyer, Caribou Kennels, Shelley, Idaho.

sort or another, and had raised a few Cockers when Joe talked of getting a hunting dog. At the time, the Dyers still had one nice male Cocker, but all the same, they started studying the various dog publications, looking at pictures, and reading about all the various qualifications of the different breeds.

Until then, the thought of a Samoyed had never occurred to them. But the more they read and looked at pictures, the more thoroughly they were convinced that this was the most beautiful dog of all, with, from what everyone said, personality to match.

The next step was letters from the Dyers to the various breeders inquiring what might be available for sale. Finally it was decided that they would purchase a grown bitch who supposedly had been bred previously to that time, with puppies soon due. Excitement was high until the day the bitch arrived, in an apple box after a five-day trip by rail, and she was in season, obviously *not* pregnant. In spite of their disappointment, the Dyers decided that they would work on training their new acquisition for obedience, at the same time trying to find a nice male to whom she could be bred next season.

Shortly thereafter Joe Dyer, who is an electrician, went to work in Idaho Falls, which meant a move there for the family. There they discovered that Emil Moore, at Idaho Falls, had a male Samoyed. By coincidence, the Dyers were driving downtown one day when they noticed a car with a big, beautiful white dog looking out. In no time at all, they introduced themselves to Emil Moore and to King, the Samoyed.

King had come, Mr. Moore told the Dyers, from a fellow who bred Sams in Salt Lake City, Utah. The Dyers found out, too, that there were obedience training classes held at Salt Lake, so off they went, together with their Samoyed, to become acquainted with Tom Ralphs, from whom King had been purchased. They found Mr. Ralphs definitely the type of gentleman who was cordial and helpful to newcomers in the breed, and when the Samoyed bitch was ready to breed, they mated her to Mr. Ralphs's Champion Williwaw, C.D.X. There were three puppies in the resulting litter, one of which did not survive. The Dyers kept the two remaining males, and when they were just five months old started them in obedience class in Idaho Falls. Mable joined the Upper Snake River Valley Dog Training Club and did very well with the puppies who eventually gained their C.D. degrees, with one going on to C.D.X.

By then interest in the conformation judging and breed shows had started to take hold, and so the Dyers started entering in both obedience and conformation for those shows to which they could travel. One of the males wound up with several points but never finished. The other was great in obedience but did not fare well as a show dog.

The more they learned about showing dogs, the more thoroughly convinced the Dyers became that this they really wanted to do, their goal becoming to own really good Samoyeds and raise puppies in which they could take pride.

Studying everything they could find on the breed, they soon decided that they liked (and still do) the Samoyeds with the broad muzzles rather than the ones with more wolfish heads. Also, they liked good balance, ears of correct size, etc. So again they started searching for a Samoyed, the goal being to get better stock with which to carry out their "Caribou Kennel" plans.

Meanwhile they continued in obedience and conformation with the three dogs they had originally. Their daughter, Bonnie, showed the dam in obedience where she took her to earn her C.D.; and Joe and Mable showed the pups.

Later on a lovely bitch which had been bred to Champion Winter Trail Blazer was purchased from Bob and Dolly Ward. This was Capella, who had to have a C-section in order to have the puppies in a litter of 11! Three of the 11 were born dead; the remaining eight turned out very nicely. The Dyers kept the male whom their son, Kenny, trained and showed in both obedience and conformation doing well with him. When Kenny switched his interest from Samoyeds to basketball, this puppy, "Blazer," was sold to Donna Yucom of Tsiulikagta Kennels, for whom he became Champion Kenny's Blazer Boy of Caribou, C.D.X.

The Dyers kept in touch with Tom Ralphs who had become a friend, and when he was unable to keep his Champion Minishka, C.D.X., he let the Dyers have this wonderful Best in Show dog.

In 1962 a bitch puppy from Helene Spathold in California was added to Caribou Kennels. Mable Dyer describes this little girl as having been "everything we had ever wanted in a puppy; lovely broad head and muzzle, good bone, terrific coat and lots of personality." Registered as Shondra of Drayalene, she was shown, then bred to Champion Minishka C.D.X. From the litter a male was kept.

In 1964 Shondra went from open class at the National Specialty (Samoyed Club of America) in Montecito, California, to Best of Breed! Owner-handled by Joe Dyer, this was truly a day of days for these dedicated fanciers.

In September 1964, Mable went with friends to the Colorado Dog Show, where she finished Shondra under Bob Ward at Denver. That same year, the male whom they had kept from Shondra's litter went Best in Show, all-breeds, in Utah with Tom Ralphs. This dog was Champion Bauzuhl of Caribou.

In 1965 Champion Shondra was Best of Opposite Sex to her litter brother, Champion Shaloon of Drayalene at the National Specialty in Seattle, Washington.

The Dyers have always tried to keep some of the bloodlines of Shondra, Minishka and Bauzuhl of Caribou to continue their breeding program as these produced the type of Samoyed they prefer.

Various lines have been added, of course, along the way, including Kondako, and the Dyers have been extremely proud of the results. Caribou puppies have been shipped to new owners, happy ones, all over the United States (including Alaska) and Canada. Also, a few years ago three grown dogs went to Costa Rica for breeding stock. One of these, a female named Rory of Caribou, became a Best in Show winner there.

One of the Dyers' pleasures is keeping in touch with the people who have purchased their dogs.

The number of Samoyeds at Caribou has been cut back, now, and very few puppies are raised there in comparison to "the old days." But the old Caribou lines are still very much existent, and the Dyers definitely plan to continue breeding and showing but on a more limited basis.

Several Caribou dogs are with Judi Lindsay in Texas. Charles and Lucinda Johnson, Windriver Kennels, in Wyoming, have some lovely ones of Caribou breeding, too.

DANICA

Danica Samoyeds, at Bloomsburg, Pennsylvania, are owned by Dr. John and Judy Kovitch, who started as Samoyed owners back in 1975 when they purchased their first one who was intended to be just a pet. She was Marcliff's Misty Moonlight, a super "family dog" with an outstanding temperament and loving nature. A neighbor encouraged Dr. and Mrs. Kovitch to try their hand at showing her. It did not take long for them to realize that she was, indeed, a pet, not a show dog; and so a watchful eye was cast about for a real nice show type puppy. The result of their search was to become Champion Weathervane Simply Smashing, their puppy who "loved the game."

By the time Simply Smashing was six months old, she was ready to take Reserve Winners Bitch at the P.V.S.C. Specialty, quickly taking as well a three-point major, and a Best of Breed from the classes over a Group-placing dog.

John now needed a dog of his own to show, so again it was puppy hunting time. Their "find" was a little bundle of fur who became the Group winning and placing Champion Danica's Russian Roulette, a "package of dynamite" who had been bred by Renete Frey. At six months old he won his first points; and his first major at eleven months. This was a dog who loved being in the ring, and even though he was close to eight years old when he died, he had never lost his zest for the shows, winning his final Group just two months prior to his untimely death.

On the way to his championship, "Shane," as this great dog was called, was always novice-handled by John Kovitch, and always took Best of Winners. He completed his Canadian title undefeated in the classes in four days with multiple Bests of Breed.

When he had matured, Shane was specialed by his co-owner Sue Grasley. For three years he was ranked in the Top 15 winning Samoyeds in the country, a consistent breed winner as well as Group winner and placer. He was stud dog winner at the 1981 P.V.S.C. Specialty, and at over seven years, he won his last Group.

Shane was usually bred to Danica bitches, siring some outstanding Group winners and Group placement dogs. There is also a Canadian Champion and several other kids have their major points.

Most of all, however, Shane is remembered by his family as a very special dog, relating as well to people as he did to other dogs. As Judy Kovitch says of him, "no matter where he was, he enjoyed life to the fullest."

Russian Roulette and Simply Smashing were bred to one another, producing several champions and Group placing dogs, among them Champion Danica's Russian Foxfire and Champion Danica's Gallant Russian Bear. This breeding combined the Sam O'Khan, Kondako, and Silver Moon lines behind both of these dogs.

Ch. Aurora's Moon Dancer, bred by Renate Frey, by Am. and Can. Ch. Weathervane's Double Trouble ex Am. and Can. Ch. Weathervane's Hot's Hit, finished in seven weekends with three majors. Her first litter by Am. and Can. Ch. Nordika's Polar Barron, C.D., included pointed pups. Dr. John and Judy Kovitch, owners.

Russian Roulette was also bred to Marcwood's Suzuki Seabreeze, adding a little English and Kendara to the Kondako and Sam O'Khan behind both of them. This combination produced several nice dogs, most notably American and Canadian Champion Danica's Silver Echo of Shane.

Recently the Kovitches have taken their two Roulette—Simply Smashing daughters to American and Canadian Champion Nordika's Polar Barron, C.D., to blend the Silver Moon within both lines. Both breedings have produced exceptional pups. At present four from the first litter and two from the second are pointed. Danica's Kila Kalisa, the one and only bitch from the first breeding, has just produced her first litter by American and Canadian Champion Weathervane's Trouble Maker, who is her great-uncle (Shane's brother); the promising puppies are four months old.

Showing and breeding are a hobby for Dr. and Mrs. Kovitch, but the dogs have become an integral part of their lives. Samoyeds swim with them, go on picnics, sledding, or just for a ride. They have been to nursery school and nursing homes acting as ambassadors of the breed. All Danica Samoyeds are raised in the house, spending time each day outside for exercise. Because the Kovitches feel that family life is of prime importance for the dogs, this has been used as a criterion when placing puppies. It is just as exciting to see a happy pet who can be a baseball team mascot, fly in his family's plane, or go backpacking, as it is to see one take a major, these folks firmly feel. Of course, it is also rewarding to see some of these dogs finish their championships with newcomers to the breed as handlers!

John and Judy Kovitch believe that understanding the Samoyed is paramount in living with one. Therefore, when placing puppies, they try to match the personality of the puppy with that of the prospective new owner. They try to be of assistance in the event of any problems, encourage the use of crates, and basic obedience. Because of this care and their policy, they have had very few dogs returned to be placed in new homes.

Recently a new dimension has been added to the Danica Samoyed activities. Several bags of fur have been spun into luxurious yarn. Their logo is now completed, with the Sam pup of real Samoyed fur. Judy has a vest, and a scarf is the next project.

After 11 years, the Kovitches bred their third Samoyed generation. It is their hope that, as they have done in the past, they will

Ch. Nordic's Kameo of Windsong, Hotshot's dam, owned by Mary Kistner and Charlotte Koehler.

continue in the future to improve with each generation. Danica is the Russian word for "Morning Star," and it has symbolized a bright side to the lives of these folks. Showing and breeding have led them to travel to places they would never have seen otherwise, and to meet many people whom they would never have known. It is their aim to give each of the dogs as much in return as the joy these lovely Samoyeds have given to them.

FROSTYACRES

Frostyacres Samoyeds, owned by Karen McFarlane, Kearney, Missouri, officially came into existence with the purchase of Champion Karalot's Hotshot of Windsong as a two-and-a-half-year-old finished champion, and then almost immediately purchased Champion Frostyacres I've Been Samkist (the first of the Bark Star progeny at Frostyacres). They became the foundation Samoyeds for the McFarlanes, and through their three breedings have produced an entire new line.

Champion Karalot's Hotshot of Windsong was a very unique type of Samoyed. He was known for the excellence of his head quality, and for the single tracking rears that he consistently threw in his progeny. He was used very sparingly at stud, but still managed to be in the Top Ten Sires during 1982, *Canine Chronicle*, *Kennel Review*, and *Samoyed Quarterly* ratings.

That same year Champion Frostyacres I've Been Samkist, "Cricket," was tied with her grandmother at first place for Top Brood Bitch.

Hotshot himself became a multiple Group placer. He produced many Group placing and Group winning offspring, including the Hotshot-Cricket daughter, American and Canadian Champion Frostyacres Noel to Westwind, owned by Tim Malueg; in addition to his Best in Show son, American, Canadian, and Bermudian Champion Karalot's Jak Frost of Westwind. Jak Frost, in turn, produced Champion Windsong's Jak Pot O'Pomirish, who is presently one of the leading sires in the breed.

Hotshot also has a Best in Show brother, Champion Windsong's Yankee Doodle Daddi, and a multiple Best in Show grandson, Champion Risuko's Mister Moonlight. Frostyacres now has a Champion Windsong's Jak Pot O'Pomirish son, Champion Frostyacres Dbl Eko O'Westwind, from Champion Frostyacres Noel to Westwind, who is linebred on the Frostyacres line.

Champion Frostyacres I've Been Samkist is the first of the three puppies from Ima Bark Star. She is the dam of many champions and Group winning Sams, and is herself a Group placer and Specialty Show winner, including a Merit Award at the 1982 National, and first in the Brood Bitch Class that same year. She spent most of her time in the whelping box, leaving the show biz to her famous litter sister, Champion Moonlighter's Spark of Bark, the Group winning multiple Specialty Best of Breed winner, Best of Opposite Sex at the National Specialty and the Best of Breed from the Veterans Class at the 1985 National. Cricket was very dominant as a producer of correct type. One of her loveliest daughters was Champion Frostyacres Carbon Classic who was by American and Canadian Champion Kristik's English Autumn.

Mrs. McFarlane's second "Bark Star" progeny is Champion Sugarok Kismet O'Frostyacres, co-owned with Linda Marden. Kismet is from Champion Kipperic Sugarok Margaritka who is a Kandi-Anoka daughter. Keeping in the tradition of crossing the Hotshot and Bark Star lines, Kismet was bred to Hotshot's brother, Best in Show winning Champion Windsong's Yankee Doodle Daddi.

The third, and last, of the Bark Star sons came to Mrs. McFarlane from Kondako Samoyeds in California. He is Champion Kandako's Bzy Brk O'Frostyacres, who finished his championship in keen competition at the Greater Milwaukee Samoyed Specialty. Already there is a lovely daughter of his out of Frostyacres Ima Moonlighter (Ch. Cricket and Ch. Quicksilver's Razz Ma Tazz).

GREY GHOST

Grey Ghost Samoyeds are owned by Wayne and Janet Heffington at Saline, Michigan.

From the very beginning, the Heffingtons set eight as the maximum number of Samoyeds they could personally love and care for at optimum. Under this system these dogs have survived and thrived on an intense program stressing health, quality, and sincere follow-up to monitor development and quality of adopted offspring since the kennel was started in 1970.

The Heffingtons are not "unilateral" breeders, basing most of their breeding program on one or two generations all descended from one favored stud. As Janet Heffington remarks, "Such practice has been beneficial to our breed at certain times in certain areas, but we ourselves have been multi-generation breeders, carefully tracing our gene-pool and solidifying desired characteristics, mainly through aunt-nephew and uncle-niece breedings." The success of this method speaks for itself, as Grey Ghost quality is now represented by 27 champions through eight generations. A handful of these Sams have become, as well, the foundation for several current breeder-exhibitors; but the interest of the Heffingtons has actually centered around breeding top quality "pets"!

Easily 90% of the Grey Ghost puppies are placed into pet homes—neutered and obedience trained—as the Heffingtons council each family. To achieve their goal of making their Sams "Ambassadors of the breed," each puppy within a litter costs no more than any one of the litter mates. Thus every puppy is available to every family on reservation. The pups are selected for each family by personality and desired characteristics rather than by quality or affordability. So an "easy champion" is neutered; instead of sitting in a kennel being seen only at dog shows, that pet is walked, taken on family outings and vacations, etc. The public will thus see what quality Sams are like in behavior and appearance. And others learn how to find a similar specimen when looking for a pet.

In 1982, at the huge Detroit Kennel Club show, of the 40 Samoyeds entered, Grey Ghost produced the largest turnout for a single breeder entry in Sam history for that important show. Four of their own and nine "pets"—all under the Grey Ghost banner and display, two of them American and Canadian Champions including the seven-year-old Best of Breed winner that day; and five others who since have become foundation stock, of whom four have now also earned their titles.

Although the Heffingtons work diligently with novices such as those mentioned above who are entering showing and breeding, they still prefer to recommend spaying and neutering. For many years they offered rebates on the operation's costs to encourage public acceptance of this practice. So well was this accomplished that when, in the mid-1970's they encountered a genetic predisposition to sub-aortic stenosis, upon contacting all owners of siblings to the affected dogs, they discovered that 90% of all females and nearly 50% of all males purchased from Grey Ghost had been neutered. The Heffingtons likewise neutered the few they had who were potential carriers, and by relying on their pedigree work, any great familiarity of their own gene pool eradicated the problem within one generation.

In the mid-1970's, Janet became an A.K.C. licensed handler. She has now had a top-ranked Chow Chow and a three years top-ranked Pomeranian, but she and Wayne have never felt that any one of their Sams deserved that much more than any of the others, to campaign one or another of them to a "top spot." Instead they find it preferable to work with all their Sams as a team. They even trained and exhibited some of them in Malamute Club sponsored weight-pulls.

Years ago, when the Heffingtons became aware that dog fanciers were becoming persecuted, they became determined to make the Grey Ghost Samoyeds something in which the community could take pride, as well as to introduce to the public the magnificence and purpose of the Samoyed breed. In the name of their dogs, they became active participants, sponsors and financial supporters of local and country-wide activities. Teams, clubs, and fund raisers were organized. Also a bill was lobbied into Michigan law, the intent of which is to protect the health and stability of pets offered through pet retailers. Michigan was only the second state to enact such legislation. Two dozen other states now have used the Michigan law as a pattern.

Janet and Wayne's greatest pride has been their all-Champion Sled Team, whose appearance was always commanded for local parades, and which became the highlight of the Jaycees Annual "Happiness Fair" for mentally and emotionally retarded children.

The ultimate goal has just recently been achieved when Janet

Am. and Can. Ch. Jac-Lin's Tibrand of Grey Ghost, foundation stud for Grey Ghost Samoyeds, winning Best of Breed at Lima, Ohio in 1974. At age 10½ years, he won the Greater Milwaukee Samoyed Fanciers Specialty. Bred by Jack Aldred. Owned and handled by the Heffingtons.

Ch. Silvertips Snow-Mac Heritage, by Am. and Can. Ch. Shaloom of Draya-lene ex Am. and Can. Ch. Silvertips Dixie Fascination. The foundation bitch for Heritage Samoyeds, owned by Nelda and T. J. Dendinger, Dr. Erv and Phoebe Faulmann, Gainesville, Florida.

received American Kennel Club approval to judge Samoyeds, already enjoying several large record-setting and quality filled assignments, even during her provisional period.

HERITAGE

Heritage Samoyeds are owned by Phoebe Castle Faulmann, who acquired her first of the breed in 1971 while she was still living in Mississippi. Now the kennel is located in Gainesville, Florida, where Phoebe contemplates the fact that she has bred or owned 30 champions.

The first Samoyed was quite definitely pet type; but Phoebe loved her anyway, and together they become the best of friends while completing an obedience class together.

In 1973, Phoebe decided that she would like to try breeding this bitch. It was suggested that she contact Nelda and T. J. Dendinger regarding the possibility of doing so and an appointment was made for the Dendingers to come see her. Their recommendation was not to breed her, but to get a real nice bitch or two specifically for breeding since by then Phoebe was enthusiastic at the prospect of doing so. From the Dendingers during the next year, Sister and Jenny were purchased, who became Champion Silvertips Dixie Heritage and Champion Silvertips Snow-Mac Heritage. These two bitches together have produced a total of about one dozen champion progeny, very definitely leaving their mark on Heritage Kennels and on the breed.

For the first breedings of these two girls, Champion Nachalnik of Draylene, known as Chief, was selected. By him Sister produced three champions: these included an International Champion, a Mexican Best in Show winner, and a Group winning bitch. Eventually Sister produced six champions, with two more daughters not yet shown.

Jenny, with Chief, produced three champions from a litter of four. Among these was Champion Heritage Chien Blanc, who won the Samoyed Club of America Puppy Dog Sweepstakes at the 1975 Specialty, then was Reserve Winners the following day from the junior puppy class over 60 dogs. He finished quickly; then his show career ended as his owner really wanted him principally as a companion. Another of Jenny's puppies, Canadian Champion Heritage Chief Tonka, was purchased by Ruby Orr in Canada and is now behind many of her principal winners, while Champion

Heritage Portrait of Jenny was the Samoyed Club of America's third Top Winning Bitch for 1975 with wins scored from the puppy classes. Now Jenny also has become the dam of six champions, plus three additional progeny in the ring who should finish with ease.

With Sister and Jenny and the puppies from her first two litters, Phoebe was all set to really embark on her breeding program. She has kept the Drayalene line active in her own bloodline, combining it with Silveracres' stud dogs, who have seemed to work out especially well with her bitches. As she points out, the majority of her first 25 champions were sired by one or the other of the Silveracres' sires. One of the outstanding examples of this success is Champion Relska's Dixie Heritage, by Champion Silveracres Trademark from Jenny, which gave her Heritage's first homebred Group winner.

Phoebe Faulmann is a lady who places great emphasis on the importance of the bitches. Early in the game she became quite impressed with Champion Silveracres Charm and American and Canadian Champion Kipperic Kando of Suruka Orr. So she is especially pleased at having a Charm great-grandson, Champion Silveracres Mac Heritage, and a Kandi kid, Champion Kipperic K.C. Heritage, two boys which have also produced well.

When asked which one, structurally, she considers her favorite of the bitches she has owned, Phoebe's reply is Champion Devonshire's Cameo Av Cloud, whom she purchased from Jan Russel after seeing her at the 1977 National in Detroit. Cameo is the dam of four champions.

Phoebe Faulmann has never cared much for pushing a big specials career on a dog. She is more interested in class competition, showing puppies, and taking them to their titles. Her favorites? Puppy bitches.

All of the Heritage dogs are personally handled by their owner; also sometimes Phoebe handles for others if they are dogs she has bred or are sired by her stud dogs.

Recently Phoebe has re-married, becoming Mrs. Faulmann. Her husband this time is one who likes dogs (Phoebe learned about that in her previous marriage), and is quite contented to share their home with some 14 Samoyeds and half a dozen or so Chihuahuas. When Phoebe was 22 years of age, she started showing Samoyeds. As is the case with most of us who truly love and enjoy our dogs "for the pleasure of their company," her lifestyle has been shaped around them.

ILLUSION

Illusion Samoyeds are owned by Arlene Heffler at Crystal Lake, Illinois. This is a very small hobby kennel which was established during the late 1960's and which has actually produced only four litters for a total of 17 puppies. What has been limited in quantity has surely made up for that fact by the amount of quality, however, as one can see from show achievements and obedience credits.

American and Canadian Champion Silvermist's Winter Blizzard, C.D.X., is a notable member of this kennel. "Stormi" was the Hefflers' first show dog, who started collecting points as a puppy with a Best of Breed from the classes at only 11 months old. He was shown in both conformation and obedience and completed his American championship and C.D. degree in a four-week span, attending just five shows. Stormi won a *Dog World* Award for his C.D. having been completed in just three trials with scores of 195 and above on each occasion, and completed again, in only three trials, placing in the Open A Class at each. He won many High Samoyed and Champion of Record Awards at trials, but his career in obedience was summed up at the North Shore Obedience Club Trial where he was in the Veterans Obedience Class at 9+ years of age and took first place with a score of 199½ (from a possible 200).

Stormi is the sire of the only brother-sister Tracking Title Samoyeds to his owners' knowledge. They are Celestial Storm Sirius, C.D., T.D.; and Celestial Storm Grand F'nale, C.D., T.D.

Stormi was 12½ years of age when he died but sired his best puppy when he was almost 12.

Illusion's Storm Revelation, known as Emilee, by Winter Blizzard from White Hope's Grand Illusion, owner-handled by Arlene Heffler, has not been shown extensively although she obviously has tremendous promise. She is one of only a handful of living Stormi puppies as he was close to 12 years old when she was born. It is an interesting side note that she was bred by artificial insemination, and that she was the only puppy in the litter born by C-section and entirely hand raised, her dam having been lost when the puppy was three days old. Arlene comments, "she is probably the closest thing one can get to a 'test tube puppy.'"

Champion Celestial's Optical Illusion, C.D., by Champion Gentle Giant of Snowcountry ex Celestial Stormi Grand F'nale, C.D., T.D., known to friends as "Isaac," is a Stormi grandson who started winning the moment his nine-and-a-half-week-old self hit the show rings. His owner comments, "It amazes me how puppies that young, ears not even up, can still show their little hearts out." At age six-and-a-half months he gained his first points, and completed his championship just ten months later, going through to Best of Breed over specials at the same time. Sad to say, Arlene Heffler lost this splendid dog at a mere eight years of age, which I am sure was heartbreaking for her.

Champion Illusion's Velvet Rose and Champion Illusion's Mystic Traveller were littermates by Champion Totala's Wizard of Celter ex Ch. Luv 'N Fun's Winter Illusion. They are homebreds. The male of these two, Mystic Traveller (called Eli) is a multiple Best of Breed winner and a multiple Group placing champion. Still very immature, big things are hoped for from him as he does display tremendous promise.

JUBILLIE

Jubillie Samoyeds are the result of Carol and Andy Hjort, who, in their early 20's and living in Tennessee, purchased their first Samoyed as a pet in December 1975. They were so pleased with the breed that they decided they would like to have more; and so a good quality bitch was sought out who could perhaps someday be used for breeding. One of their priorities was to locate a bloodline which was linebred, stable, and consistently producing healthy animals with good temperament.

The Hjorts purchased their foundation bitch, Kobe's Jubilee of Encino, in 1977 from the Kobe of Encino bloodlines of Mrs. Margaret (Billy) Tucker, a breeder with 40 years' experience in successfully breeding outstanding Sams. The Kobe of Encino line combined many of Agnes Mason's best White Way champions and sled dogs combined with imports from the noted Kobe Kennels of England.

Jubillie was selected as their kennel name by the Hjorts in 1979, combining the name of their foundation bitch, Jubilee, with that of "Billy" Tucker as a tribute to the lady who had bred her.

In 1979 the Hjorts chose as the foundation sire for their kennel the handsome Champion Kondako's Sun Dancer, owned by Dave and Connie Richardson in California. Sun Dancer was a two-time Specialty winner, a Group winner, and a Top Producer for the breed who brought in the Drayalene and Silver Moon lines, balancing out Jubilee with both substance and frosting. Today all of the Samoyeds with the Jubillie prefix carry these two Sams behind them in their pedigrees.

Another male who has had beneficial influence on the Jubillie breeding program is a Sun Dancer grandson, American and Canadian Champion Moonlighter's Ima Bark Star, owned by Wayne and Jeanne Nonhof of Wisconsin. "Bark" is a five time Specialty winner, a Best in Show winner, and in 1984 became an all time Top Producer for the breed. The Hjorts bred their Sun Dancer-Jubilee daughter (Jubillie's Native Dancer) to him in 1982 (a nephew/aunt linebreeding on Champion Kondako's Sun Dancer) and in doing so developed a strain consisting of nine consecutive generations of Group or Best in Show winners, nine consecutive generations of Top Producers, and six consecutive generations of Specialty winners.

Jubillie Samoyeds have been located in three different states—Tennessee, New Jersey, and Michigan—since their inception, and will soon relocate again due to a transfer by Andy's company, Du Pont. Since the Hjorts are always likely to be transferred, they have made it a point to avoid "fad" breeding to styles that are popular only in particular areas of the country. Carol and Andy feel that the "living art" of striving to breed a better show dog is a challenging, interesting and sometimes frustrating hobby. But with persistence, hard work and good luck, they hope to remain successful in the years ahead.

KENDARA

Kendara Samoyeds, owned by Mary A. Frederick at West Chicago, Illinois, have some very outstanding dogs and bitches in which to take pride for their quality and for their achievements.

The list is headed by American and Canadian Champion Kendara's Tora Togiak, by Kendara's Winter Lion ex Bell of Brierbrook. "Togie" is the sire of eight American and six Canadian Champions, plus the only "search and rescue" dog, Champion Kendara's Tops of White Thunder, C.D., T.D., in the history of

Jubillie's Mystical Maverick, born January 1985, pictured winning at age nine months. Bred by Ron and Judi Schold; owned by Carol and Andy Hjort, Jubillie Samoyeds, Temperance, Michigan.

Left: Ch. Celestial Optical Illusion, C.D., by Ch. Gentle Giant of Snowcountry ex Celestial Stormi Grand F'nale, C.D., T.D., bred by Anne Copeland. Owned by Arlene Heffler, Illusion Samoyeds. *Right:* Ch. Kendara's Most Happy Fella, by Ch. Rob's Frost Sam of Caribou ex Hazel and Ken's Hello Dolly.

this breed, we are told.

"Togie" also numbers among his progeny American and Canadian Champion Czartu of Kendaraland, Champion Kendara's Frederick The Great (sire of Group-winning offspring), American and Canadian Champion Dajmozek's Tavaresh O'Kendara, American U.D. and Canadian C.D.X.; American and Canadian Champion Czartu of Kendaraland; and American and Canadian Champion Kendara's Czarina of Taiga.

The first homebred champion at this kennel is Champion Kendara's Most Happy Fella.

Then there is Champion Kendara's Star Dustin of Kobe, by Champion Kendara's Hundred Proof ex Edan's Ms. Boo Jangles. This splendid dog is the sire of the youngest Group winning puppy bitch, owned and handled by Jean Yeskey, Champion Gem-Mar's Charm of Jasmine, who carried off Group 1 at exactly four days past six months' age, this her first dog show.

The newest bright star is a puppy bitch, Kendara's Scheherazade, who placed Group 2nd at Chicago International when six-and-a-half months old.

KIPPERIC

Kipperic Samoyeds are owned by Don and Dot Hodges of Poynette, Wisconsin, where a male puppy, registered as Ku Techi and known as "Kip," was purchased for companionship and obedience competition by the Hodges in 1966. This was their first Samoyed.

Kip began attending obedience trials a couple of years later, and while the Hodges showed him in obedience, their interest in conformation competition was growing.

Two more Samoyeds joined the Hodges's household before long, Astro of Rivido J and Asta of Rivido J, and in 1968, after completion of Kip's C.D., the Hodges entered the conformation ring for the first time.

Beginners' luck, to quote the Hodges, bestowed a Best of Breed, a Group 1st, and a close encounter with Best in Show on the Hodges's entry that day. Needless to say, they immediately were "hooked" on "this conformation stuff," and within six months they had a new champion, several Bests of Breed, and a couple of additional Group placements.

In 1970 two bitch puppies were purchased: Kipparic Kandu of

Suruka Orr and Kipparic D'Lite of Frost River. They were to be the foundation for a breeding program carefully planned by the Hodges, following travels around the country to a lot of kennels and dog shows. The first Kipperic litter was whelped in 1972.

Because of the rather auspicious start they had made in conformation competition, the Hodges have quite heavily slanted their Samoyed activities and interests in that direction, with an eye on Best of Breed, Group and Best in Show levels. Obviously, if one is to pursue these goals, one must first complete championships. But the emphasis at Kipperic has been on showing to championship only those dogs believed by them to have some important contribution to make to the breed, dogs who would not just make another champion, but who have potential for higher goals.

As testimony to their success, it is a matter of record that of the 28 champions owned or bred by the Hodges, 14 have competed successfully against other champions in Best of Breed competition; 10 have placed in the Working Group (five of these having Group 1sts); and two have won Best in Show at both All-Breed events and National Specialties. Three of the Kipperic Samoyeds have had at least 50 Bests of Breed, all three of these having placed in one or more rating systems for Top Winning Samoyeds in the United States.

American and Canadian Champion Kipperic Kandu of Suruka Orr, C.D. won Best of Breed at the National Specialty in 1973, which had 243 Sams in competition. Subsequently she won two all-breed Bests in Show, and was Top Winning Samoyed in the United States under all systems for 1974. The Hodges tell us that no other female Samoyed in the history of the breed had equalled this record.

Even though the Hodges have not emphasized completion of large numbers of champions, one of their foundation bitches, Champion Kipperic Kandu of Suruka Orr, C.D., in addition to her show ring successes did receive the Kennel Review Award as #1 Top Producer in the breed and #3 (which was a tie) Top Producer in the Working Group in 1980, based on number of champion progeny in one year. Altogether she produced five champions including a Group winner.

The Hodges's other foundation bitch, Champion Kipperic D'Lite of Frost River, C.D., also produced a Group winner and four champions. Many second generation descendants of these two Sams have also achieved championships, Group wins and Group placements. Additionally, eight Samoyeds owned or bred by the Hodges have gained C.D. degrees in the obedience ring.

The emphasis the Hodges have placed on the Best of Breed competition area has resulted in a special niche for their kennel, which can claim National Specialty and all-breed Best in Show wins on two different Samoyeds. They are additionally proud of the fact that four of those five wins came owner-handled.

KRISKELLA

Kriskella Samoyeds, owned by Geoff and Brenda Abbot at Pine, Colorado, had their start in 1978, although the first breeding did not take place until 1980. Between 1972 and 1977, Brenda had owned-handled to championship two male Samoyeds, Champion Silveracres Bronco Beobear and Champion Silveracres Sunshine Boy.

It was in 1978 that Geoff and Brenda purchased the five-month-old puppy bitch who was to become Champion Blue Sky's No Options (by Champion Sulu's Mark of Distinction ex Champion Blue Sky's Honey Bun) and the foundation dam of Kriskella. While several stud dogs have contributed to the Kriskella breeding program, over half of all puppies carrying this kennel name are descended from Champion Silveracres Sunshine Boy, and he and his progeny figure very strongly in the future linebreeding plans.

Sunshine Boy has been bred to six different bitches and has sired 18 show age puppies. He has produced four A.K.C. champions with four others major-pointed. In addition, three have obedience titles.

For three different litters, Sunshine Boy was the stud selected by Mary Jo and Doug Ragsdale to whom their bitch, Champion Tushina Snow Star was bred. That particular combination "clicked" for quality every time.

A Sunshine Boy son, Kriskella's Adam Up Again, C.D., was the winner of the first Sled Dog Class held at a Samoyed Club of America National Specialty, this in 1982.

Champion Blue Sky's No Options produced only a total of eight offspring by four sires between 1980 and 1983. She is the dam of Champion Kriskella's Peg O' My Heart, Champion Kriskella's

Ch. Gebaa Sun-Dee of Kipperic, by Ch. Nordic's Wynter Sunniglo (Best in Show winner) ex Ch. Kipperic D'Lite of Frost River, C.D., bred by the Hodges, now owned by Anne Koffenberger and the Hodges. Sun-Dee also has two Group-placing sons.

Ch. Blue Sky's No Options, by Ch. Sulu's Mark of Distinction ex Ch. Blue Sky's Honey Bun. Geoff and Brenda Abbott, owners.

Melody of Carlar and three other major- or minor-pointed young-sters. Two of her sons have earned obedience degrees. Her daughter, Kriskella's Wild Irish Rose, when bred to a Sunshine Boy son (Champion Evenstar's Earendil) produced Kriskella's Tatiana, who was Reserve Winners Bitch at the 1985 National Specialty and is now nearly finished. Champion Kriskella's Peg O' My Heart, when bred to her cousin Champion Blue Sky's Breaking Away, produced Kriskella's Run For The Roses who at age 18 months has three major wins towards her championship.

From the very beginning, the Kriskella Samoyeds have been sledding show dogs. In the winter of 1979, Geoff Abbott drove the top OWS (Organization for the Working Samoyed) Sled Team, composed of champions, a pet quality Samoyed, and one mixed breed bitch who was just a house pet. This oddly assorted team, led by Champion Sunshine Boy, competed on sheer heart, guts and enthusiasm; there was nothing scientific or even planned about the make-up of this team. Then followed a few years of planned breedings and the development of the Abbotts' "own" ideal dual purpose Samoyed. Puppies were chosen and sled training developed some continuity from year to year.

Finally, in 1984, this time with an entirely purebred team of Samoyeds, Geoff Abbott again drove the Top OWS Sled Team. This team has the added distinction of also winning the first Samoyed Club of America Award offered for a top sled team. This team also ranked 55th of the 186 mixed breed and purebred (Siberian Husky) teams, earning the ISDRA (International Sled Dog Racing Association) points that season at sanctioned races. To the Abbotts' knowledge, no other Samoyed team has ever achieved a ranking this high in the sled dog racing world.

The future breeding plans of Kriskella will involve a blend of the lines represented by their two foundation dogs with occasional outcrossings to other fine animals.

MITHRIL

Mithril Samoyeds came into being in March 1973 with the purchase (by Frances E. Trojan and her family, Wisconsin Dells, Wisconsin) of a three-month-old puppy bitch who was destined to become Gimli Mithril Cotton, C.D., and the foundation of Mithril. Although Gimli's first litter, sired by Crystal Snow, pro-

60

duced their first Companion Dog, Gimli's Snow Shadow, C.D. and their first Champion-Companion Dog, Champion Conan Mithril, C.D., neither were used for breeding.

Gimli's two other litters were sired by American and Canadian Champion Moonlighter's Ima Bark Star. These litters produced five U.S. champions, a Canadian champion, three Companion Dog titlists, and a registered Therapy Dog. Champion Mithril's Star of Keledzaram (Kheli), Champion Mithril's Star of Earendil, C.D. (Randi), and American/Canadian Champion Desertsnos Mithril Star, C.D. These have formed the nucleus for the future of Mithril Samoyeds.

Kheli was bred to Champion Kondako's Sun Dancer, Silveracres Nachalnik, Champion Kolinka's Quilted Bear, and twice to Champion K-Way's Omen of Destiny, C.D.X. From these breedings came American and Canadian Champion Mithril's Mirror of Celebrant (Sun Dancer), who was a multiple Group-placing male; Mithril's Gilgalad, and Mithril's Sunshine Destiny (Omen), Best Puppy and Reserve Winners Dog at the 1985 Manitoba Specialty.

American and Canadian Champion Mithril's Polar Prince II (Sun Dancer), a Group winner and Specialty Best of Winners, and Mithril's Cherbu of Indian Valley went to Jerry and Carolyn Golias, Monticello, Illinois, where they have formed the foundation for Indian Valley Samoyeds.

Champion Kolinka's Kelsey of Mithril, Best Puppy at the 1983 Samoyed Club of America National Specialty, is co-owned by M. Baird and Joyce Curtis at Phoenix, Arizona. American and Canadian Champion Mithril's Rio Di Janeiro (by Omen), 1984 Samoyed Club of America National Specialty Grand Sweepstakes winner and 1984 Manitoba Samoyed Specialty Winners Bitch, went to Pat and Gary Griffin, Lakeville, Minnesota, to be the foundation bitch for their Millcreek Samoyeds.

Mithril Cheers Samtara On (by Omen) has gone to Kathy Kersten, Green Bay, Wisconsin, where it is hoped she will become the foundation bitch for Kathy to help carry on the Samtara Kennel name.

Mithril Hart of the Woods (by Omen), first in the 6-9 Puppy Dog Class at the 1984 Samoyed Club of America National, is owned by Kathy Carr of Rockford, Illinois, and has been bred to that owner's 1985 Samoyed Club National Specialty Winners Bitch, Champion Moonlighter's Krystal Image.

Randi was bred to Champion K-Way's Omen of Destiny, C.D.X., American and Canadian Champion Mithril's Mirror of Celebrant (Kheli son), and Champion Kipperic K.C. Heritage. Due to a serious bout with pyometria, Randi's breeding potential was diminished so far as quantity is concerned, but the Trojans feel that the quality will be of importance to future breeding programs. Three bitches, one from each litter, remain at Mithril: American and Canadian Champion Mithril's Ninquelote (Omen), who was Winners Bitch at the 1983 Manitoba Specialty; Mithril's Baranduin O'Caebryn (Brant), pointed in both the United States and Canada; and Champion Mithril's Star of Elendil (K.C.). Mithril's Lady of the Snows, C.D., by Brant, is owned by Sandy Elam of Atlanta, Georgia.

American and Canadian Champion Desertsnos Mithril Star, C.D., who was Winners Dog and Best of Winners at the 1983 Manitoba Samoyed Specialty, has sired two litters at Mithril. The first, from Kipperic White Lilacs (a Silveracres Nachalnik daughter), produced KUSA Champion Americ of Caebryn, owned by Irene Rowe of Harare in Zimbabwe, Africa; Ch. Americ was once Top Sledge Puppy for South Africa, is a Group winner, and has numerous additional Group placements in South Africa and in Zimbabwe. He now has begun his show career in Zambia, where he is placing in group competition.

From the above litter, Mithril's Blue Star has gone to Randy and Kathie Lensen, Cascade, Wisconsin, to be part of their My Way Samoyeds.

A second litter by American and Canadian Champion Desertsnos Mithril Star, C.D., this one from American and Canadian Champion Ninquelote, produced three youngsters who, it is felt, will be of consequence to the future. They are Mithril's Anduril O'Luin and Mithril's Belthil O'Luin, both owned at Mithril; and Mithril's Satin Starr, co-owned with Jane Huff, Sciota, Illinois.

Ninquelote, who is a Randi daughter, whelped a litter of eight on February 25, 1986 for Mithril's first *third* generation litter based on their original Bark Star-Gimli breeding. Time will tell what the future holds in store for them!

The goal at Mithril has from the beginning been to produce top quality Samoyeds by breeding dogs of compatible bloodlines, at the same time being willing to share what they consider their best with other fanciers.

Ch. Desertsno's Mithril Star, C.D., born June 1978, by Ch. Moonlighter's Ima Bark Star ex Gimli Mithril Cotton, C.D. Owned by Tim and Frances Trojan, Wisconsin Dells, Wisconsin.

MY WAY

My Way Samoyeds, which are owned by Kathie and Randy Lensen and situated at Cascade, Wisconsin, began in 1976 with the purchase of a puppy from the Nonhofs. It was the Lensens' first encounter with the world of purebred dogs and show dogs. They waited several years for their first puppy because they had concentrated very hard on choosing just the right one from the many Sammy breeders in their area.

Huggi Bear, as he was called, was his new owners' "learn on it dog." He became their first champion and first Group winner, all owner-handled. His patience and love of the show life is still with him at almost ten years' age. He will never be replaced, but his sons and daughters carry on his love of life. Officially Champion Moonlighters Ima Huggi Bear, this handsome dog is a son of Eng-

Ch. My Way's Lil Bit O'Frosty Acres, by Ch. Karalot's Hot Shot of Windsong ex Ch. Frosty Acres I've Been Samkist. Owned by My Way Samoyeds, Kathie and Randy Lensen, Cascade, Wisconsin.

lish, Canadian, and American Champion Delmonte This Is It from Champion Moonlighter's Ice 'N Spice. He was bred by Wayne and Jeanne Nonhof, is a multi-breed winner with many Group wins and placements, and his owners have never for one moment regretted the time that they spent waiting for just the right puppy!

While Kathie Lensen learned on Huggi Bear, a puppy bitch was acquired from the Sunkist Kennels of Sharon Kremsreiter for Randy to play with. Sparkle did a great deal more than play, and has truly become My Way Samoyeds' "claim to fame." She is Champion Moonlighter's Ima Spark 'O Bark, she is a daughter of American and Canadian Champion Moonlighter's Ima Bark Star ex Champion Samkist's Classy Chassis, and she was bred by Sharon Kremsreiter. A Top Winning Bitch, she has multiple Group wins and placements to her credit. Plus Best of Breed at the Greater Milwaukee Samoyed Specialty in 1982, Chicago-Land Samoyed Fanciers Specialty 1984, Samoyed Club of America National Specialty from the Veterans Class in 1985—not to mention Best of Opposite Sex at the National Specialty in 1983.

All of Sparkle's wins have been owner-handled except for one, the latter due to Randy's dislike of flying. Her first time in the ring, at age six months, she won Best in Sweepstakes at the Greater Milwaukee Samoyed Fanciers Specialty.

Needless to say, Sparkle is Queen of the Lensen household.

Others of the My Way family include Champion Mauyak's English Star of My Way, known as B.J., a multi-Best of Breed winner who was bred by Elaine Valentine; and Champion My Way's Lil Bit O'Frosty Acres.

All of the Samoyeds at My Way are owner-handled, as the Lensens' principal emphasis is placed on their enjoyment so far as being in competition is concerned. They have done occasional breeding, more, recently, than in the past. And they now anticipate more enjoyment in the future from showing in the "Bred-by" class. Their goal is to produce sound working dogs that maintain the breed type and look and function as true Samoyeds, with special emphasis on maintaining that sweet Sammy temperament.

NORTH STARR

North Starr Samoyeds have, since the mid-1960s, been a busy and rewarding hobby for Dr. Robert J. and Mrs. Patricia Hritzo, and their family, in Hubbard, Ohio.

Through breeding and showing dogs, they have come in contact and formed lasting friendships with interesting people from many other countries as well as from all over the United States. Breeding has been a continuing challenge to achieve perfection in their Samoyeds, while exhibiting has provided a level of competition that rivals any major league sport.

The Hritzos first Samoyed, Ch. King Olaf's Ivory Katrina, was purchased as a family pet. While training her for obedience work, the Hritzos were introduced to the conformation ring. When Trina easily finished a C.D. degree and became North Starr's first champion, her owners were bitten by the proverbial bug and began seriously applying themselves to the betterment of the breed and the quest for blue ribbons.

They kept that "special" puppy, who grew up to become Ch. Kalamara of the North Starr, from Trina's only litter. In turn, Mara produced, from her single litter, the Hritzos' foundation bitch, Group-placing American and Canadian Champion Archangel of the North Starr. She became the #6 AKC Top Producing Bitch of All Breeds in 1973 and the Top Producing Samoyed Bitch in the history of the breed, with 17 AKC and ten foreign championship titles for her puppies and with both Best in Show children and grandchildren to her credit. More than that, Angel was always the loving and unchallenged head of the North Starr herd.

In order to expand their breeding program, the Hritzos next purchased Karelia, a four-month-old bitch from the West Coast. Due to an unfortunate accident, she died at two-and-a-half years of age with 12 championship points including both majors; but not before giving her owners a litter of three champions out of four puppies, including the great American and Canadian Champion North Starr King's Ransom, an all-time stand-out in the breed.

Ransom earned his championship as a puppy in eight shows, handled by then ten-year-old Kathy Hritzo. He finished with three majors and two Bests of Breed over specials. He was first shown primarily as a Junior Showmanship dog, hopelessly out of coat on many occasions before his owners learned about campaigning a special. He went on to win ten Bests in Show (All-Breeds); a Samoyed Specialty; and 85 Group placements, including 43 combined Working/Herding Group Firsts. Ransom was the first Samoyed in more than 20 years to place in the Top Ten Working Dogs in the United States, being #5 two years in a row.

Ransom was also a consistent producer of exceptional quality puppies, a sire of 33 champions to date from a total of 99 puppies. These include four Best in Show winners, nine Group winners, and two Specialty winners, with more pointed get to undoubtedly finish soon.

Together, Ransom and Angel produced the breed's only litter of All-breed Best in Show winners. Their most notable children include the Hritzos fourth-generation Best in Show winner, American and Canadian Champion North Starr's Heir Apparent, a multiple Best in Show and Best in Specialty winner who has produced champion offspring. Blu, as he was known, also won very large Veterans Classes at two Samoyed Club of America National Specialties and, from an entry of 400, was one of two finalists for Best of Breed at the 1983 National. Blu was also one of five Veteran Finalists at *Kennel Review*'s Show Dog of the Year Tournament.

Blu's littermate, Champion North Starr's Heir Line, was sold originally as a pet and was purchased at age five years by Bob and Judy Underwood. In spite of so late a start, Heir Line became a champion with ease, won a Best in Show and a Best in Specialty Show, and has produced another generation of champions.

In Italy, Champion North Starr's Dushka is a Best in Show winner with multiple Best in Show offspring dominating many of the European shows.

In South America, Champion North Starr's Swiss Patrol is an All-breed Best in Show winner and an American, Colombian, and Santo Domingan Champion. North Starr's Bo'sun became the Top Winning Dog in Colombia, after being shown only seven times in the United States, and ranked as #6 Top Winning Samoyed.

Although the Hritzos have never campaigned a specials bitch, they have had four win Group placements from the classes while completing their championship titles.

Since their first puppies were whelped in 1966, the Hritzos have bred 26 litters, and to date 56 champions bear the North Starr prefix, including the current contenders, Champion North Starr's Lucky Break, who is about to embark on his special career in the Midwest with his new owners, Lou and Susan Hoehn; and Santo Domingan and Puerto Rican Champion Stinyhill F'Lar of North Starr, whose Group placements from the Open Class included a first on the Caribbean show circuit. F'Lar is owned by Sr. Jaime Mota of Santo Domingo.

Not only have North Starr dogs produced champions and consistent winners, but they have also provided the companionship and team work necessary for the Hritzo children to achieve in the Junior Showmanship ring. All three of the "younger generation" Hritzos have gained friends and learned sportsmanship and responsibility through the Junior Classes. The culmination of this facet of their dog activities came when Kathy won the Leonard Brumby Memorial Award for first place in the National Junior Showmanship Finals at the Westminster Kennel Club's 100th Anniversary Show.

The Hritzos have shared the pleasure of their Samoyeds with their community while enjoying it themselves. Over the years the dogs have participated in numerous programs for senior citizens and grade school children; the team of nine Samoyeds has delivered Santa Claus in their city's holiday parade; they have competed in weight pulls and in sled races; and they are in demand for "guest appearances" at fashion shows in the Youngstown and Pittsburgh areas.

NOR'WOOD

Nor'Wood Samoyeds were founded in 1980 by Chuck and Lorraine Waldes at River Vale, New Jersey, after they had owned the breed for an eight-year period prior to that time. This is a kennel whose sole purpose is the breeding and showing of Samoyeds.

Major accomplishments include three Champions of Record, two of whom are multiple Group placing dogs. In particular, Champion Nor'Woods White Magic has gained considerable acclaim, having been ranked in the Top Ten nationally (Rutledge System) for his breed. Also he received an Award of Merit at the 1983 National Specialty where he was Winners Dog and Best of Winners, the only dog to defeat him there having been the #1 Samoyed in the History of the Breed.

Nor'Wood Samoyeds are bred "true to the traditional standard" by which is meant that the original or traditional standard was based on the historical function for which the Samoyed was intended. Accordingly, the Samoyed as both a herding and a draft animal must be a medium-sized dog with sufficient bulk and strength to haul, while at the same time displaying enough agility, speed and stamina to enable it to run while herding. To this end, in addition to correctness of structure, movement, eye color and attitude, Nor'Wood as a kennel places special emphasis on the fact that the Samoyed is a medium-sized breed, not to exceed 23½ inches.

Being a small kennel, the Waldes can enjoy showing their dogs, whom they consider to be fun members of the family, while still keeping it strictly a hobby.

ORION

Orion Samoyeds, owned by Jim and Sharon Hurst of Auburn, California, were established in 1967 with the purchase of the first *show* puppy. But the Hursts had owned Sams for several years at that time. It was attending her first dog show "just to look" that triggered Sharon's enthusiasm. She noticed that the dogs in the ring looked far superior to hers, and that despite being A.K.C.

North Starr King's Ransom at ten months. Completed title with three majors and two Bests of Breed over specials in one month. Bred and owned by North Starr Samoyeds.

Ch. Nor'Wood White Magic, Winners Dog and Best of Winners at the Samoyed Club of America National Specialty for 1983. Owned by Chuck and Lorraine Waldes.

registered, the latter was definitely pet type only.

Then the search to find the perfect show puppy got under way. The "find," and eventual purchase, was of future Champion Frost River's Omar of Orion, who joined the Hursts at age three-and-a-half months despite his exceedingly long ears and legs at that gangly stage. It did all come together magnificently later on!

The very first match the Hursts attended with their new purchase resulted in his winning a Group 1st under the noted A.K.C. judge Mrs. Helen Wittrig. This was a source of great amazement to Sharon, who had never before been on the end of a show lead, and had been told just a few days previously that the handler conducting the class which she had joined hoped she was not entered in the match, as she obviously did not have her puppy under control. After receiving a few suggestions on improving her technique, Sharon took the puppy home and *worked*—obviously with good results, from the win she achieved with the puppy so short a time afterwards.

When Omar completed his championship, the Hursts purchased two beautiful bitches from the White Krystal line, plus another from Frost River. All three were bred when ready (combining the Silver Moon, Williwaw, and Snow Ridge heritage) and producing an imposing number of champions, all owner-handled. As breeders, the Hursts point with pride to their having produced the Top Winning Bitch in the Nation over two years consecutively during the early 1970's, Champion Orion's Mishka of Marcomar, and a very high percentage of champions from their various litters.

Orion has owned and/or produced an imposing number more who have gained titles. And in January 1986 they experienced that once-in-a-lifetime thrill of winning their first Best in Show, this with their beautiful, loyal and loving Omi, more formally Champion Sansaka's Omarsun of Orion.

Temperament and soundness, along with correct type, are the breeding aims at Orion. Both dogs and bitches get on well together, and bring an enormous amount of pride and pleasure to their owners.

POLAR MIST

Polar Mist Samoyeds came into being and are located at Libby, Montana, the result of Lynette Hansen having acquired her first

Sam in 1965 as a pet. Interest in the showing aspect of Samoyed ownership gradually grew on her, and in 1971 she made her first important purchase of a show Samoyed, who was to become Champion McKenzie's Polar Mist Nikki. Later a second bitch was purchased, Polar Mist Baerstone Nishka. These two became the foundation for a kennel which now has owned, bred, or co-bred approximately 40 champions, including foreign champions and the dog who is the breed's Top Winning Owner Handled member of the breed to date.

Nishka acquired ten points, including both her majors, but "due to my inexperience," to quote her owner, decided she didn't like dog shows, so was never finished. She did do her bit for the kennel's future, however, when she was bred to Champion Silver Raffles of Misty Way; she produced three champions, one Canadian, the other two American.

Champion McKenzie's Polar Mist Nikki, an inbred bitch doubling up on Champion Rokandi of Drayalene, was bred to Champion Kalmarli's Lord and Master, a combination of Williwaw and Kubla Khan bloodlines. This produced Champion Polar Mist Ain't She Sassy. Three of Sassy's champion daughters are still at Polar Mist. They are American and Canadian Champion Polar Mist Ain't She Foxy, who tied for Top Brood Bitch in 1984 and is the dam of 11 champions with others major pointed, seven of these offspring being Group placers and one having been Best of Winners at the 1984 National Specialty. Another of Sassy's daughters is American and Canadian Champion Polar Mist Ice Vixen, who has done extremely well, starting by winning her puppy class at her very first dog show, the 1982 National, from where she has gone on to become a Group placer, winner of Best of Opposite Sex at two Specialty Shows, and the dam of two champions to date.

Pride of place at Polar Mist must belong to the great, highly successful and much admired American, Canadian, and Bahamian Champion Polar Mist Dr. Pepper, who has become the Top Winning Owner Handled Samoyed in the history of the breed, with a record of 13 Bests in Show, 135 Group placements, and seven Specialty Bests in Show. He is handled by his co-owner, John Ronald, and lives with the Ronalds. Bred at Polar Mist and co-owned by his breeder, Dr. Pepper is by Champion Beleya Sergeant Pepper ex American and Canadian Champion Pepsi Kola of Polar Mist, who was by Champion Silver Raffles of Misty Way ex Polar Mist

Am. and Can. Ch. Polar Mist Ain't She Sassy, by Ch. Kalmarli's Lord N' Master ex Ch. McKenzie's Polar Mist Nikki. Bred and owned by Lynette Hansen, Polar Mist Samoyeds.

Baerstone Nishka from the first litter of Nishka's which produced three champions including Kola and the bitch upon whom Timberline Samoyeds was founded, Champion Polar Mist Ain't She Somethin'.

Champion Polar Mist Ain't She Foxy has been a tremendous asset to Lynette Hansen, producing an all-champion litter by Champion Ice Way's The Ice Breaker, a breeding which was, needless to say, repeated. Now at Polar Mist there is a combination of the two foundation girls in the background, this in the form of American and Canadian Champion Polar Mist Naughty Angel, sired by Dr. Pepper from Champion Polar Mist Heartbreaker who is a daughter of Ain't She Foxy. Angel, by the age of seven months, had become a multi-Group placer. She now has her first litter, sired by her grandsire, Champion Ice Way's Ice Breaker, all show quality puppies, all hopefully destined to follow in the family tradition.

Lynette Hansen has followed a combination of linebreeding, inbreeding and outcrossing. Her goal is a beautiful Samoyed with outstanding movement and maintaining the wonderful disposition and other essential breed traits.

QUICKSILVER

Quicksilver Samoyeds are owned by Danny and Chris Middleton of Houston, Texas, who purchased their first Sam in 1972, two days following their marriage. In fact, as Chris notes, they still have her, at age 14 years. She was just a pet. As so many others have done, the Middletons became interested first in obedience, then from there went into conformation and showing.

Of course the pride of this kennel, and standard bearer of the present day for the Samoyed Fancy, is the justly famous Champion Quicksilver's Razz Ma Tazz, Top Winning Samoyed in the History of the Breed. This splendid homebred dog, who was campaigned under the co-ownership of his breeders, the Middletons and Eugene and Joyce Curtis of Phoenix, Arizona, was handled by Roy Murray. His total list of awards included: 54 All Breed Bests in Show; 141 times Group 1st; 202 Group placements (including the 141 times 1st); 232 times Best of Breed; National Specialty Winner, 1983 and 1984; #1 Working Dog, 1983 and 1984; #2 All Breeds in 1983; #3 All Breeds in 1984; #1 Samoyed in 1983 and 1984, all systems; and Quaker Oats Award Winner, 1983 and 1984.

Born in 1981, by Champion Kolinka's Quilted Bear (Champion K-Way's Omen of Destiny-Ch. Silvercreek's Rustic Charm) from Champion Quicksilver's Lucky Starr (Champion Quicksilver's Red Baron-Champion Silvercreek's Puddin O'Sitkin), "Tazzy" is a fourth generation champion for his breeders-owners, the Middletons.

His son, Champion Kolinka Quicksilver Jazzman, is the fifth generation coming into its own. He is by Tazzy from Champion Kolinka's Crystal Reflection (a litter sister of Quilted Bear). This was an aunt-nephew breeding.

Jazzman is starting out well in his sire's paw prints, being a Best in Show winner; a multiple Group winner; and a two-time National Specialty Award of Merit winner, the latter in 1984 and 1985. Along with the Curtis's Champion Kolinka's Quilted Bear, Best in Show winner, the three boys represent three generations of Best in Show winners.

The Middletons are planning to continue both breeding and showing their Samoyeds, although as Chris says, "for the moment dog activities are on the back burner because we have young children just starting school and that makes travelling every weekend difficult." This is just a temporary situation, however, and you may be sure that once the children are "settled into" their activities, their parents will have their gorgeous Samoyeds back in the ring again.

SAMOYEDS OF SEELAH

Samoyeds of Seelah at Waukee, Iowa, are owned by Merrill and Rowena Evans, by whom they were officially established in 1972 with the purchase of two female Samoyed pups who formed the foundation of their very successful breeding program.

These were Champion Snow Fire's Bo Peep, C.D. and Champion Snow Fire's Miss Muffet, both of whom finished their A.K.C. championship, and who were descended from the bloodlines of White Way and Kobe.

In 1974 Champion Snow Fire's Bo Peep, C.D., was bred to the Samoyed Club of America National Specialty winner, American and Canadian Champion Oakwood Farm's Kari J'Go Diko, and from this litter came the first of the Seelah great show dogs, Champion Di Murdock of Seelah, who was born in December of 1974.

Murdock's powerful movement, unsurpassed beauty, and obviously correct type made him a "once in a lifetime dog." During his show career he established the following winning record: Multiple Best in Show winner; Multiple Specialty winner; Multiple SCA Merit Award winner; SCA Top Winning Dog in 1979 and 1980; 216 Bests of Breed; 100 Group placements; and, in 1982, SCA Top Stud Dog, Sire of Champions.

In 1979, Champion Dor Kei's Pepeta was bred to Murdock, the combination producing Champion Murdock's Marauder of Seelah, who was born on May 22, 1979. In just limited showing during his career, "Bucky," as Marauder is known, has gained the following: 5 Best in Show wins; 168 times Best of Breed; 75 Group placements; Samoyed Club of America Top Winning Dog in 1982; Samoyed Club of America Merit Annual Award winner.

Bucky started his initial show career at age six months on the tough Florida circuit by winning three consecutive 4-point major wins in his first four shows. He completed his A.K.C. championship as a puppy at age nine months.

The original Seelah brood bitch, Champion Snow Fire's Bo Peep, C.D., was named the Samoyed Club of America Top Brood

74

Bitch for 1982 and for 1983.

An unforgettable occasion for the Evans was the Annual Meeting of the Samoyed Club of America in the fall of 1983 when their dogs received a "grand slam" in awards for the calendar year 1982. SCA Top Winning Dog was Bucky; Top Stud Dog, Murdock; Top Brood Bitch, Pepeta; and Merit Award winner, Bucky.

Seelah has now completed title on their newest winner, Champion Dusha's Keno of Seelah, born July 29, 1984. Keno is from their brood bitch Champion Murdock's Mykola of Seelah and Champion Windsong's Jak Pot O'Pomirish. He possesses all the attributes of truly a great Samoyed so excellent as to make his owners feel that in him they have come close to breeding a "perfect" Sammy, distinguished by more handsome head, smiling face, gentle disposition, and show spirit which should make him a future "great."

At Seelah a very carefully controlled breeding program is practiced, providing for only one or two litters to be whelped each year using Murdock and Bucky as their principal sires. Seelah puppies are sold worldwide, including Canada and Mexico. They have produced 22 champions to date from this breeding program.

All of the Sammys at Seelah Kennels are truly *enjoyed* by their owners. The Evans continually show in Iowa and adjacent states throughout the year, concentrating heavily upon the puppies. The "profit" to which their breeding program is directed is towards overall improvement of the breed. Hardly a week ever passes without one of their dogs going to obedience school or to conformation in the show ring.

SANSASKA

Sansaska Samoyeds, owned by Mr. and Mrs. Derek Gitelson at Concord, California, had their beginning in 1970 with the purchase of a Samoyed from the local pet shop. Friends talked them into showing the puppy at matches, where they soon realized that he was a poor breed specimen. But the "dog show bug" had bitten them, and the search was started for a "good one."

In 1972 this search ended at the Kubla Khan Kennels of Pat Morehouse. By Pat they were sent to see a litter from American and Canadian Champion Tsonoqua of Snow Ridge, sired by Champion Sam O'Khan's Kubla Khan, these puppies owned by Margo Gervolstad. The result of this was to be the Gitelsons' pur-

Ch. Norgemar O'Khan's Milka, Winners Bitch at the 1978 Samoyed Club of San Diego Specialty. She is the foundation bitch at Sansaska, a daughter of the great Ch. Sam O'Khan's Kubla Khan ex Ch. Tsonoqua of Snow Ridge. Bred by Margo Gervolstad. Owned by Derek and Marilyn Gitelson.

chase of future Champion Norgemar O'Khan's Milka, a Specialty Winners Bitch and a breed winner from the classes.

Next came the future Champion Frostriver's Toy Drum; Champion Rickshaw's Subatai O'Sansaska; Rickshaw's Sundara O'Sansaska; and Hyland's Shalimar of Hilltop, a two-year-old bitch that came to be bred to Toy Drum in 1976.

All of the above dogs had the Silver Moon line in common. Two were strongly crossbred to the Williwaw line; and one had much of the old Snow Ridge sledding lines.

Three breedings over the years have been of particular importance to the development of the "Sansaska look," noted for typey, pretty dogs and bitches that move like working dogs and have great personalities. First, in 1975, Rickshaw's Sundara O'Sansaska

(Champion Rickshaw's Suntori-Champion Scherezade of Kubla Khan) was bred to Champion Samursis Sumo of Rickshaw (Champion Sam O'Khan's Kubla Khan-Champion Rickshaw's Mandarin Lady), resulting in two pups. The one the Gitelsons kept was Sansaska's Sherman T. (Tank). The next breeding, in 1976, was of Champion Milka to Champion Rickshaw's Subatai O'Sansaska (Champion Sam O'Khan's Kubla Khan ex Williwawa Byelei Sosulka), which produced Champion Sansaska's Oscar Meyer and Sansaska's Czarina Mouschka. Then Mouschka was bred to Tank in 1978, resulting in probably the best known of the Sansaska dogs, Best in Specialty Show Champion Sansaska's Mark of Evenstar, Best of Breed at the Samoyed Club of Los Angeles Specialty in 1984, a multiple Group placer, and three-time Specialty Stud Dog winner.

Last, Toy Drum was bred to Shalimar in 1976, with these pups being bred to Champion Subatai and Champion Mark. All Sansaska dogs today are a combination of these breedings, resulting in many champion progeny down through several generations. The combination is very tight Silver Moon/Snow Ridge/Williwaw.

Currently sons and daughters of Champion Sansaska's Oscar Meyer are being bred back into the line via Snowpaw and Moonshadow, with still young but very promising puppies.

Sansaska has bred/owned 20 titlists, of which three are obedience degreed, and 17 bench champions. They include two Bests in Specialty; a Mexican Best in Show dog (Champion Sansaska's Omarsun of Orion), two Specialty Bests in Sweepstakes, two Specialty Best Puppy in Show winners, and even a Best Brace in Show.

The emphasis at Sansaska has almost always been on class dogs rather than on Specials. The Gitelsons enjoy seeing a constant stream of quality dogs who continue to win in preference to the occasional big winner. Also, Mrs. Gitelson notes, the attitude of exhibitors seems to change when one specials a dog, while for the most part showing in the classes is fun, with people really enjoying having their dogs in the ring.

SEA-SUN

Sea-Sun Samoyeds, owned by Rosemary Jones at Bothell, Washington, in 1986 marked an impressive 25 years of Samoyed ownership. They started back in 1961 when a registered three-year-old male needing a home, Sam by name, joined the family. He had been chained all his life; his ruff was gone; his coat in terrible condition. His temperament, however, was superb! He became the 4-H project of the Jones's daughter, who spent two years in conditioning to transform him into the beautiful dog he became. Tragically, Sam was killed by a train in 1963.

In February of 1964, Mrs. Jones attended the Seattle Kennel Club Dog Show for the purpose of contacting some Samoyed breeders and owners. She joined the Northwest Division of the Samoyed Club of America (SCA) in April 1964, and is a charter member of the Samoyed Club of Washington State, Inc. (SCWS). She has held office and remained a member in good standing of both these organizations since first joining them.

The first Samoyed bitch puppy that Rosemary Jones and her family raised, hoping for showing and breeding, introduced them to the heartbreak of Hip Dysplasia. She was, as the result, spayed and kept as a family pet until well past 15 years of age. With caution and an HD guarantee (i.e. the puppy guaranteed against development of this disease), Rosemary Jones purchased a promising bitch puppy in 1968 who became her first owner-handled champion. She was American and Canadian Champion Steffi-Luna's Troika of Sea-Sun by Joli White Knight ex Bel-Ora's Kira Vam and she had been bred by the late Ethel Stefanik. Troika won her American and Canadian Championships by taking the points at eight out of nine consecutive shows.

In 1968 Rosemary Jones bred Sea-Sun's Dama Sho-Shanna to Champion Joli White Knight, keeping from the litter Sea-Sun's Shann Tavyk. This handsome dog had eight points towards the title plus, from the classes, a Working Group placement at the Tacoma Kennel Club Show, June 11, 1972. Then tragedy struck again, this time in the form of Troika's dam having gone blind, affected with Progressive Retinal Atrophy (PRA). The verdict was that both Troika and Tavyk would become affected. Deeply shocked at this development, Rosemary Jones curtailed all breeding activities in 1971 and stopped showing in 1973 while she sought to find answers.

During February of 1979, the SCWS had veterinary ophthalmologist Paul F. Dice, V.M.D., M.S., give a program to their group on eye diseases. Then the SCWS Eye Research Project, under the direction of Dr. Dice, Ethel Stefanik and Rosemary Jones

78

Ch. Snow Fire's Bo Peep, C.D., bred by Richard and Sandra Hipson, owned by Dr. Merrill and Rowena Evans, Waukee, Iowa.

Am. and Can. Ch. Steffi-Luna's Troika of Sea-Sun, the first owner-handled champion at Sea-Sun, Mrs. Rosemary Jones, Bothell, Washington. Taking Best of Opposite Sex at the Samoyed Club of Washington Specialty Show at Renton, Washington, August 1972.

was initiated. In 1974 the SCWS hosted the SCA Rotating Specialty Show. An eye clinic was held and an eye booklet, "A Discussion of Some Canine Eye Diseases" by Dr. Dice was published by SCWS as a gift to benefit the breed. Breeders were urged to have routine annual eye exams by a board certified ophthalmologist. The results of the SCWS Eye Research Project were published in the September 1978 SCA "Bulletin." Additionally, a professional article was published by Dr. Dice in the January 1980 "Modern Veterinary Practice."

In 1977, Rosemary acquired Oakwood Farm's Silver Echo on a co-ownership with Joan Lueck of Oakwood Farm Kennels. In 1982, Echo was bred to Oakwood Farm's Diko Tijano, producing Champion Charok's Extra Terrestrial, "E.T.," who was bred and is handled by Judy Cooper. In attaining his championship in limited local showing, E.T. gained one of his majors by winning first in the Working Group at Tualatin Kennel Club in July 1985.

An acquisition by Rosemary during 1982 was that of Oakwood Farm's Diko Rasha, who in 1984 was bred to Leahi Kii of Kaleoloka owned by Joann Morse. From this litter she selected Sea-Sun's Poli 'Ahu Mokihana who gathered up 12 points during 1985, shown sparingly under the handling of Judy Cooper. She was Best Puppy in Sweepstakes at the SCWS Specialty Show, August 3, 1985—an elegant, balanced, sound bitch whom Rosemary feels is a "rich reward following a long dry spell. And a new beginning."

Sea-Sun continues to strive for quality and soundness, and Mrs. Jones is an active supporter of Orthopedic Foundation for Animals and Canine Eye Registration in all their endeavors. The goal here is to pass a beautiful, sound, healthy heritage to the future.

SILVERACRES

Silveracres Samoyeds, located at Morrison, Colorado, are owned by Harold and Doris McLaughlin, who purchased their first member of the breed in 1954. She was an adult who had been running free and was caught chasing sheep, so was in need of a fast new home before the farmer shot her. She had been seen several times running with a coyote pack. She was the bitch who later became Champion Fancy of Critcell Creek, and she turned out to be a good show bitch, finishing in six shows with Doris McLaughlin as her, at that time, very novice handler. Shown a total of 13 times, Fancy took Best of Breed on three of these occasions. As Mrs. McLaughlin comments, "She had to be good, what with teaching me to handle." There is none of her bloodline at Silveracres in the kennel today.

The McLaughlins speak of their "foundation stock" as being Chief and Jinks. "Chief" was Champion Nachalnik of Drayalene, who was purchased from Helene Spathold as a young boy of about nine months' age. The McLaughlins were delighted with him upon arrival, via United Air Lines, that long ago night. He had light biscuit ears and biscuit freckles, something which still appears in the Silveracres Sams to this very day. He excelled in temperament and good sound construction and was truly a breeder's dream. Not as flashy as a lot of dogs, but with mighty few hereditary problems. As his owner comments, "Even today there have been no eye problems from Chief kids, nor grandchildren. We were very lucky to get him at a time when we were in need of a good stud."

As indeed they were! Chief was the Top Stud Dog in the Samoyed Club of America for ten years, 1973-1983, with a total of 45 American Champions, including a Best in Show daughter, 11 Canadian Champions, and six Mexican Champions which included a Best in Show son. Chief lived at Silveracres from the time he arrived, at nine months, until he passed away in 1976.

The other half of the McLaughlins' foundation pair was Champion Cnejinka, known as "Jinks," who produced one litter of three girls with Khatangas Toby, C.D., of which two became champions, one in both the States and Canada.

Jink's next four litters all were sired by Chief, and produced a total of 12 puppies of whom eight became A.K.C. champions, one was never shown, and the other three were major pointed. Today all of the Silveracres dogs come down from these foundation dogs. To date the McLaughlins have bred the very imposing total of 52 champions! They are to be found in all parts of the United States, plus some others in several foreign countries.

Mrs. McLaughlin tells us that now Silveracres are down to only seven Samoyeds, although at one time there were always 14 to 16 "in residence."

The Silveracres Samoyeds are not presently standing at stud, and their owners are now having "maybe" one litter of puppies a year.

Silveracres Skala with daughter and grandson. Representative of the type and beauty of the Silveracres Samoyeds who have contributed so noticeably to this breed over the years. Harold and Doris McLaughlin, owners.

STERLING SAMOYEDS

Sterling Samoyeds are owned by Dr. Marion M. Jerszyk at Mendham Park, New Jersey, whose first quality Samoyed was Nordic's Quicksilver Kodiac, C.D., acquired from Gail Mathews of Nordic Samoyeds.

Kodi achieved his C.D. degree with all scores in the 190s, and his beauty along with his intelligence prompted Dr. Jerszyk to want to start showing the breed in conformation.

Gail Mathews helped her to obtain the foundation bitch, from similar breeding developed from the long standing quality of the Tsiulikagta Kennels established by Donna Yocum. The puppy grew up to become Champion Nentsi's Nordic Mia-Kis. She had been bred by Teddy Thuma, sired by Champion Tsiulikagta's Kabloona from Champion Nordic's Kismet of Nentsi.

Mia was only bred twice, and from her total of seven pups she proved an outstanding producer of quality. Her first litter was by American and Canadian Champion Kristik's English Autumn, consisting of five puppies. One of these was unfortunately killed in an auto accident before having the opportunity to prove his potential. The others include Champion Sterling's Silversmith.

Regarding Silversmith, Dr. Jerszyk brings up a point of such interest and so frequently misunderstood that I am going to quote her remarks directly in an effort to clarify the situation. She says about it: "Smitty is a fine example of a Sam with intriguing biscuit shadings through his coat. Showing a biscuit Samoyed drew a lot of attention and comment, and, unfortunately, curiosity and questions regarding its properness for the breed. So few dogs are shown that have the classic biscuit coloring inherent in the breed that I found myself educating many on this attribute *which is definitely part of the Samoyed standard*. Please emphasize the correctness of this characteristic as it has unfortunately become an oddity or 'problem' to many of those new in Samoyeds."

Silversmith's littermates include two other Sams who are working on their titles: Sterling's English Piper and Sterling's Silver Frost.

Ch. Sterling's Silversmith, by Am. and Can. Ch. Kristik's English Autumn ex Ch. Nentsi's Nordic Mia-Kis. Bred by Dr. Marion M. Jerszyk, co-owner with Ellen A. Selin.

Mia's second breeding was to Champion Aladdin's Dominator, bred and owned by Joe and Joyce Johnson. Only two puppies this time, both males—Sterling's Lord Chumley and Sterling's Nathan Hail. Chumley started his show career by placing in his Futurity Class out of 13 entries at the Samoyed Club of America National Specialty in Maryland in 1983, his first show when just six months' age. Nathan Hail is currently being shown. An early highlight for him was Best of Winners at Westminster in 1985 under judge J. D. Jones.

Dr. Jerszyk is a firm believer in the versatility of the Samoyed, and has endeavored to incorporate this into her breeding program. Backpacking, obedience, sledding, and showing are activities shared by all her Sams which they do seem to enjoy.

Chumley and his niece, Sterling's Little Dickens, won 2nd place in the two-day Senior Division at the Connecticut Valley Siberian Husky Club Sled Dog Race in the winter of 1984.

Mia's first granddaughter, Sterling's Little Dickens, was the result of a linebreeding of Sterling's English Piper to Tsiulikagta's Tawa'Pah. Major pointed, she has a Best of Breed over a special in her new show career, and has also produced two pointed offspring from her first litter, a linebreeding to Chumley.

Windward's Sterling Legacy was pointed from the puppy class. Windward's Zaks Fifth Avenue has accumulated 5 points as a puppy. All in all, Dr. Jerszyk is well pleased with the early careers of these third generation Sterling linebred kids.

Sterling Samoyeds have produced four litters in 12 years.

SULU

Sulu Samoyeds were founded in 1969 by Lewis and Susan Hoehn, being located at Lowell, Indiana. Mr. Hoehn, from 1971 until 1976, was an all breed professional handler. After that he became an American Kennel Club approved judge for the Arctic breeds until 1981, at which time he resigned due to the assumption of the presidency of a dog food company.

Samoyeds produced by the Hoehns have contributed significantly to the increased breeding and exhibiting of Samoyeds in the Midwest. Additionally, many current breeders throughout the United States started their successful kennels based upon dogs and bitches from Sulu.

The entire breeding program at Sulu was predicated on three

highly influential lines: Baerstone, which was principally from the Kobe dogs of England; Samtara, which was from Snowland; and Sassillie, which traces back to Champion Starchak who was owned by Bob and Dolly Ward.

Sulu's first champion was Samtara's Sugar Koko, who was by Champion Saroma's Polar Prince ex Champion Samtara's Sugar N Spice. This dog was then used on a half-sister, which produced Tsartar's Somewhere My Lara who ultimately became the Samoyed Club of America Top Brood Bitch for 1977.

Next the Hoehns obtained, from Baerstone Kennels, the puppy who was to become Champion Sulu's Karbon Kopi O'Baerstone; Kopi's dam, Silver Sonnett of Gro-Nil, was the Samoyed Club of America Top Brood Bitch for 1973.

Champion Sulu's Karbon Kopi O'Baerstone amassed a most enviable record as a youngster, becoming #4 Samoyed in 1972 and #2 in 1973, all while still under two years' age. His winning record, the Hoehns note, was surpassed only by his prepotence as a sire. His stud dog record stood at Top Stud Dog, Samoyed Club of America, for the years 1976, 1977 and 1978. Especially successful was the breeding to him of the Hoehns' bitch, the aforementioned Tsartar's Somewhere My Lara, who produced seven champions of which four bitches were multiple Group placers. Champion Sulu's Fascinatin Rhythm was Best of Opposite Sex at the 1974 San Diego Specialty at age ten months. Champion Que Sera's Karaimee was Best of Breed and the Samoyed Club of America Top Winning Bitch for 1978. Champion Que Sera's Vicki O'Larathor was Top Winning Bitch in Canada in 1978. And Champion Sulu's Honkin Hogan of Sulu was an all-breed Best in Show winner and received an Award of Merit at the 1979 National Specialty.

A bitch from the West Coast, Champion Sassillies Shasta, was acquired by the Hoehns for a breeding to Karbon Kopi. Notable results of this breeding included Champion Sulu's Mark of Distinction with whom the Hoehns, breeder-owner-handled, won Best of Breed at the Samoyed Club of America National Specialty in 1979 over an entry of 361 which included 71 specials! This splendid dog became a multiple Group winner. Additionally Mark became the favorite of Lou Hoehn, owing to his outstanding personality and untiring eagerness to always please his master. When bred to Karbon Kopi daughters, Mark produced a number of no-

Ch. Sulu's Mark of Distinction pictured going Best of Breed at the 1979 Samoyed Club of America National Specialty. This is the *only* breeder/owner-handled Samoyed National Specialty winner! By Ch. Sulu's Karbon Kopi O'Baerstone ex Ch. Sassillies Shasta. Bred and owned by Lewis and Susan Hoehn.

table winners, one of which was Champion Blue Sky's Pound Cake, an all-breed Best in Show winner.

The Hoehns' current winning male is Champion Sulu's Poetry in Motion. This multiple Group placing dog has been used on a lovely bitch acquired from Kendara Kennels, and Lewis and Susan Susan Hoehn are anticipating that the puppies from these two will provide the foundation for Sulu's breeding program of the 1990's.

Since acquisition of their first Samoyed in 1964, the Hoehns have experienced many changes in the breed, they note. It is their feeling that more knowledgeable breeders exist today, the end result being greater overall quality in the dogs than ever before.

SUNSET

Sunset Samoyeds at Grand Junction, Colorado, are owned by Eleanor Lohmiller (known to close friends as "Tommie") who is a really excellent example of a lady who enjoys her dogs in every possible way, from the hobby of spinning their hair from which she creates most beautiful shawls and other lovely items, through outstanding success in the show and obedience world.

86

Pride of place at this kennel, goes to a bitch called "Spicey," whose full name and titles are Champion Trailblazer's Yukon Sunset, U.D. Bred by William E. Graessle and Judy Mears (by whom she is handled in the show ring), Spicey completed her championship in ten shows, which included her taking three 4-point majors in a row and three Bests of Winners. She was, additionally, first in the Junior Bitch Class at the 1980 National Specialty in California.

In obedience, Spicey completed her C.D. degree in four trials even before she ever entered the conformation ring. Her scores were all 192. On the way, she scored two High Scoring Samoyed awards and two second places.

She finished Open in three trials, one first and two second places, consecutively. Then came Utility, where again she scored with her degree in seven trials, one third and one fourth place.

Spicey was Highest Scoring Samoyed in the Rocky Mountain Obedience Association competition in 1980 Novice, 1981 Open, and 1982 Utility.

It was Spicey's distinction to be featured in the Samoyed Club of Southern California calendar for 1983. Also, she was #6 ranked Samoyed for the year 1981, Delaney System.

Spicey is about to embark on a new career as a registered Therapy Dog.

There are two additional Sams at Eleanor Lohmiller's kennel. These are Trailblazer Star at Sunset, C.D. (Star), and Novaskaya Icezones Prinzes Andromeda (Holly) from England. Star and Holly will not be shown because arthritis has made it difficult for Mrs. Lohmiller to travel. However, she is really looking forward, with very keen anticipation, to their Therapy Dog work. And, of course, all of the Samoyeds take their turns donating fur to the spinning wheel.

SUZUKI

Suzuki Samoyeds, at Farmingdale, New Jersey, came into being during the summer of 1974 when 14-year old Jimmy Kirms, son of Mrs. Patricia Kirms, fell in love with one at a local dog show.

After spending some time doing research into the breed, it was decided to purchase a puppy bitch from Adrienne Israels' Windom Kennels. On the way home, Jimmy named her Windom's Suzuki Snowstorm after his second favorite thing, his Suzuki dirt bike, and thus the kennel name was born.

"Suke" was a great-granddaughter of Champion Sam O'Khan's Kubla Khan and went back to all the great Kobe English dogs. She was Jimmy's constant and beloved companion until her death from cancer in 1984. She was bred once to the Kirms's Champion Silversea Winkies Denver, and twice to National Specialty winner, Champion Kristik's English Autumn. Out of 13 puppies she produced five champions, including Champion Suzuki's Final Edition, who finished from the puppy class in seven shows and was Best of Opposite Sex at the 1979 Samoyed Club of America National Specialty in 1979. Also she was the dam of a well-known obedience "star," Suzuki's Miss-B-Havin, C.D.X., owned by Genevieve Deltieure, who gained her degree in three consecutive shows, including the Samoyed Club of America National Specialty in 1980. She then took High Samoyed in Trial at the San Diego Specialty the following day. In 1981 she completed her C.D.X. in three consecutive shows, finishing her title by going High in Trial at the Samoyed Club of America National Specialty. She was also a Gaines Regional finalist.

Champion Suzuki's Autumn Elegance, Suki's granddaughter, was Reserve Winners Bitch at the National Specialty in 1981, and was Best of Opposite Sex to the Grand Futurity winner.

Suki herself was winner of the Brood Bitch Class at the Potomac Valley Samoyed Specialty in 1980.

The current champion at Suzuki is from Mark and Jan Russell's Devonshire Kennel. Champion Devonshire's Sudden Stop was second in his Futurity Class and first in Sweepstakes at the National Specialty in 1983. He is now co-owned and shown by Lynda Zaraza of Autumn Samoyeds.

Patricia Kirms comments: "It has always been our policy to breed only sound, OFA-certified dogs with super temperament and no genetic problems, to our knowledge, because we feel that the bottom line in breeding and selling dogs is that people are entitled to a healthy, loving puppy to enjoy when they buy a dog to be part of their lives for many years to come. If the puppy develops into a great show dog also, that is a bonus."

The Kirms have bred or owned 12 Samoyed Champions in the past 11 years. In addition, Mrs. Kirms has had the fun of finishing three Chihuahuas as well, including Champion Pittore's Miz Mini Mouse, a smooth coat black and tan, whom she owner-handled to a place among the country's Top Ten Chihuahuas two consecutive

Merry Christmas, Samoyed style! Windom's Suzuki Snowstorm makes Santa welcome at the home of owner, Patricia Kirms, Farmingdale, New Jersey.

years and to Best of Breed in two Chihuahua Specialties.

There is also a large black Labrador Retriever beauty in residence here, Champion Mijan's Barnegat Buot, who was the youngest dog to go Best of Breed at the Labrador Retriever Club of the Potomac Specialty in 1983 and was the country's #7 Labrador.

Pat Kirms adds that "altogether, we feel that our association with these dogs has greatly enriched our lives. The family has moved three times to better accommodate both the dogs and the neighbors, and we are now living on three acres in Allaire State Park near the Jersey Shore, and we look forward to many more years of fuzzy white babies and smiling Sammy faces."

TARAHILL

Tarahill Samoyeds are owned by Cheryl Wagner of South Lyon, Michigan, who has been showing Sams since about 1973 and breeding them for just a slightly shorter time.

The foundation bitch here is Champion Monteego's Lady in White, C.D., who, bred to Champion Star Wind's Khan of Kazakh, started the kennel off well when she produced Champion Tarahill's Impossible Dream and Champion Tarahill's Arctic Delight, C.D. In her second litter, bred to Champion North Starr's King's Ransom, she added to her winning progeny with Champion Tarahill's Elusive Dream and Champion Tarahill's Tribute to Kim; then in her last litter, by Kazakh's Themir-Tau, came Champion Tarahill's Casey Can Do, Champion Tarahill's Last Edition Shada, C.D.X., and Champion Tarahill's Rave Review. Certainly a most impressive group when one considers the quality and success of these Sams!

Champion Tarahill's Elusive Dream, when bred to Champion North Starr's Special Edition, became the dam of Champion Tarahill's Limited Edition. Then in 1985 she was bred to Champion Tarahill's Casey Can Do; from this outstanding litter hopes are especially high for Tarahill's And Tigger Too.

Mrs. Wagner usually keeps about eight or ten Samoyeds at home. Currently, Casey Can Do is out to the shows, being campaigned by Nancy Martin, with two Bests in Show already to his credit. Mrs. Wagner notes that Casey wound up #2 Samoyed for 1985, to which she adds, "of course we hope this year to be better."

T–SNOW STAR

The start of T–Snow Star Samoyeds, owned by Mary Jo and Doug Ragsdale at Conifer, Colorado, undoubtedly was the direct result of Mary Jo, one day during 1976, having stopped to admire a handsome white Samoyed whose beauty had caught her eye. Actually this was the beginning of a romance as well as of a new Samoyed kennel, as the dog's owner was Doug Ragsdale and the couple very soon after their meeting were married.

Doug's birthday/engagement gift to Mary Jo was a Sammy puppy of her own, and her selection became the foundation bitch of T–Snow Star Kennel, Champion Tushina Snow Star.

Champion Tushina has been an exceptionally consistent producer of the qualities so essential for the continuing success of the Ragsdales' kennel. Of her four litters, totalling 16 puppies, five have become champions; five more are pointed, three of whom are *major* pointed. Champion Tushina's breeding to Champion Ri-

Ch. Tarahill's Casey Can Do winning the Working Group at Indianhead K.C. in August 1985. Nancy Martin handling for owner Cheryl A. Wagner, South Lyon, Michigan.

suko's Dancing Demon produced the top winning bitch special, Champion T-Snow Star's Name of the Game, known to her friends as "Fame."

Fame is a multiple Group winning/multiple Group placing/multiple Best of Breed special at just three years' age. At two years, she was the 1984 Samoyed Club of America National Specialty Best of Opposite Sex. That same year she also received the Samoyed Club of America Award of Merit. This lovely bitch's winning ways are a direct reflection of the balance, structure, temperament and style that her dam, Champion Tushina Snow Star, exemplifies.

Champion T–Snow Star's Valhtar began his show career early, at the Samoyed Club of Colorado Specialty Fun Match. With an entry of 14 puppies, Champion Valhtar won Best Puppy in Match with Champion T–Snow Star's Name of the Game, his littermate,

Ch. T–Snow Star's Tulkas, by Ch. Silveracres Sunshine Boy ex Ch. Tushina Snow Star, taking Best of Breed over seven specials at age three years. Colorado K.C. 1983, bred and handled by Mary Jo Ragsdale, co-owned by Doug Ragsdale.

Ch. T–Snow Star's Xenith, by Ch. Risuko's Dancing Demon ex Ch. T–Snow Star's Xanadu. Bred and owned by Mary Jo and Doug Ragsdale.

taking Best of Opposite Sex. By the time he had reached eight months' age, Valhtar had also obtained five points towards his title and a Best of Breed from the classes.

Since 1979, the T–Snow Star kennel has completed seven championship titles, six of them breeder-owner-handled. They are Champion Tushina Snow Star, Champion T–Snow Star's Tulkas, Champion T–Snow Star's Xanadu, Champion T–Snow Star's Yoda, Champion T–Snow Star's Name of the Game, Champion T–Snow Star's Xenith, and Champion T–Snow Star's Valhtar.

Representing the T–Snow Star Kennel in the obedience ring, T–Snow Star's Wintermagic, C.D., attained her Companion Dog degree with three consecutive scores over 195, expertly handled by her owner, Emily Krokosz.

In 1981, at Mary Jo's very first Samoyed Club of America National Specialty, Champion T–Snow Star's Tulkas delighted her by coming home with first place Futurity Dog, 12-15 months; Best in Futurity, 12-15 months; first place, 12-15 month dogs; plus an array of beautiful trophies. Then the following day, at the Greater Milwaukee Regional Specialty, he took first place, 12-18 month dogs; and second place in Sweepstakes. While at the same Samoyed Club of America Specialty, littermate Champion T–Snow Star's Xanadu won third place in the Futurity 12-15 months and third place in Sweepstakes. These two littermates went on to take Winners Dog and Winners Bitch four shows in a row under all different judges during their trip to championship. They became Mary Jo's and Tushina's "double delight," both finishing their titles while under two years of age.

Champion T–Snow Star's Yoda, a littermate to Champion Tulkas and Champion Xanadu, finished his championship with a Best of Breed over specials at only his ninth show.

Presently being campaigned for his championship title is T–Snow Star's Liv'n Legend, a promising young dog from a repeat breeding of that which produced Tulkas, Xanadu and Yoda. "Logan," as he is called, started out by gaining six points including a four-point major within his first three shows.

Champion T–Snow Star's Xanadu, Champion Tushina's daughter, so far has produced Champion T–Snow Star's Xenith and T–Snow Star's Wintermagic, C.D. Champion Xanadu's most recent breeding to Champion Risuko's Mister Moonlight, a Best in Show and Best in Specialty Show winner, has produced a promising third generation. These new "stars" of tomorrow are T–Snow Star's Enterpris'n Times, T–Snow Star's Shining Brite, and T–Snow Star's All That Glitters.

Mary Jo and Doug Ragsdale have recently built their dream home on 43 acres in Conifer, Colorado, and are sharing their home and hearts with 12 Samoyeds.

The T–Snow Star Kennel was named in honor of Champion Tushina Snow Star. Balance, structure, temperament and style are the key components for which the Ragsdales strive in the development of their lines—goals which their beautiful dogs are fulfilling admirably.

WESTWIND

Westwind Samoyeds, owned by Timothy J. Malueg at Oostburg, Wisconsin, started in 1976 with the whelping of American, Canadian, and Bermudian Champion Karalot's Jak Frost of Westwind.

Jak Frost was bred at Karalot Kennels, owned by Eugene and Joanne Hilbelink. Sired by Champion Karalot's Hotshot of Windsong, who was later to be named a Top Producer, and out of Champion Karalot's Kit N' Kaboodle.

Jak started off his show career with a bang, taking Winners Dog with four points, Best of Winners, and Best of Breed over specials; and five shows later finished with a Winners Dog, again Best of Breed from the classes, then on to first in the Working Group, winding up the day with Best in Show. Then at age 20 months he had added to this "Canadian and Bermudian Champion," thus had his title in three countries, and was a Group winner and multi-Group placer in them all. Very nice going! Jak was owner-handled throughout his career, and one of the few owner-handled ("if not the *only* Best in Show winner *from the classes*") to these honors.

As a producer, Jak has two *all champion litters*, another fact in which to take special pride. His owner tells us that 30% of all Jak's total get reached their titles, with among them eight Group placers, and four Specialty winners, more to come. Jak has been named a Top Producer in both the United States and Canada. Jak passed away of bloat on Christmas Eve in 1984.

Jak was followed by the purchase of his half sister, American and Canadian Champion Karalot's Katy Did of Westwind, who was also bred by Eugene and Joanne Hilbelink at Karalot Kennels, being from the same dam as Jak.

Katy's first points and her first show at 6½ months came simultaneously with her going Winners Bitch for four points, Best of Winners, and Best of Breed over five specials including several Best in Show dogs. Again an auspicious start for any show prospect puppy! Along the way to her title, Katy was Winners Bitch at the Greater Milwaukee Samoyed Specialty.

As a producer, Katy had five puppies, of whom three are champions and one pointed. These include an all-champion litter sired by Champion Karalot's Hot Shot of Singsong.

Next to join the troop at Westwind was American and Canadian Champion Frostyacres Noel To Westwind. Known as "Mindy," she was bred by Karen McFarlane of Frostyacres Samoyeds, and was sired by Champion Karalot's Hot Shot of Windsong out of Champion Frostyacre's I've Been Samkist. In Mindy's first three all-breed shows, she won 11 points (3-3-5), Best of Winners each time, Best of Opposite Sex likewise, and *all from the puppy classes*. After changing from her puppy coat, Mindy was entered in Open, and won three points plus Best of Winners and Best of Breed her first time in the Open Class. Next show, Winners Bitch and Best of Winners for four points, to finish with Best of Breed over five specials, then on to win the Working Group at age 14 months. In 1981, Mindy became a multi-Group winner, and the top Owner-Handled Bitch that year.

Following her litter in 1982, Mindy returned twice to the show ring, winning the breed and placing in the Group both times.

American and Canadian Champion Karalot's Katy Did of West-wind's puppies were the next from this kennel to hit the show rings. This was Katy's all champion litter, which speaks for itself regarding the success which these youngsters met. Champion Westwind's Too Hot To Handle is now a multi-Best of Breed winner. Champion Karalot's Jeti Master took four majors and Best of Winners at each, owner-handled. And the sister from the litter, Champion Westwind's Wish Upon A Star, C.D.X., is a two-time High in Trial at Specialties including the 1984 National.

Gambler was the next dog to be shown under the Westwind banner, more formally known as American and Canadian Champion Windsong's Jak Pot O'Pomirish. Gambler was bred by Mary Kistner and Charlotte Koeppel of Windsong Samoyeds. Gambler is out of Windsong's Koko Puff and sired by American, Canadian, and Bermudian Champion Karalot's Jak Frost of Westwind, Best in Show winner.

Westwind puppies at eight weeks; two dogs on outside, two bitches on inside. Owned by Timothy J. Malueg, Westwind Samoyeds.

Am., Can., and Bda. Ch. Karalot's Jak Frost O'Westwind, noted Best in Show winner. Owned by Timothy J. Malueg.

Gambler was a multi-breed winner from the classes, Best of Winners at Milwaukee Specialty, multi-Group placer, and is now coming into his own as a stud dog.

Upon Jak's sad early death, the owners of Norwood Samoyeds gave Tim Malueg a puppy dog who became American and Canadian Champion Westwind's Jumpn Jak O'Norwood. "J.J.," at age two years, did very well with a Best in Sweepstakes over more than 60 puppies, four majors with Best of Winners each time, and twice Best of Breed, along with multi-Group placements from the puppy classes. Now he is just starting on a second career as a special, with multi-Group placings his first few weekends out.

The newest "star" at this kennel is a Gambler daughter, sired by American and Canadian Champion Windsong's Jak Pot O'Pomirish from Karalot's Kristen. Major pointed, she is Champion Westwind's Wild Card of Pomirish, called "Lucky." Finished at age 20 months with four majors, all Bests of Winners, and Best of Opposite Sex if not Best of Breed. Lucky finished *all the way from the American-bred class*, as her owner did not accept what he had been told about it being impossible to finish a dog from American-bred alone. He certainly proved his point, as Lucky wound up with some very impressive wins as well as her title.

Chapter 4

The Samoyed in Canada

Canada had long been aware of the attributes of the Samoyed, and this is another country where the breed has gained prestige. We have, in fact, read that early in the 1960's, Samoyeds were introduced to work along with the St. Bernards in the hauling of supplies; now they are being used almost exclusively for this purpose on small loads and for messenger service during the frozen seasons.

Canada, as did the United States, imported numerous Samoyeds from leading British kennels to be used in establishing their breeding and show strains. Farningham Samoyeds went there, as did those from other leading breeders, to be well used.

The Canadian Standard for Samoyeds is based primarily on that used in England.

Among the outstanding Canadian winners of the present day in Samoyeds is Canadian and American Champion Baretta of Kara, #1 Samoyed of 1984, a consistent breed winner during 1985, and a Best in Show winner in 1984, plus a Group winner, 1983-1985. Carl Kaarsemaker, Waterdown, Ontario, is the breeder-owner of this splendid dog, who has been handled to these successes by Lory Ross.

Facing page:
Top: Can. Ch. Ker-Lu's Iceray of Kobe, imported, by Eng. Ch. Zamostar of Kobe ex Lealsam Lorraine of Kobe. Bred by Irene Ashfield. Owned by Shirley Curzon. Photo courtesy of Mrs. Betty Moody. *Bottom*: (*Left*) Ch. Glokon's Star Fire, winning Best of Breed at the Canadian National Sportsmen's Dog Show in 1978. Bred by Mrs. Islay Aitchison, Glokon Samoyeds. (*Right*) Ch. Aurora's Moon Dancer, by Am. and Can. Ch. Weathervane's Double Trouble ex Am. and Can. Ch. Weathervane's Hot's Hit. Bred by Renate M. Frey, Aurora Samoyeds. Owned by Dr. John and Judy Kovitch.

We have also noted a lovely Sam from Katimavik Kennels handled by the noted Jennifer McAuley. This one is Champion Katimavik's Taz, by Champion Moonlighter's Ima Bark Star ex Champion Katimavik's Ooomik, bred and owned by Ruby J. Orr-Milligan at Mt. Forest, Ontario. This dog has been doing extremely well in Group competition with numerous placements and wins. A worthy representative of the breed!

Roy and Gloria Borstad of Grande Prairie, Alberta, can well take pride in the achievements of their American and Canadian Champion Karon's It Has Ta Be Shasta, who having just a short few months after arrival in Canada in 1985 won Best in Show at one event, along with consistent Working Group placements. Carol Graham handled Shasta.

We tell you on the following pages the stories of several successful Canadian Samoyed breeders.

AURORA

When asked during the mid-1970's, by her husband, what breed of dog she would like for a birthday gift, without a second's hesitation Renate M. Frey of Boisbriand, Quebec, replied "a Samoyed." Thus the Aurora Kennel was born!

Having lived in Montreal for 18 years prior to a move to Connecticut, Renate had seen numerous Samoyeds and loved them dearly. So the first dog to come into her life was Weathervane's Double Trouble. It had been decided that Renate wanted the pick of the litter dogs; thus they searched for a Samoyed breeder. They found the kennel, but then Trouble found them, as when they went to arrange for their puppy at the kennel, it was Trouble who took their eye—and their hearts. As Renate says of him, "he is and always will be, a regal gentleman of the Samoyed breed." Trouble grew up to become American and Canadian Champion Weathervane's Double Trouble, the first of his all-Champion litter born November 2, 1975, to gain his title. Incidentally, this is only the second time in the history of the breed that an entire litter of seven had finished. The sire was Best in Show American and Canadian Champion Scandia's Kejsare, who was in a tie as 1980 Top Producer, *Kennel Review* System, from Champion Weathervane's Katie-Did, who won the Samoyed Club of America 1978 Top Producing Bitch award. Unfortunately, this breeding was never to be repeated.

Trouble, at seven months, in June 1976, went 2nd in Puppy Sweepstakes at the Colorado Samoyed Club cf America Specialty. He became the first Grand Futurity Winner at the Samoyed Club of America Specialty in 1977; won his Canadian title at the Samoyed Association of Canada Specialty in 1979, going Best of Winners both days for two 5-point majors plus one other win under another judge; was the 5th Top Producer, American Kennel Club *Gazette*, for both Jan/Dec 1981 and Jan/Dec 1982. He was #4 Samoyed under the *Samoyed Quarterly System* 1, and #9 Samoyed, *Quarterly System2*, Spring Issue 1982.

Trouble's show record includes multiple Group placements, 22 Best of Breed wins in 31 shows, and he had reached the #4 placement in four months of campaigning, May 16th to September 27, 1981.

Being convinced that good things come in pairs, six months after the purchase of Trouble, the Freys bought a second Samoyed, this one Weathervane's Hots Hit, known as Foxy. Not yet having learned about pedigree lines or how to critique a puppy, they went on good feeling, and chose this spunky, pretty little bitch. Renate comments, "her name suited her to a T, but of course the American Kennel Club would not register the name, so the 's' was removed from the second name and was added to the first." After a few harrowing experiences of these two puppies sneaking out of their designated yard, the Freys then fenced in the entire property with chain-link, flush to the ground; installed automatic door closures on all doors leading to the street, and never left them outside in the yards without total supervision. When you're new at the dog game, it takes a while to learn all about dog-proofing your surroundings.

Foxy was slow maturing, so at the age of one-year-and-a-half it was decided to breed her to Trouble prior to sending her out on the show circuits. She presented her owners with a Christmas day litter. She proved to be a wonderful mother to her babies, and in the spring of 1978 she was ready for the show ring, becoming American and Canadian Champion Weathervane's Hots Hit with ease, going Best of Breed from the classes along the way, but quite steadily placing Best of Opposite Sex to Trouble, and to her son, Trouble Maker. She was the 2nd Top Producing Bitch, according to the American Kennel Club *Gazette*, for both Jan/Dec 1981 and Jan/Dec 1982.

101

Foxy and Trouble together produced two litters of 13 puppies which have included six champions. They make an ideal combination of soundness, beauty and showmanship, and a tight linebred pedigree of some of the grandest ancestry in the breed. Their champion offspring includes:

American and Canadian Champion Danica's Russian Roulette, owned by Dr. John and Judy Kovitch, Danica Samoyeds, co-owned and handled by Sue Grasely. This dog was the first in the litter to finish title, and went on to multiple Best of Breed and Group wins during his career. A grand showman, a heart of gold, a great credit to Foxy and Trouble.

American and Canadian Champion Weathervane's Trouble Maker (Mongi) stayed at home with Renate M. Frey, for whom he attained his American championship with four majors and Best of Breed over specials. His Canadian title took five shows, with him going on to Best of Breed over leading Canadian specials. Jean and Ernie Palumbo, Diamondbrook Samoyeds, as handlers, were responsible for Mongi's dual championship in seven weekends straight. Pulled out of early retirement at age eight years, Mongi proved himself still a show dog, and has won Bests of Breed and a Group placement, handled exclusively by Sue Grasely. He also has sired four litters during this same time span, but hopes are high for their future accomplishments. Mongi is now residing with a cousin and nieces at Danica Samoyeds.

Some other notable Samoyeds from Aurora include Champion Weathervane's Blue Bayou, who won a Group placement at only 14 months of age on the way to her championship, then, sad to report, died as the result of a horse kick to her chest. She was owned by Laufman, Creekway Samoyeds, who also is the owner of Champion Aurora's I'm Trouble Too.

In the beginning, Renate had used Weathervane as the identifying prefix on her dogs, doing so until she decided that she would prefer to become Aurora Samoyeds.

Born and raised for her first nine years in Austria, Mrs. Frey has been a country girl at heart ever since. Subsequently her entire family emigrated to Montreal, Canada, where she met and married a Swiss engineer, Peter Frey, after which the Freys moved to Hartford, Connecticut, where his electronics company was located. Having been a secretary previous to their marriage, Renate volunteered to become his office manager, to learn to use a word processor, as well as to assemble electronic prototypes, circuit boards, and hybrids. Acquiring all these skills, there was no longer need for the outside office, and thus it became possible for her to remain at home and concentrate on her breeding program. In 1980, the Freys sold the company, moving to an island outside of Montreal. During the interim of this move, Jean and Ernie Palumbo of Diamondbrook Samoyeds skillfully handled Foxy to her Canadian championship, Dancer to her American championship, Mongi to his American and Canadian titles, and Trouble to his #4 standing.

All of the Aurora Samoyeds are house dogs, who will always be regarded as being children who grow old but never grow up. In this instance, the priority in the Frey household is safety, health and happiness. All the Sams are treated as equals (young and old). Guidelines, rules, and regulations are set from puppyhood on, and are re-enforced daily. Mrs. Frey is now looking at four generations of heritage behind Foxy and Trouble. Their elegance, grace and style are being carried on through their offspring.

At this point in time, says this dedicated breeder, she has had the pleasure of owning, loving, breeding, and showing over a period of years, and she has enjoyed every moment along the way. She notes that she is a believer in hip X-rays and eye check-ups in order to validate her breeding stock as early as possible. As long as the dog is genetically sound, happy, healthy, and moves correctly she is satisfied.

GLOKON

Glokon Samoyeds are owned by Mrs. Islay Aitchison, Seeley's Bay, Ontario, who, when she started breeding them, was amazed at all there was to be learned. As a registered nurse, she had her physiology, anatomy and genetics background, but still she bought the best books that she could find, studying the text hard and long, then moving on to the pictures, pedigrees, and all the various dogs of the breed whom she could manage to see on her schedule. As she read and studied, she learned better about what the breed needed for improvement; and where the dogs who could do the job might be located.

Then she proceeded to get together certain bloodlines and dogs with which she felt she could work well. Imported by her then were Silveracres Sir Glokon, Silveracres Jana of Glokon, Bowlsam's Echo, Bowlsam's Flammett of Glokon, and Champion's K-Way's Tabor Reveille.

Two Canadian-breds, Champion Silver Storm of Kombo and Glokon Bowling King Pin were most influential added in lines.

In commenting on them, Mrs. Aitchison notes that the above dogs all had exceptional lay back of shoulders, and correct stifle angulations, thus produced Samoyeds who moved exceptionally well. They were used extensively at stud, by both long time and newer breeders, thus proved beneficial to Samoyeds by providing splendid foundation from which others could work. Mrs. Aitchison takes pleasure and satisfaction in seeing so many Sams in the show ring who descend from generations of Glokon dogs, or are linebred to Sir, King, Storm or Echo. All dogs at Glokon are and always will be descendants of these abovementioned dogs.

Linebreeding to Reveille is yet to come, but he has already proven himself an excellent producer of heads, which are of such importance in the breed.

WHITE SPIRITS

White Spirits Samoyeds are owned by Charlotte and Archie Baillie, located at Sault Ste. Marie, Ontario, Canada. Mrs. Baillie purchased her first Samoyed in the mid-1970's, since which time she has gained five conformation champions, four C.D. degrees, and a C.D.X.

The kennel divides its interest between the conformation shows and obedience competition. The kennel's top show winner at the moment is Canadian Champion White Spirit's Canadian Kayak, who is also on his way in the United States and has, as well, a major towards the title in Bermuda.

Kayak had earned his Canadian Championship when only eight months old. He is by American, Canadian, and Bermudian Champion Samover's True Grit (a Best in Show winner and former Top Canadian Samoyed) ex Champion Kristik's Snow Sabrina, C.D., of White Spirit (daughter of Champion Kristik's Satin Sultan, also a former Top Canadian Samoyed).

Kayak, handled by Richard Paquette, on his first visit to the United States in 1983, went from the classes through to Best of Breed and a Group fourth at Oakland County, and was a Group second winner at the big Met event in Toronto with 440 dogs com-

Ch. Glokon's Nepachee Paper Doll, by Gloken's Bowling King Pin ex Ch. Thea's Chanel, is now at Cusona Kennels.

peting in the Working Group—both accomplishments when only eight months old.

As we write, Kayak is starting work towards his C.D.X. On the way to his C.D. he earned top score on two occasions. As his owner comments, "Who says Sams are not smart!"

Kayak's dam, Champion Kristik's Snow Sabrina, C.D., of White Spirit, is also the dam of Champion White Spirits Merry Meeko, C.D.X., who recently has whelped a litter by her half brother, Kayak. There are also some especially promising puppies, by Champion Kristik's Jasper of Wenrick ex Sabrina, who look extremely promising.

The Baillies enjoy sledding with their dogs "just for the fun and exercise," doing so on many weekends but not competitively. They are keenly involved with obedience work, too, as one notes from the titles on their dogs!

Chapter 5

Samoyeds Down Under

Samoyeds have been known in Australia and in New Zealand since the early explorations of Amundsen, Borchgrevink and Shackleton, all three of whom left dogs there when returning from their expeditions. Interest in the breed, and in Sled Dogs generally, has long flourished, as there was ample access to these dogs.

Carsten F. Borchgrevink, although Norwegian by birth, lived in Australia and had more than 100 Samoyeds with him in 1904 when he started out on an exploration to the Antarctic. Two Samoyeds from the Borchgrevink pack were especially well-known.

We have read in an article about Samoyeds written by Mr. E. Kilburn-Scott that he had taken an appointment at the University at Sydney in Australia early in the 1900's. On a visit to the Sydney Zoo, he was surprised to find a handsome Samoyed there, and to learn that it was one which had been left there by Borchgrevink upon his return from the 1904 expedition. When Mrs. Kilburn-Scott and the family joined her husband for the remainder of his time in Australia, they became frequent visitors to the Zoo and to see the splendid Samoyed called Antarctic Buck. Needless to say, on their return home to England, this dog accompanied them. Once through quarantine, Buck became a popular stud dog in England, and he was the winner of a cup for Best Dog when it

Facing page:
Top: (*Right*) Aust. Ch. Donest Star Eve, by Fairvilla Tsarovitch (U.K. import) ex Donesk Diosma, bred by Mr. and Mrs. C. Donnan, owned by Monalyto Kennels, Victoria, Australia. (*Left*) Aust. Ch. Monalyto Sono Royal is by Aust. Ch. Wynadlon Royal Mystere ex Kalina Imperial Museta. A homebred from Monalyto Kennels, he was a top contender while being shown and has also been a tremendous asset as a stud dog. *Bottom*: Monalyto Miss Muffett, by Aust. Ch. Monalyto Sono Royal ex Aust. Ch. Donesk Star Eve, one of the lovely Monalyto Samoyeds.

was decided to try showing him. Thus he became part of the background of Samoyeds in England.

The other dog mentioned above became well known and also wound up in England. He was Trip, who became part of the Ernest Shackleton 1907-1909 expedition, eventually winding up in England with Lieutenant Charles Adams.

Considerable friendship and rapport has developed during recent years between fanciers of purebred dogs in Australia and in the United States. Our judges and theirs now travel frequently between the two countries, fulfilling judging assignments, and it is interesting to see the splendid quality in Australian kennels and dog shows. They are doing an excellent job there as breeders, with their efforts to raise top quality in many breeds definitely successful.

There are numerous Specialty Clubs now dedicated to the Samoyed in various parts of Australia. The earliest was the Samoyed Club of Victoria in 1948, followed ten years later by the Samoyed Club of New South Wales. Both of these remain strong and active, and as interest in the breed has escalated, so has the formation of new clubs.

Samoyeds in Australia are classified as a Non-Sporting breed and compete in the Non-Sporting Group. The breed standard is based on the English Standard for the breeding and judging of Samoyeds in Australia.

Studying Australian pedigrees, it seems very apparent that much of the finest stock there today goes back to importations from the famous Kobe Samoyeds in Great Britain. Literally dozens of them have been noted as "imp.UK" and they have been used to good advantage, as have importations from other British and from some American kennels; but Kobe seems to stand quite firmly as the dominant one behind the greatest number of successful Australian Sams.

We bring you on the following pages resumés of some of the winning Australian kennels of the present.

MISS ROSSLYN C. CORR

Another breeder in New South Wales with Samoyeds of quality is Miss Rosslyn C. Corr, who is located at Annangrove. She has been especially successful with the notable bitch, Australian Champion Camkobe Vanessa, C.D., who is still winning now at ten months past 12 years of age.

Vanessa was bred by W. E. Reeves and is a daughter of Corshaw Krucio ex Kotlas Sinner, C.D. She has won 60 Challenges and over 800 Challenge Points. Some of her outstanding wins include twice Best in Show at the New South Wales Samoyed Club Specialties; once Runner Up at this event; two Challenges at the Sydney Royal Easter Show; five times Challenge Bitch at the New South Wales Samoyed Club, three of them successfully, September 1975, 1976, and 1977, having made her the first Samoyed in the Club's history to retire a Perpetual Trophy from competition.

Additionally, Vanessa has one Reserve Challenge from the New South Wales Specialty.

Her talents also include obedience work, and Vanessa also was Obedience Dog of the Year in 1976 and Bitch Pointscore Winner, 1976/77 and 1978/79.

Additionally this splendid bitch has also won numerous In Show and In Group Awards under judges from many countries, but probably the most noteworthy of these, says her owner, was the 1976 Spring Fair where she took Challenge and Runner Up Best of Breed under a Norwegian judge, Australian Bred in Group under an American judge, and finally Australian Bred in Show under an English judge.

There is a most handsome grandson of Vanessa's now making good records in the show ring for Miss Corr's kennel. This is a young dog, Keftiu Arctic Legend, son of Champion Tax The Caliph ex Champion Keftiu Rose Mellay, and he is a homebred.

"Ben" at age 14 months was already well on his way to his Australian Championship, his early wins having included Best Baby Puppy in Show, New South Wales Samoyed Club Parade, July 1985. Best of Breed, North of the Harbour Kennel Club at only six months and four days old. Best Minor in Breed, Dalwood Championship Show. Best Minor in Show and Reserve Challenge Dog; Runner Up in Show, and 1st in Gait Class, New South Wales Championship Show in 1985; Best of Breed at the Non-Sporting Dog Club of New South Wales; Runner Up Best of Breed, Blacktown Kennel Club, 1985; and Best of Breed at Camden Show Society in 1986.

Both Ben's sire and dam are Best in Show winners at breed Specialty Shows, and he is especially strong on his dam lines with winners of high awards.

CRYSTALFERN

Crystalfern Kennels belong to Kerrie A. Carter and they are located at Eaglevale, New South Wales, Australia.

This very enthusiastic fancier and breeder first became interested in Sams in the mid-1970's from a photo in a dog book. This was the first she had seen of the breed—and it was "love at first sight."

At the end of 1976, Kerrie Carter had purchased what was to become her foundation bitch—a lovely one named Crisam Charisma who now has an outstanding show career to her credit, and who is still adding to her honors. She won countless Bests of Breed, numerous "in Group and Veteran In Show" awards, and achieved the distinction of gaining Challenge Bitch at the prestigious Sydney Royal Easter Show in 1983 under English judge Mr. R. Gadsden. She gained her Australian title at age 16 months, and has retained it many times over.

Charisma is a daughter of Australian Champion Kalina Silver Troika (Aust. Ch. Kalina Silver Blaze—Kalina Imperial Zarena) from Australian Champion Snosheen Sadi Sally (Aust. Ch. Tarnova Imperial Sabre ex Australian Champion Snosheen Debutante). At age three years she was bred to Australian and New Zealand Champion Kalina Imperial Ureka, owned and bred by Mrs. Yvonne Sydenham-Clarke of Kalina Kennels in Victoria, Australia. The mating produced a litter of four beautiful puppies, so nice a litter that their picture appeared on the front cover of the *National Dog Magazine,* which is distributed throughout Australia and New Zealand.

A dog and a bitch puppy were kept from this litter. They are Australian Champion Crystalfern White Khan, who completed title at age 18 months and whose wins include many Bests in Breed, in Group, in Show, and Sweepstakes awards; and Australian Champion Crystalfern April Snow, who earned her title by 20 months' age. Her show successes have included Reserve Challenge Bitch at the 1984 Canberra Royal Show under New Zealand judge Mr. D. Brown, and Challenge Bitch and Best Open in Show at the 1985 New South Wales Samoyed Club's Golden Anniversary Champion Show under international judge Mr. E. Schache of New Zealand.

Prior to attaining her championship, April Snow was the Runner-up Best Bitch, Best Open, Best Headed Bitch, Best Feet and

110

Feathering Bitch at the New South Wales Samoyed Club's 1983 Parade under Mr. R. Besoff of N.S.W. She also has the distinction of winning Best Headed Bitch Class at almost every New South Wales Samoyed Club Championship Show and Parade since the start of her show career.

At the height of April Show's show career, it was decided that she should be bred, and a conference regarding the best possible choice of dog for her was held between Kerrie Carter and Mrs. Y. Sydenham-Clarke, the breeder. Kalina Silver Samover was the one selected, by Australian Champion Kalina Silver Troika ex Kalina Silver Zala. The choice proved to be an ideal one, with a litter of three handsome puppies of which a dog and a bitch remained at Crystalfern. These are Crystalfern Snow Lord and Crystalfern China Doll. At age six months, Snow Lord had won three Sweepstakes and two times Best Baby Puppy in Group, while China Doll had won four Sweepstakes, seven times Best Baby Puppy in Group, and two times Best Baby Puppy in Show.

One notices that Crystalfern breeding is based primarily on the Kalina and Snosheen lines. These two kennels are the largest for Samoyeds in Australia, and go directly back to the outstanding Kobe Kennels, the latter dogs being the foundation for all Australian Samoyeds.

Kerrie Carter has been showing Samoyeds for ten years and breeding during four of them, so she is relatively new to "the breeding game." The person with whom she confers and whose advice she values in regard to crossing bloodlines and matching them correctly is Mrs. Y. Sydenham-Clarke, a noted international judge who brought the first Samoyed imported into Australia and is very knowledgeable regarding the breed.

Kerrie does not want to flood the market with surplus puppies. She likes to have her bitches back in show coat and condition as quickly as possible, which means that she refrains from breeding them frequently. As already noted, her eldest bitch is now age eight years, and still going strong in the show ring, which speaks well in support of her method.

MONALYTO

Monalyto Samoyeds are at Preston, Victoria, Australia, where they are owned by Mrs. Mary Scanlon and her two daughters, Mrs. Judy Scanlon Bacon and Mrs. Maree Scanlon Wakelin.

Aust. Ch. Donesk Star Eve, by Fairvilla Tsarovitch (U.K. import) ex Donesk Diosma. Owned by Monalyto Samoyeds, Victoria, Australia.

Aust. Ch. Sikandi Noble Czar, by Aust. Ch. Kalina Silver Viking ex Novaskaya Tina Lafay (U.K.), owned by Mrs. V. E. Williams. Photo courtesy of Mrs. Betty Moody, Novaskaya Samoyeds.

SILVASAM SAMOYEDS
AUST. CH. SIKANDI NOBLE CZAR.

The kennel was established in 1967 with the purchase of a dog from the Wyndalon Kennels, which has long been associated with the Samoyed breed.

Success in the show ring with their first Sammy inspired the Scanlons to go on and purchase their first brood bitch from the world-renowned Kalina Kennels to complement the bloodlines of their dog. The two of them combined some very strong English blood from the unforgettable Kobe Kennels, and success with their progeny started the Scanlons on a long association with Sammys.

Over the years, litters were bred and bitches purchased from very carefully selected kennels to strengthen their own lines and to breed true-to-type puppies. Although they have not bred a vast number of litters, the Scanlons have, at all points, aimed their program towards long term results and what they would be doing in ten years' time.

Judy Scanlon Bacon is currently the chief handler of the Sams and has held various positions with the Samoyed Club of Victoria, of which she currently is Assistant Secretary. This is the oldest Samoyed Club in Australia.

Maree Scanlon Wakelin is not as active now as formerly, being the mother of three young future handlers. She is, of course, involved in all decisions regarding breeding and other aspects of running the kennel and the dogs.

Mary Scanlon is a licensed judge for Groups 6 and 7 in Australia, and has judged one of the largest Samoyed Parades ever held in Victoria. She has held various positions on the Samoyed Club of Victoria Board, and is presently the Overseas Liaison Officer as well as being one of the Life Members of the Club.

Some of the Samoyeds which have helped to make Monalyto so famous in the breed are as follows:

Australian Champion Wyndalon Royal Mystere, by English and Australian Champion Imperial Rebel of Kobe (U.K. import) ex Australian Champion Wyndalon Kara Lea. Bred by Mrs. N. Thompson, Royal was a consistent winner in his breed and Group, with many Best in Show wins in his age groups along the way. One of his last wins in his show career was that of Best Exhibit in Show at the Samoyed Club of Victoria's Annual Specialty, which is the largest Samoyed Show in Australasia. He won numerous Best Exhibit in Show awards, and in his semi-retirement was selected as the Best Veteran a number of times. Royal was selected by Monalyto for his excellent English bloodlines, which included some of the all-time Great Samoyeds anywhere in the world.

His sire, English and Australian Champion Imperial Rebel of Kobe, was himself a multi-in-Show winner at some of the most prestigious dog shows around Australia, where he has left an unforgettable stamp on the breed. He was brought to Australia by Kalina Kennels.

Australian Champion Monalyto Sono Royal, by Mystere from Kalina Imperial Musetta, was bred and owned by the Scanlons. Always a top contender in the breed, with many big Group awards, he was placed 4th in the K.C.C. Guineas Final judged at the Royal Melbourne Show, which is the largest dog show in Australia averaging approximately 7,000 entries. Still king of the yard in his retirement, "Casey" at 14 years of age looks and acts far more like a two-year-old. He was bred from the Scanlons' foundation dog, thus is especially strong in Kobe lines. He is a double grandson of the well-known English and Australian Champion Imperial Rebel of Kobe.

Australian Champion Donesk Star Eve, by Fairvilla Tsarovitch (U.K. import) ex Donesk Diosma, was purchased, from the long-established Donesk Kennels, for the valuable lines she carries. Preferring the back yard to the dog show ring, "Casey" has only been sparingly shown; despite this fact she was as well always a top contender in the ring.

Monalyto Miss Muffett is by Australian Champion Monalyto Song Royal ex Australian Champion Donesk Star Eve. A homebred, she took Best of Opposite Sex in Show at the Samoyed Club of Victoria's annual Parade, and twice the Best Australian-bred Samoyed at the same show which is the largest Samoyed Parade in Australia, Mrs. Scanlon points out. She was a Best Exhibit in Show at a young age, and won numerous awards in her age group at the all-breed shows.

Muffy was the Top Samoyed Puppy Bitch of the Year, and her list of top awards is most impressive.

Monalyto Mystere, Musetta, and Millennium are young littermates by New Zealand and Australian Champion Kalina Imperial Ureka ex Monalyto Miss Muffett. Now about to begin their careers in competition, they are puppies of superb lineage and im-

Aust. and N.Z. Ch. Novaskaya Silva Yaravitch, by Novaskaya Alexander ex Novaskaya Katya. Reserve Best in Show, all breeds, sire of Aust. Ch. Kossov Kara Nova; N.Z. Ch. Leegalina Pearlonna; and N.Z. Ch. Sevina Pearlonna. Owned by Fran Wilson in New Zealand. Photo courtesy of Mrs. Betty Moody.

Aust. Ch. Kalina Silver Reward, daughter of Aust. Ch. Kalina Silver Blaze, was bred by Mrs. V. Sydenham Clarke. Owned by Monalyto Kennels. Titled at an early age, she was presented to Maree Scanlon Wakelin as the reward for achieving Best Junior Handler.

pressive quality. Their sire, Ureka, now past 11 years of age, was chosen by the Scanlons for his imposing pedigree which contains so many noted English names. He has been used at stud all over Australia and is known as one of the truly great sires, passing on so many of the breed's most desirable features.

Australian Champion Kalina Silver Reward, daughter of Champion Kalina Silver Blaze, was so named as she was the reward in a long competition for the Best Junior Handler in the Samoyed Club, and was presented to Maree for her achievements in the ring as well as sportsmanship. "Minnie" gained her title very young, having been one of the top winners of her time. She was the Top Puppy and Junior winning bitch and was awarded, among other notable wins, Best of Opposite Sex in Show at the Samoyed Club of Victoria's Annual Specialty.

She brought success in the show ring and even greater pleasure to her family at home.

OMIK

Omik Samoyeds at Liverpool, New South Wales, are owned by Norm and June Carter, whose first Samoyed was adopted by them in 1977. This was a male named Ptashka Nezhin, by Australian Champion Sayantsi Pouska ex Chichester Cherakoba. Because he needed some company, other than his humans, in 1978 the Carters found their second Sam, a bitch, in Australian Champion Siralet Solo Shewins, C.D., daughter of Triargo North To Alaska ex Siralet Onewin Too. Unfortunately, Ptashka died of pancreatitis at only 18 months of age, at a time when the Carters were still learning what the dog show world was all about.

Late in 1979 the Carters obtained their second male, Australian Champion Snowvink Silver Arrow, by Australian Champion Laureloakes Bonblaze ex Australian Champion Parlevink Snow Angel. He was a Christmas gift from Norm to June and was found under the Christmas tree wrapped in gift paper. Both Arrow and Solo (known to her friends as "Solitare") were successfully campaigned to their Australian championships.

Solitaire is a petite bitch; however, at 20 inches, she reaches the maximum height limit for the breed in Australia. She has been well admired by the judges, nonetheless, having won a Bitch Challenge from the Sydney Royal Easter Show in 1981. She also completed her Companion Dog degree, top scoring on the day and tying up the Obedience Dog of the Year Pointscore which she won for two consecutive years, during that same Easter period.

Arrow was winning Challenge Certificates even as a puppy and has also met with success at Specialty events, including the New South Wales Samoyed Club where he was Runner Up to Best in Show.

In November 1981, these two produced their first litter for the Carters. Unfortunately only two of the six puppies survived, mainly due to the prolonged labor endured by Solitaire. But, as the Carters say, "at least that one male and one female were strong and healthy." The bitch became Australian Champion Omik Solo Samica with a satisfying amount of success, including wins at Group level along with Specialty shows.

A repeat mating produced in November 1982 a litter of two males and one female. This time everyone survived, with two shown to their titles. They became Australian Champion Omik Ice Sanie (male) and Australian Champion Omik Cie Krystaly (female), both having proven highly successful in the ring. The Carters are anticipating the time when these two young homebreds should be reaching their peak of performance, as it should be a good period for exhibiting them.

TAZ

Taz Samoyeds are owned, at Greenacre in New South Wales, by Mr. Robert and Mrs. Clara Willis who are long-time breeders now, having obtained their first Sam in 1961. Since that time, they have bred about 20 litters for a total of probably 110 to 120 puppies.

Many of these puppies have gone to folks who were already Samoyed owners. About one-fifth of them became champions and ten have also gained titular honors. Especially the Willises are proud of the fact that at Samoyed Specialties, 17 of their dogs have been Best Exhibit or Runner Up (Australia does not have a "Best of Opposite Sex award" at shows in New South Wales), gaining these awards on a total of 41 occasions between them. The greatest number of these went to Australian Champion Taz The Caliph, who on six occasions has been Best Exhibit and four times Runner Up. Next is Caliph's dam, Champion Marydell Regal Angel whose score stands at twice Best Exhibit and four times Runner Up.

Australian Champion Taz The Caliph was born September 1, 1977, by Fair Villa Tsarovitch ex Ch. Marydell Regal Angel. He is a homebred dog whose contribution to his breed has been considerable—between 1978 and 1984 he has had a long list of prestigious wins at both all-breed and Specialty events under many knowledgeable judges.

Canadian Champion Kristik's Satin Silhouette came to Taz as an import from Canada, where he was bred by Harold and Marguerite Kritsch. He is co-owned by the Willises with Pat and Dennis Hosking, and the first year he was in Australia he earned the position of Top Samoyed Stud Dog there. He is by Canadian Champion Kristik's Satin Sultan ex Canadian Champion Kristik's Snow Panda.

The great Ch. Taz The Caliph, by Fair Villa Tsarovitch ex Ch. Marydell Regel Angel, at the Sydney Royal in 1981. Co-owned by Mrs. Clara Willis (breeder) and Robert Willis (Taz Kennels).

This lovely drawing by A. Smith is of Aust. Ch. Taz Tamara The Taro, one of the outstanding Samoyeds owned by Robert and Mrs. Clara Willis.

Australian Champion Taz Tamara The Taro is a famous winner of the early 1970's from this kennel, from Victoria bloodlines, by Champion Kozhva Rouski ex Champion Kalina Tatjana.

Australian Champion Taz The Challenger has been doing well in the 1980's. Bred by the Willises, who co-own the dog with the Hoskings, Challenger is by Champion Tamce The Trademark ex Champion Kotlas Sunaura Lady. This Sam has won Best Exhibit in Show on several occasions at the Samoyed Club of New South Wales Specialty.

Chapter 6

Samoyeds in South Africa and Zimbabwe

The following information regarding Samoyeds in South Africa and Samoyeds in Zimbabwe has been compiled for us by Mrs. Lieselotte Egeler, who has done research for us at the Kennel Union there in order to gather the necessary information and statistics. Mrs. Egeler owns the Ikwezi Samoyeds at Cape Town and is a highly enthusiastic fancier of this breed. We truly appreciate her efforts in compiling South African Samoyed history for us!

A.K.N.

Although there are rumors that Samoyeds from Captain Scott's expedition to the Antarctic in 1911 had been left behind in South Africa, I had not been able to trace a single one.

According to the Kennel Union of Southern Africa's Registration books dating back to 1891, the first Samoyed registered was a bitch in 1947 by the name of Simba Quana, bred by Miss E. Murray of Snowland Kennels in England.

During the 1940's and the 1950's another five Samoyeds, also imported from England, were registered as follows: 1948, Ch. Pongo of Kobe. Dog. Breeder, Mrs. D. L. Perry; 1949, Snowland Moscow. Dog. Breeder, Mrs. I. A. Westcott; 1949, Ch. Nishka of the Arctic. Bitch. Breeder, Miss M. Keyte-Perry; 1954, Gayling

Facing page:
Top row: (*Left*) So. Afr. Ch. Whitewisp Snow Courier of Annan (U.K.), owned by Mrs. D. Edmondson, Kempton Park, South Africa. (*Right*) Ch. Annan Polar Adventurer, another famous South African winner owned by Mrs. D. Edmondson.
Bottom row: (*Left*) Ch. Wolwedans Zillah as a 12-week-old. One of the outstanding Samoyeds owned by Mrs. L. Egeler, Cape Town, South Africa. (*Right*) South African Ch. Annan Polar Light, owned by Miss J. Liddicoat, Kempton Park, South Africa.

121

Gaylove of Shadowrick. Dog. Breeder, Mrs. B. Beech; 1956, Shadowrick's Gayling Giana. Bitch. Breeder, Mrs. K. Pyle. The latter two of these Samoyeds went to Bulawayo, Rhodesia (now Zimbabwe).

Five puppies from these first imports were registered in 1952, 1953, 1958, and 1962.

In 1952 an important event took place when Mrs. Ivy Kilburn-Morris immigrated to South Africa, bringing with her a Samoyed male, Polar Bado of the Tower, from Australia. Mrs. Kilburn-Morris also brought another Samoyed back with her from her visit to England in 1964, this one Polar Ice of Kobe. Both dogs were shown, but never bred from in South Africa, as Mrs. Morris was then concentrating on the breeding of Scottish Terriers.

During the early 1960's, a male and a female Samoyed, Karabou of Kobe and Kouria of Kobe, bred by Mrs. I. Ashfield in the U.K., were imported to Lusaka, Zambia. The owners obviously took their dogs with them down south, as puppies were born in Malawi and sold later to people in Rhodesia (Zimbabwe) and South Africa. It is from this breeding that the majority of puppies of the breed from the early 1970's were produced.

During the 1970's there were 11 Samoyeds imported to South Africa. From New Zealand, in 1971, came a bitch, Baroness of Middlemarch, bred by Mrs. M. Renneberg. From Holland, in 1974, came Quinny van Tamadejo, also a bitch, bred by Mr. H. de Jonge.

From the United States, in 1973, came a dog, Droomhoekie Se Alexi, bred by Frank Koch; and the following year a bitch, Droomhoekie Se Tanya, bred by Kenneth and Judith Anderson.

From Israel, in 1978, there came the dog, Sasha Gesher Haziv, bred by A. Ziv.

While from England, during this period, a dog, Tannu of the Midnight Sun, bred by Mr. C. Robertson, came to South Africa in 1972; a bitch, Champion Carwood Snow Natasha, bred by Mrs. G. Varney, came in 1973; another bitch, Champion Grendonna of Snowcryst, bred by R. Lewis and I. Munday, came in 1974; another dog, Izzken Guy Fawkes, came from Mr. M. Cordy in 1975; and two more dogs, Champion Samont Loyal Lad and Champion Whitewisp Snow Courier, bred by Mr. and Mrs. Pont and Grounds/Rivers respectively, came in 1976 and 1979.

These last named four Samoyeds all went to one person, as they were imported by Mrs. Denise Edmondson of Johannesburg, who established her Annan Samoyeds Kennel with them. Mrs. Edmondson's is, up to the present time, the most successful Samoyed kennel in Southern Africa. A side note about Mrs. Edmondson is that she has been the only importer of Samoyeds to South Africa from 1976 to 1986 and has bred about ten litters thus far, evidently having none of the difficulties placing puppies in Johannesburg, as some of the breeders have in the Cape Province, which has caused several to give up breeding. Mrs. Egeler at this time is the only breeder and exhibitor remaining active in the Cape.

Interest in the breed was growing steadily during the latter part of the seventies, registrations of puppies rising from seven in 1975 to an average of 50 annually by the last few years of that decade. Champion Grendonna of Snowcryst, by Champion Grenadier of Crensa ex Champion Snowcryst Fair Madonna; and Champion Whitewisp Snow Courier, by Whitewisp Arrogance ex Lodenski Larissa of Whitewisp, proved to be the most influential sire and dam in the breed. Sadly, Snow Courier died before reaching two years' age of a massive bacterial infection. He left behind in his children and his grandchildren so much of himself! Terrific temperament, beautiful heads and expressions, and his soundness. His son, Champion Annan Polar Adventurer, is carrying on the tradition with five Group wins and numerous Group placements.

During the early 1980's, Mrs. Irene Rowe, Caebryn Samoyeds, Harare, imported two males into Zimbabwe.

The latest Samoyed arrivals in South Africa have been two males, primarily of Whitewisp and Novaskaya breeding. They are Champion Leader of Hilsar, by Astutas Aladin Hilsar ex Tansy Code of Hilsar, bred by Mr. and Mrs. Ames, U.K.; and Silversams Adventurer, by Novaskaya Silva Starsun ex Silversams Salana's Pride, both of these imported by Mrs. Denise Edmondson for her Annan Kennels. Obviously the imports have been vital to the improvement of the breed in South Africa, and it is hoped that these two will carry on, as indeed should be the case considering the excellence of their background.

Dog showing in Southern Africa is not anywhere near as big an activity as in the United States or the United Kingdom. South Africa is a large country with a comparatively small population. Goldfields, the biggest show, attracted 2,652 entries in 1985, of which 20 were Samoyeds.

A Specialty Club for Samoyeds was founded during 1985, with about 70 members in less than a year. Also there is a club which caters to Alaskan Malamutes, Eskimo Dogs, Samoyeds and Siberian Huskies.

We are happy to bring you some kennel stories from South Africa which will further elaborate on what breeders are doing there.

ANNAN

Annan Samoyeds, located at Kempton Park in the Republic of South Africa, were started in 1973 when Mrs. Denise Edmondson acquired her first Sam from Dr. Loots of Pretoria. This was Champion Navon of Mirny, who carried entirely Kobe bloodlines on his dam's side and a mixture of England, New Zealand, and Australian bloodlines on his sire's. Although not a glamorous dog, he was shown with some success, and in years to come it was found that with him in the immediate background, soundness predominated. In October 1974 he was joined by the English bred bitch Grendonna of Snowcryst, by Champion Grenadier of Crensa (a one breed Challenge Certificate record holder in England) from Champion Snowcryst Fair Madonna, and bred by Mrs. I. Munday and Mrs. R. E. Lewis. She contributed size, bone, and pigmentation to the breed. Their descendants have dominated the show ring in South Africa to the present day.

Champion Navon of Mirny and Champion Grendonna of Snowcryst produced two litters, from the second of which came Champion Annan Snow Imp of Royana owned by Mrs. A. Baynes who in Zimbabwe attained numerous Group placements and two Bests in Show at all-breed championship events. From the first litter of Navon and Grendonna came an outstanding bitch, Champion Annan Kareena, who was successful both as a show dog and as a producing matron. Kareena's first breeding was to an English import, Champion Samont Loyal Lad of Annan (by Champion Fairvilla Fairfax ex Champion Fairville Katrina) bred by Mr. and Mrs. E. T. Pont. They produced Champion Annan Krystina of Royana, who has proven a most valuable brood bitch.

It was, however, Kareena's second and last litter that made the biggest impact on the breed. Another male was imported from the U.K. specifically for Kareena, this one Champion Whitewisp

124

Snow Courier of Annan, a most glamorous and beautiful dog. He sired only three litters prior to his tragic death before even reaching two years' age. He was a son of Whitewisp Arrogance ex Champion Lodenski Larissa of Whitewisp and bred by Mr. and Mrs. Grounds and Mr. and Mrs. Rivers. Only three of that litter were shown, but they were quickly made up into Champions Annan Polar Adventurer, Annan Polar Light, and Annan Polar Leader.

Champion Annan Polar Adventurer has brought Denise Edmondson tremendous pleasure. He has been the top all-time winner in the breed in South Africa, having won five Working Groups, twice Best in Show, and 15 Group placements at Championship Shows. He was sledge dog of the year for four consecutive years, and has sired numerous champions.

Champion Annan Polar Light, owned by Miss J. Liddicoat, has won important awards country-wide, including 13 Bests of Breed at Championship Shows, and has been runner-up sledge dog of the year for two years. Several of her progeny also have attained championship status.

Breeding at Annan slowed down for a few years, due to problems in finding the ideal dogs to import from U.K. to complement existing bloodlines. Then in 1984, after a sightseeing trip to the U.K., by Mrs. Edmondson, the first of two new imports arrived. Champion Leader of Hilsar, by Astutas Aladdin Hilsar ex Tansy Code of Hilsar (mainly Whitewisp and Novaskaya breeding), bred by Mr. and Mrs. Ames and exported by Misses Styles and Breeze. He arrived in October of that year and quickly attained his championship status during 1985 at six shows, winning five Challenge Certificates, one Reserve Challenge Certificate, two Bests of Breed, and third Best in Show at a Working Group Championship Show. At the end of that show season he went Best in Show at a Sledge Dog Club Show with 71 dogs entered.

In March 1985 came Silversams Adventurer of Annan, by Novaskaya Silva Starsun (a predominant U.K. sire) ex Silversam's Salanas Pride (a daughter of the well-known Salana of Kobe). His first litter is most promising.

Denise Edmondson is a founder-member of the Samoyed Club and its policy is to breed for quality rather than quantity. Therefore members are encouraged to breed only from the best basic stock available.

CAEBRYN

Caebryn Samoyeds, at Chisipite, Zimbabwe, are owned by Irene Rowe, who really started out as a Pomeranian breeder, then "discovered" the Samoyed, this in 1979 when she purchased her first Sam bitch in South Africa, while attending some dog shows. This lovely four-month-old puppy had been bred by Mrs. Clucas, and grew up to become South African Champion Redmond Sonya of Caebryn, which title she completed in 1981. Along the way, during 1980, she won a Best of Breed; and also was bred for the first time that year, presenting Irene Rowe with a litter of nine puppies. One of these was exported to an American living in Nairobi, Kenya. Of the others, six are now champions. Mrs. Rowe kept two bitches from the litter, who now are Champion Caebryn Silver Mist and Champion Caebryn Silver Spray.

In 1981, Mrs. Rowe imported, from Mrs. Cawtera of Lireva Kennels in England, the dog who became South African Champion Lireva's Karakov of Caebryn. Unfortunately, this magnificent Sam died of kidney problems in 1985.

Mrs. Rowe also imported a dog from Frankie Trojan of Mithril Samoyeds in Wisconsin, U.S.A. in 1981. She describes him as "one of the most beautiful Sams I had ever seen," who did very well in show competition for his South African owner. But again misfortune struck and this lovely puppy, within one third of a point of his championship, died just a week after his first birthday. His sire was Silveracres Nachalnik, owned by Doris and Harold McLaughlin of Colorado; and his dam was Champion Mithril's Star of Kheledzaram. Irene Rowe became good friends with the Trojans and with the McLaughlins, and after the death of the original gorgeous young dog, who was Mithril's Chief of Caebryn, she asked them to select another for her.

Thus it was that in 1982 Mithril's Americ of Caebryn, at age six months and during December of that year, was flown to Irene.

Americ was shown both in Zimbabwe and in South Africa, and was a champion before reaching his first birthday, with many Bests of Breed and Group placements. He was Best Samoyed Puppy and won the Challenge Certificate under American judge Nancy Riley, then went on to win Best Puppy in the Working Group and was third Best Puppy in Show at the Witwatersrand Kennel Club, South Africa, in May 1983.

Americ was also Sledge Dog Puppy of the Year (South Africa),

Ch. Mithril's Americ Caebryn, multiple Best of Breed and Group-placing Samoyed owned by Jack and Irene Rowe, Caebryn Samoyeds.

scoring the highest points for wins over all other Sledge dogs (Sams, Malamutes, Siberian Huskies, etc.). Irene Rowe feels that he is following in the pawprints of some of the great dogs in his pedigree, such as American and Canadian Champion Moonlighters Ima Bark Star; English, Canadian, and American Champion Delmonte This Is It; Champion Nachalnik of Drayalene, Champion Saroma's Polar Prince, and lots more. Americ's sire is American and Canadian Champion Desertsno's Mithril Star, C.D., and his dam is Kipperic White Lilacs.

Silver Mist was bred to Americ in 1983, producing a litter of seven. One of these, Caebryn's Chip O'Mithril, was Best Puppy in Show and won his first Challenge Certificate at age six months, after which he was exported to South Africa. Of the other six, two are now champions and two more are pointed.

Irene Rowe comments, "The first Samoyed was brought into Zimbabwe in 1978, so I feel we haven't done too badly considering all the problems we have had in this country. So many people left the country after I had imported my dogs. That is why I have only bred two litters, as I am very particular about the homes to which my puppies go.

"When you go back to all the Samoyed pedigrees, you will find that they all originate from the first few to be taken back to England. Sonya has the Fairville, Kobe, and Sword-Dale lines, plus Lealsam. Americ also has the Lealsam lines and Sworddale among the English ones. I have traced all of my stock way back through Nansen of Farnigham of Snowland to the very early dogs, with one in particular, Antarctic Buck, there in the background."

IKWEZI

Ikwezi, meaning "Morning star" in the Zulu language, is the kennel name for the Samoyeds belonging to Lieselotte Egeler at Cape Town in South Africa.

It was in 1981 when Mrs. Egeler purchased her Samoyed bitch, Champion Wolwedans Zillah, by Annan Silva Sam of Wolwedans ex Samerste Elizabeth of Kleinwolwedans. Zillah's sire was bred from the two English imports Champion Samont Loyal Lad ex Champion Grendonna of Snowcryst. Thus the pedigree reaches back to include some famous Samoyeds representing the finest bloodlines in the breed.

Zillah has been shown successfully for three years, during which time she has attained four Group placements, plus 18 times Best of Breed. She was qualified for the "Dog of the Year" competition at Goldfields Kennel Club in 1984 and 1985—a valued honor as only one pair of each breed is invited.

So far, Zillah has produced two litters. Ikwezi Natasha, from her first litter, this one sired by Champion Mirny's Nicholas of Samerste, emigrated with her owners to the United States, living now in Fort Collins, Colorado.

Zillah's second litter was by Nordvik Gay Voyager, a Champion Whitewisp Show Courier grandson. There are some lovely "young hopefuls" in it who will be coming out soon.

← Overleaf:

Janet Heffington, Grey Ghost Samoyeds, with some of the "girls" who helped establish this kennel in Saline, Michigan. To her *right*, Am. and Can. Ch. Grey Ghost's Patent, known as "Punkette," who has provided foundation stock for several currently successful kennels. To her *left*, Punkette's dam, Am. and Can. Ch. Grey Ghost's Sissy of Shiloh; in *front*, Sissy's dam, Am. and Can. Ch. Ghost-O-Princi's Ladies Ninki. Note the refinement of eyes (color and shape), ear set, length of neck, etc. Photo by Tom Mac, Saline. Michigan.

1. Ch. Luv N'Fun's Winter Illusion, by Ch. Gentle Giant of Snowcountry ex Luv N'Fun's Magic Trinket. "Mother dog" at Illusion Samoyeds and dam of two champions, Ch. Illusion's Valerie Rose and Ch. Illusion's Mystic Traveller. Illusion is now retired from both show ring and motherhood, having contributed well through both. Arlene Heffler, owner, Illusion Samoyeds, Crystal Lake, Illinois.

2. Ch. Nordika's Polar Barron, C.D., winning the Working Group at Belle City in 1985. This noted sire and winner is owned by Barbara and Dan Cole, St. Charles, Missouri.

3. Ch. Me Too of Bubbling Oaks, Top Samoyed Bitch in 1983 and 1984, No. 5 and No. 4 Samoyed respectively. A Specialty and all-breed Best in Show winner, a multiple Group winner, and winner of the Windsong Challenge Trophy. Owned by Jack and Amelia Price, Bubbling Oaks Samoyeds, Commack, New York.

4. Ch. Autumn Rainbow Connection, by Am. and Can. Ch. Kristik's English Autumn ex Am. and Can. Ch. Kristik's Modesty Blaze, bred, owned, and handled by Linda Zaraza, Autumn Samoyeds, Southbury, Connecticut. Shown taking Best of Winners at Taconic Hills K.C. in 1982 under international judge, Mrs. Agnes Buchwald, São Paolo, Brazil.

5. Ch. Blue Sky's Pound Cake winning Best in Show at the 1983 Northern California (San Francisco) Specialty. Was also Samoyed Club of America Top Winning Bitch for 1979. Pictured at age six years. Judge, Helen Miller Fisher. Owners, Dr. P. J. and Elizabeth Hooyman, Pine, Colorado.

6. Ch. Sundune Caribou Choo-Choo, born December 1981, bred by Mable Dyer. By Chandar's Chatter of Caribou, this dog is a multi-Best of Breed and group placer. Owned and handled by Judi Lindsey, Canyon, Texas. Photo courtesy of Mable Dyer.

WORKING GROUP

⟵ **Overleaf:**

1. Grey Ghost's D'Incomparable taking Winners at Medina in 1985. Born May 1982 weighing only four ounces (thus not expected to survive), this lovely son of Am. and Can. Ch. Grey Ghost's Son-ova-Gun ex Grey Ghost's Dixie Melody represents the sixth generation at this kennel, which is now in its eighth. Wayne and Janet Heffington, co-owners, Saline, Michigan.

2. Am. and Can. Ch. Kendara's Czarina of Taiga, by Am. and Can. Ch. Czartu of Kendaraland, finished both titles before reaching nine months' age. One of the breed's youngest Group-placing bitches, having taken a Group 4th at six months and one week old. Mary A. Frederick, Kendara Sams, West Chicago, Illinois.

3. Am. and Can. Ch. Weathervane's Trouble Maker winning a Group placement at Onondaga K.A. in 1985. By Am. and Can. Ch. Weathervane's Double Trouble ex Am. and Can. Ch. Weathervane's Hot's Hit. Bred by Renate Frey. Dr. John and Judy Kovitch, owners, Danica Samoyeds, Bloomsburg, Pennsylvania.

4. Ch. Devonshire's Cameo Av Cloud, by Ch. Lelia's Lord White Cloud ex SamKist's Shining Victory, is a foundation bitch for Heritage Samoyeds. This dam of champions and Group-placing daughters gained title with only one defeat and had a Group placement from the puppy class. Bred by Sharon Kremsriter and Maria Farr. Owned by Heritage Samoyeds, Gainesville, Florida.

5. Ch. Jubillie's Native Star, by Am. and Can. Ch. Moonlighter's Ima Bark Star ex Jubillie's Native Dancer, bred and owned by Carol and Andy Hjort, Jubillie Samoyeds, Temperance, Michigan. Pictured taking Best of Winners, Dayton 1984.

6. Ch. Sugarok Kismet O'Frostyacres is by Am. and Can. Ch. Moonlighter's Ima Bark Star ex Ch. Kipperac Sugarok Margaritka (who is Kandi-Anoka daughter). Kismet is co-owned by Karen S. McFarlane, Kearney, Missouri, Frostyacres Samoyeds, and Linda Marden.

1. Ahdoolo's Polar Storm, by Ch. Ice Mist's Silver Lightning ex Ch. Ahdoolo's Grotsia Tashi-Ling, at Bryn Mawr in 1985. Owned by Marie M. Gemeinhardt, Cedar Grove, New Jersey, and Wayne and Ann Berg, Saugerties, New York.

2. Am. and Can. Ch. Mithrils Mirror of Celebrant, born August 1979, by Ch. Kondako's Sun Dancer ex Ch. Mithrils Star of Kheledzaram. Winning a Group placement here for owners Tim and Frances Trojan, Wisconsin Dells, Wisconsin.

3. Suzuki's Storm Kist of Cinnabar was sired by Am. and Can. Ch. Suzuki's Happy Digger ex Ch. Silversea Sham's Kismet. Owned by Pat Kirms, Suzuki, Farmingdale, New Jersey.

4. Winterways Legacy, by Ch. Winterways Mr. Wonderful ex Winterways Wayward Wench, a young dog of beautiful type owned by Phoebe Faulmann and Audrey Lycan, bred by Audrey and Glen Lycan.

1

2

WORKING GROUP

3

4

1

2

3

← **Overleaf:**

1. "Like father, like son." This stunning dog is Ch. Kolinka Quicksilver Jazz-man, son of the noted Razz Ma Tazz, from Ch. Kolinka's Crystal Reflection. He is a Best in Show and multiple Group winner, twice the winner of the National Specialty Award of Merit. Owned by Danny and Chris Middleton, Quicksilver Kennels, Houston, Texas.

2. Am. and Can. Ch. North Starr's Heir Apparent at age 11 years. Veteran Finalist in *Kennel Review* International Dog Show of the Year Tournament, 1985. Owned by Dr. and Mrs. Robert J. Hritzo, Hubbard, Ohio.

3. Am. and Can. Ch. Moonlighter's Ima Bark Star, TT, noted Best in Show winner and outstanding sire is the son of Eng. and Can. Ch. Delmonte This Is It ex Ch. Moonlighter's Ice N Spice. Always breeder-owner handled, Bark Star was the Top Winning Samoyed in the nation, and the Top Producing Stud Dog of all time. Sire of 50 champions, Bark Star is a double winner of the Samoyed Club of America Award of Merit. Moonlighter Samoyeds, Wayne and Jeanne Nonhof, breeder-owners, Walso, Wisconsin.

1. Ch. Charok's Extra Terrestrial ("ET") by Oakwood Farm's Silver Echo ex Oakwood Farm's Diko Tijana, winning the Working Group at Tualatin K.C., July 1985. Bred, owned, and handled by Judy Cooper. Photo courtesy of Rosemary Jones, Bothell, Washington.

2. Am. and Can. Ch. Polar Mist Ain't She Foxy, by Ch. Silver Raffles of Misty Way ex Am. and Can. Ch. Polar Mist Ain't She Sassy, en route to title in 1981. Bred and owned by Lynette Hansen, Polar Mist Samoyeds, Libby, Montana.

3. Ch. Nor'Woods White Magic at the Samoyed Club of America National Specialty in 1983. Handsome representative of the Nor-Wood Samoyeds, Chuck and Lorraine Waldes, River Vale, New Jersey.

4. Ch. Sansaska's Mark of Evenstar, multiple Group placer, Specialty Best in Show winner, and three-time Specialty Stud winner. This Samoyed, by Sansaska's Sherman T. ex Sansaska's Czarina Mouschka, was bred by Danny and Pam Russell. Owned by Derek and Marilyn Gitelson, Sansaska Samoyeds, Concord, California. Handled by Brian Phillips.

1

2

3

4

1 ◄

2 ◄

3 ◄

4 ◄

BEST OF
WINNERS
LADIES KENNEL ASSOC.
1980
SHERRY PHOTO

← **Overleaf:**

1. Sterling's English Piper, Best of Breed winner, by Am. and Can. Ch. Kristik's English Autumn ex Ch. Nentsi's Nordic Mia Kis. Bred and owned by Dr. Marion M. Jerszyk, Sterling Samoyeds, Mendham, New Jersey. Pictured taking Winners Dog at Westchester in 1985.

2. Ch. Murdock's Marauder of Seelah, born May 1979, in a limited show career is the winner of five Bests in Show, 75 Group placements, Samoyed Club of America Top Winning Dog in 1982, and Samoyed Club of America Merit Annual Award. Owned by Merrill and Rowena Evans, Samoyeds of Seelah, Waukee, Iowa.

3. Windward's Zak's Fifth Avenue, by Sterling's Lord Chumley ex Sterling's Little Dickens, bred by Mary Ellen and Thomas Fydenkevez and Dr. Marion H. Jerszyk. Owned by Pamela and James Cropley. Headed towards championship, here taking Best of Winners at the big Lehigh Valley event in 1985.

4. Ch. Suffolk Woly Baby of Oakwood, TT, littermate to Ch. Bubbles La Rue, is the foundation stud dog at Bubbling Oaks Kennels. Pictured in 1980 on the way to his title, age eight and a half years. Received his TT at 11½ years. This Guard Dog par excellence is 13 generations direct from original Arctic imports. Owned by Bubbling Oaks Kennels, Jack and Amelia Price, Commack, New York.

1. Ch. Westwind's Too Hot To Handle winning Best in Sweepstakes, Combined Specialty Clubs of Greater Milwaukee, March 1982. Timothy J. Malueg, owner, Oostburg, Wisconsin.

2. Am. and Can. Ch. Frostyacres Noel to Westwind, owned by Westwind Kennels, Timothy J. Malueg, Oostburg, Wisconsin. Pictured winning the Working Group at Winnegamie in May 1981.

3. Ch. Suzuki's Final Edition taking Best of Opposite Sex at the 1979 Specialty Show of the Samoyed Club of America for Patricia Kirms, Farmingdale, New Jersey. "Nellie" is by Am. and Can. Ch. Kristik's English Autumn ex Windom's Suzuki Snowstorm.

4. *Left*: Ch. Sansaska's Omarsun of Orion, multiple Group placer and Mexican Best in Show winner, by Ch. Tickshaw's Subatai O'Sansaska ex Sansaska's Hyland Fling. *Right*: Ch. Sansaska Mishka II of Orion, multiple Best of Breed winner, by Ch. Snodens Dusty Miller ex Ch. Sansaska's Marzipan. These excellent Samoyeds were bred by Derek and Marilyn Gitelson, Sansaska Samoyeds, and owned by Jim and Sharon Hurst.

5. Ch. Tushina Snow Star, by Ch. Silveracres Trademark ex Kiev Jewel of the Czars, is the foundation bitch for T–Snow Star Samoyeds owned by Mary Jo and Doug Ragsdale, Conifer, Colorado. She is the dam of five champions with several others pointed and on their way.

6. Ch. Tarahill's Last Edition Shada, C.D.X., receiving an Award of Merit at the 1986 Samoyed Club of America National Specialty. Also earned third leg of C.D.X. in three shows, winding up with the National. Nancy Martin handling for Cheryl A. Wagner, Tarahill Samoyeds, South Lyon, Michigan.

WORKING GROUP

SAMOYED CLUB
OF AMERCIA

BEST OF
OPPOSITE SEX

← **Overleaf:**

1. Ch. T–Snow Star's Xanadu, by Ch. Silveracres Sunshine Boy ex Ch. Tushina Snow Star, going from classes to Best of Breed, Southern Colorado K.C. 1982. Bred and handled by Mary Jo Ragsdale, co-owner with Doug Ragsdale, Conifer, Colorado.

2. Ch. Heritage Billie Jean, by Ch. Kipperic K.C. Heritage ex Ch. Silvertips Snow-Mac Heritage, is the 30th champion for Phoebe Castle Faulmann (breeder-owner) at Heritage Samoyeds, Gainesville, Florida.

3. These adorable puppies are by Ch. Whitecliff's Sarmik Karu ex Ch. Tarahill's Last Edition Shada, C.D.X. Born in 1985, they were bred and are owned by Cheryl Walker, South Lyon, Michigan.

4. Am. and Can. Ch. Danica's Russian Roulette, by Am. and Can. Ch. Weathervane's Double Trouble ex Ch. Weathervane's Hot's Hit. Bred by Renate M. Frey, Aurora Samoyeds. Owned by Dr. John and Judy Kovitch, Danica Samoyeds.

5. Am. and Can. Ch. Bubbles La Rue of Oakwood, famous winning bitch owned by Jack and Amelia Price, Commack, New York.

1. Ch. Mithril's Star of Kheledzaram, born October 1976, by Am. and Can. Ch. Moonlighter's Ima Bark Star ex Gimli Mithril Cotton, C.D. Owned by Tim E. and Frances Trojan, Wisconsin Dells, Wisconsin.

2. Ch. Nordic's Wynter Sunniglo taking Best of Breed at the 1978 Samoyed Club of America National Specialty. Handled by co-owner Don Hodges. Sunni won an all-breed Best in Show the following day, becoming the second Samoyed at Kipperic to have both all-breed and specialty Bests in Show (the only kennel of Sams in the U.S. that can claim this honor). By Tsiulikagta's Wynterwynd ex Ch. Nordic's Ketsie Tu, Sunni was bred by Dick and Gail Mathers and is owned by Leroy and Betty Anderson, Gail Mathews, and Don Hodges.

3. Ch. Moonlighter's Ima Huggy Bear, by Eng., Can. and Am. Ch. Delmonte This Is It ex Ch. Moonlighter's Ice N'Spice, winning Best of Breed in Minnesota, 1982. Bred by Wayne and Jeanne Nonhof. Owned by Kathie and Randy Lensen, My Way Samoyeds, Cascade, Wisconsin.

4. Am. and Can. Ch. Northwind's Robin Hood, winning Group and Best in Show dog, owned by Jack and Helen Feinberg, Bedford, New York. Robin Hood is a homebred son of Ch. Northwind's Running Bear ex Northwind's Black Magic, born January 1981. This outstanding Samoyed is pictured winning the 1985 Potomac Valley Samoyed Club Specialty Show.

5. Ch. Kipperic Kandu of Suruka Orr, C.D., by Ch. Nachalnik of Draylene ex Ch. Kuei of Suruka Orr, C.D., was bred by Mel and Miriam Laski; owned and handled by Don and Dot Hodges, Poynette, Wisconsin. One of two foundation bitches for Kipperic Samoyeds, "Kandi" joined the kennel in 1970. Dam of five champions and a Group winner, Kandi broke all records in the show ring by becoming the *only* bitch to win two all-breed Bests in Show and a National Specialty. Her records also include being the only bitch in the breed to have become Top Winning Samoyed in all rating systems, both sexes, which she accomplished in 1974.

6. Best in Show winning Ch. Northwind's Running Bear, No. 1 Samoyed for 1979 and 1980. Owned by the Jack Feinbergs, Bedford, New York. Pictured winning Best in Show at Greater Gainesville, April 1981.

← **Overleaf:**

1. Am., Can. and Bah. Ch. Polar Mist Dr. Pepper is a Top Winning owner-handled Samoyed with 13 Bests in Show, 135 Group placements and seven Specialty wins. These wins were accomplished with co-owners John Ronald (with whom Pepper resides) and Lynette Hansen, Polar Mist Samoyeds, Libby, Montana.

2. The great Ch. Quicksilver's Razz Ma Tazz is by Ch. Kolinka's Quilted Bear ex Ch. Quicksilver's Lucky Starr. Owned and bred by Danny and Chris Middleton, Houston, Texas.

3. Ch. Aladdin's Dominator and Ch. Aladdin's Frosted Thunder winning Best Brace in Show at Seattle Kennel Club for owners Joseph and Joyce Johnson, Kirkland, Washington.

4. *Left,* Ch. Blue Sky's Breaking Away and *Right*, Ch. Blue Sky's Calamity Jane. Owned by Dr. P. J. and Elizabeth Lockmann Hooyman, Pine, Colorado.

150

Overleaf: →

1. Ch. Quicksilver Razz Ma Tazz, by Ch. Kolinka's Quilted Bear ex Ch. Quicksilver Lucky Star, is a famous many times Best in Show dog who was winner of the Ken-L-Biskit Award for Top Working Dog in the United States in 1984. Pictured winning Best in Show under Robert S. Forsyth. Roy Murray handling for breeders-owners Mr. and Mrs. Chris Middleton, Houston, Texas. Eugene Curtis is co-owner of this great Samoyed.

2. Sometimes the water is mild enough for shirt sleeves! Geoff Abbott and his Kriskella Team are from Pine, Colorado.

BEST OF
OPPOSITE
ABILENE
KENNEL CLUB
1985
EGINI

← Overleaf:

1. Ch. Sulu's Fascinatin Rhythm, by Ch. Sulu's Karbon Kopi O'Bearstone ex Tsartar's Somewhere My Lara, pictured going Best of Opposite Sex at the San Diego Samoyed Specialty when ten months old. Bred and owned by Lewis and Susan Hoehn, Sulu Samoyeds, Lowell, Indiana.

2. Ch. Sundune Caribou Star Shontu finished in 1985 owner-handled by 18-year-old Lori Lindsay. Bred by Mabel Dyer from Jo Jo's Starbuck of Caribou ex Shondra of Caribou II. Winner of the American-bred bitch class at the 1984 National. Co-owned with Judi Lindsey, Canyon, Texas. Photo courtesy of Mabel Dyer.

3. This is a rarely seen biscuit Samoyed—an allowable, and very beautiful, color in the breed. Eng. Ch. Fairvilla Anastasia is one of very few Samoyeds actually registered as biscuit. She won her first Challenge Certificate at seven and a half months; her last Best of Breed at age 11 years; won a Best in Show at Samoyed Breeders and Owners League when 14½ years old. This remarkable and beautiful bitch, by Ch. Fairville White Phantom ex Ch. Fairville Snow Imp, was bred by Eileen Danvers.

1. Ch. Silveracres Sunshine Boy, by Ch. Polar Star's Tiger ex Silveracres Karavella, is the foundation stud at Kriskella Samoyeds. Owned by Geoff and Brenda Abbott, Pine, Colorado. Shown winning at Aspen in 1977.

2. Can. Ch. Polar Mist Zsa Zsa and Can. Ch. Polar Mist Puttin On The Ritz were sired by Ch. Ice Way's Ice Breaker ex Am. and Can. Ch. Polar Mist Ain't She Foxy. Both are Best Puppy in Show winners. Bred by Lynette Hansen, Polar Mist Samoyeds, Libby, Montana. Owned by Karin McClain.

3. Ch. Sansaska's Pandemonium, by Ch. Frostriver's Toy Drum ex Hyland's Shalimar of Hilltop, at three months. She grew up to become a Specialty Brood Bitch winner. Bred by Marilyn Gitelson and Valerie Weers. Owned by Derek and Marilyn Gitelson, Sansaska, Concord, California.

← **Overleaf:**

1. These future show stars, born February 1985, are by Ch. Tarahill's Casey Can Do ex Tarahill's Elusive Dream. Pictured with Nancy Martin. Owned by Cheryl Wagner, Tarahill Kennels, South Lyon, Michigan.

2. Ch. T–Snow Star's Name of the Game. "Fame," to friends, is a multi-Group winning, Group-placing and Best of Breed winner. Pictured taking Best of Breed at Buckhorn Valley K.C. August 1985. Handled by his breeder-owner, Mary Jo Ragsdale, co-owner with Doug Ragsdale, Conifer, Colorado. This dog was Best of Opposite Sex at the 1984 National Specialty, and earned an Award of Merit that year from the parent club.

3. Ch. Kipperic Kandita, by Kipperic Kandikid en Kipperic Peppita, bred, owned, and handled by Don and Dot Hodges, Poynette, Wisconsin. Finished title in 1984 taking three five-point majors in two weeks, including Winners Bitch at Greater Milwaukee Samoyed Specialty. This 9th Group-placing Kipperic Samoyed received three awards in May 1985. One of several Group-placing descendants of Ch. Kipperic Kandu of Suruka Orr (a Best in Show winner), Kandita already had a Group-placing son from her first litter.

1. *Left to right*: Am. and Can. Ch. Danica's Russian Roulette with two of his kids, Danica's Arctic Show Prince and Danica's Russian Ice. Breeder/owners Dr. John and Kathy Kovitch, Danica Samoyeds, Bloomsburg, Pennsylvania.

2. Can you imagine a more adorable group of puppies? These Sam babies (by Am. and Can. Ch. Nordika's Polar Barron, C.D., ex Ch. Danica's Russian Foxfile) were all pointed by the time they had become a year old, all owner-handled. Dr. John and Judy Kovitch, Danica Samoyeds, Bloomsburg, Pennsylvania.

Glen E.

1↑ 2↓

← **Overleaf:**

1. Gimli's Snow Shadow, C.D. (by Crystal Snow ex Gimli Mithril Cotton, C.D.). Owned by Tim and Frances Trojan, Wisconsin Dells, Wisconsin.

2. Ikwezi Ice Bear and Ikwezi Ice King, by Nordvik Gay Voyager ex Ch. Wolwedans Zillah, Mrs. L. Egeler, Cape Town, South Africa.

1. Eng. Ch. Novaskaya Imry Lafay, by Ch. Novaskaya Silva King ex Novaskaya Shani Lafay, was bred by Mrs. Betty Moody and is owned by Mr.
   L. Winger.

2. Ch. Novaskaya Silva Shilokan, by Ch. Silversams Polar Bear ex Novaskaya Kara, winner of the Working Group, West of England Ladies Kennel Society (WELKS) Championship Dog Show, England, 1981. Mrs. Betty
   Moody, Novaskaya Samoyeds, now at Chesapeake, Virginia.

3. Empress of Snowscape is the dam of these promising puppies owned by
   Snowscape Kennels, Jimmy and Rita Hyland, Glen of Imaal, County
   Wicklow, Ireland.

4. Eng. Ch. Sworddale Silver Minstrel of Annecy was bred by Mrs. M. M.
   Ross and owned by Mrs. M. J. Wilcock, Clayton-Le-Woods, Lancashire,
   England.

5. Eng. Ch. Novaskaya Rebel, by Ch. Golway Mr. Chan, at age ten months.
   Bred by Mrs. Betty Moody, Novaskaya Samoyeds. Owned by Mrs. Tina Ri-
   chardes.

6. Ch. Demitre of Snowscape, breed champion at Royal Dublin Society Show-
   grounds, 1983. Owned by Snowscape Kennels, Jimmy and Rita Hyland,
   Glen of Imaal, County Wicklow, Ireland.

← Overleaf:

1. Am. and Can. Ch. Weathervane's Double Trouble, by Best in Show Am. and Can. Ch. Scandia's Kejsare ex Ch. Weathervane's Katie-Did, was the Grand Futurity First Prize winner at the Samoyed Club of America Specialty in 1977. Owned by Renate M. Frey, Aurora Samoyeds, Boisbriand, P.Q., Canada.

2. Am. and Can. Ch. Weathervane's Hot's Hit, by Ch. Weathervane's Komar ex Ch. Taradawn's Snow Princess, owned by Renate M. Frey, Aurora Samoyeds.

3. Can. Ch. Glokon Zippy Go Go Girl, by Ch. K-Way's Tabor Reveille, finishing her title. Here taking Best of Winners and Best of Opposite Sex at Ottawa K.C. in 1984. Owned by Mrs. Islay Aitchison, Seeley's Bay, Ontario.

4. Can. Ch. White Spirits Canadian Kayah, C.D., taking a major at Oakland County K.C. in the United States in 1983. Kayah has already earned a major in Bermuda. Owned by Charlotte Baillie, Sault Ste. Marie, Ontario.

5. Ch. Diamondbrook's Twikki, by Am. and Can. Ch. Weathervane's Double Trouble ex Ch. Weathervane's Hope Diamond, is a homebred owned by Jean and Ernie Palumbo, Diamondbrook Samoyeds.

6. Can. Ch. Novaskaya Silva Solitaire of Ker Lu, by Ch. Golway Mr. Chan ex Ch. Morgana Tisha Lafay of Novaskaya, bred by Betty Moody. Owned by Mr. and Mrs. Roy Curzon.

1. Ch. Crystalfern April Snow (*left*) and Ch. Crystalfern White Khan were bred and are owned by K. A. Carter. Crystalfern Samoyeds, Eaglevale, New South Wales, Australia.

2. Aust. Ch. Taz The Caliph surrounded by some of his Specialty Show mementos. Born September 1977, by Fair Villa Tsarovitch (U.K. import) ex Ch. Marydell Regal Angel, he was bred by Mrs. Clara Willis. Co-owned with Robert Willis, Taz Samoyeds, Greenacre, Australia. The winner of many prestigious and important awards.

3. Aust. Ch. Monalyto Sono Royal (*right*); Aust. Ch. Donesk Star Eve (*center*); and Monalyto Miss Muffett (left). Owned by Monalyto Samoyeds, Victoria, Australia.

4. Aust. Ch. Siralet Solo Shewins, C.D., with trophies and sashes for Obedience Dog of the Year 1981; trophy for Bitch Challenge, Sydney Royal, 1981; trophy for Best of Breed, Sydney Royal, 1981; trophy for C.D title at New South Wales Samoyed Show 1981. Owned by Omik Samoyeds, Mr. and Mrs. N. J. Carter, Liverpool, New South Wales. Aust. Ch. Snowvink Silver Arrow is beneath the table.

5. Aust. Ch. Snowvink Silver Arrow on a very hot day at Armidale. Owned by Omik Samoyeds, Mr. and Mrs. N. J. Carter, Liverpool, New South Wales.

6. Ch. Camkobe Vanessa, C.D., by Corshaw Krucio ex Kotlas Sinner, C.D., bred by W. E. Reeves. She is the winner of 60 Challenges and has more than 800 Challenge points. Owned by Miss R. C. Corr, Annangrove, New South Wales.

1

2

3

4

5

6

← Overleaf:

1. So. Afr. Ch. Samont Loyal Lad of Annan (U.K.) and So. Afr. Ch. Grendonna of Snowcryst (U.K.) are two of the handsome Samoyeds owned by Mrs. D. Edmondson, Kempton Park, South Africa.

2. N.Z. Ch. Novaskaya Silva Sabya (U.K.), by Novaskaya Silva Starsun ex Novaskaya Kings Rhapsody, is dam of N.Z. Ch. Kimchatka Sun Blossom, the Top Winning Samoyed Bitch in New Zealand for 1985; and N.Z. Ch. Kimchatka Sun Emperor (also sire of N.Z. Ch. Kimchatka Sun Blossom), Top Winning Samoyed Dog in New Zealand for 1985. Bred by Mrs. Betty Moody; owned by E. and T. Maitland.

3. Special Encounter, born 1984, bred by Mr. and Mrs. P. J. Atkins. Pictured at age 15 months, he is a son of Ch. Zoox Katodzki (Ch. Fairvilla Taras Bulba–Ch. Fairvilla Katarina) ex Nenetsky Stargazer (Ch. Fairvilla Snowivan of Nenetsky–Nenetsky Omni). Owned by J. A. C. Ouwerkerk, Rotterdam, Netherlands.

4. Ch. Wolwedans Zillah, by Annan Silva Sam ex Samerste Elizabeth, bred by Mrs. M. M. de Villiers. Owner, Mrs. L. Egeler, Cape Town, South Africa. Zillah is pictured here at Goldfields K.C. Dog Show, Johannesburg Dog of the Year Competition 1984.

5. Ch. Mithril's Americ of Caebryn, Best Puppy in Working Group and 3rd Best Puppy in Show WITS Kennel Club, South Africa 1983. Also Sledge Dog Puppy of the Year 1983. By Am. and Can. Ch. Desertsno's Mithril Star, C.D., ex Kipperic White Lilacs. Owned by Jack and Irene Rowe, Chisipite, Zimbabwe.

6. Youth World Champion 1985, Bundessieger 1985 Rebecca's Olinda of Bjelkiers, owned by Werner and Ingrid Degenhardt, Bjelkiers Kennel, São Paulo, Brazil.

1. Ch. Trailblazer's Yukon Sunset, U.D., by Am. and Can. Ch. Scandia's Kejsare ex Trailblazer's Talaria, bred by Wm. E. Graessle and Judy Mears and owned by Eleanor and George Lohmiller.

2. Gimli Mithril Cotton, C.D., by De Jong of Ala Cyrss ex Luck's Patricia, bred by Wayland Luck, owned by Tim and Frances Trojan, Wisconsin Dells, Wisconsin. The foundation bitch at Mithril Samoyeds.

3. *Left to right*: O.T.Ch. Barron's White Lightnin; Am. and Can. Ch. Nordika's Polar Barron, C.D.; Kappy's Grizzly Barron; and Barron's Sparkling Chablis, C.D. Splendid example of beauty combined with brains from the Barron Kennels, Dan and Barbara Cole, St. Charles, Missouri.

1

2

3

← Overleaf:

1. Ch. Sulu's Tobo Loki, by Ch. Sulu's Karbon Kopi O'Bearstone ex Tsartars Somewhere My Lara, has multiple Group placements for the owners Newmans. Bred by Lewis and Susan Hoehn.

2. A lovely portrait of the well-known Ch. Danica's Gallant Russian Bear. By Am. and Can. Ch. Danica's Russian Roulette ex Ch. Weathervane's Simply Smashing. Bred by Dr. John and Judy Kovitch. Owned by June Smith.

1. Ch. Heritage Mischief Maker is a Group-placer by Ch. Nachalnik of Draya-lene ex Ch. Silvertips Dixie Heritage. Bred by Heritage Samoyeds, owned by Bill and George-Anne Ferguson.

2. Can. Ch. Kristik's Blaze of Autumn, by Am. and Can. Ch. English Autumn ex Am. and Can. Ch. Kristik's Modesty Blaze, owned by M. Fox. Bred by Linda A. Zaraza, Autumn Samoyeds, Southbury, Connecticut.

3. Barron's White Lightnin, U.D., by Lord Nicholas of Aurora ex Ochoas Misty Lady, taking High in Trial at Two Cities K.C., October 1982. Owned by Barbara and Dan Cole, St. Charles, Missouri.

4. Jubillie's Moonlight Dancer, by Am. and Can. Ch. Moonlighter's Ima Bark Star ex Jubillie's Native Dancer, represents nine consecutive generations of Best in Show winners and Top Producers, and six generations of Specialty Show winners. He is the result of a nephew/aunt line-breeding on Ch. Kondako's Sun Dancer. Bred and owned by Carol and Andy Hjort, Jubillie Samoyeds, Decatur, Georgia.

5. Ch.Aladdin's Dominator winning the Working Group at Mt. Baker K.C. Owned by Aladdin Samoyeds, Joseph and Joyce Johnson, Kirkland, Washington.

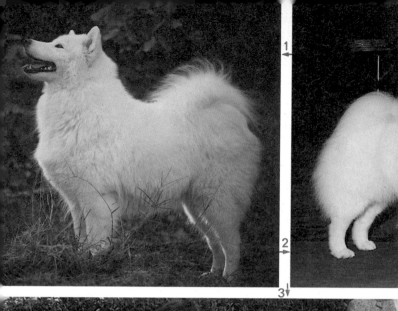

HIGH IN TRIAL
TWO CITIES
KENNEL
CLUB
16 OCT 1982

OF BREED
OYGAN K.C.
30.1978
SON PHOTO

1 ↑
2 ←
3 →
4 ↓

RESERVE
WINNERS

← Overleaf:

1. *Left*: Am. and Can. Ch. Karalot's Katy Did was Best of Breed from the Puppy Class over three Best in Show winners at her first show, age six and a half months. *Right*: Am., Can., and Bda. Ch. Karalot's Jak-Frost O'Westwind, Best of Opposite Sex. Timothy J. Malueg, Oostburg, Wisconsin.

2. Snowcrest Teddy Barron, by Am. and Can. Ch. Nordika's Polar Barron, C.D., ex Lady Snowflake XIX, born August 1981. Bred by Angie and Dave Lucia and owned by Linda Smith.

3. Ch. Kimchatka Sun Seeker, by N.Z. Ch. Sikandi Silver Joker ex Novaskaya Tina Lafay, handled here by Harvey Yamashita for owner Amy Sakata, Hawaii. Photo courtesy of Mrs. Betty Moody.

4. Jack Price with the Bubbling Oaks team in 1983. *In the lead*, Poison Ivy of Bubbling Oaks; *left point*, Ch. Bogart of Bubbling Oaks; *right point*, Deja Vu of Bubbling Oaks; *left wheel*, Ch. Camshaft of Bubbling Oaks; *right wheel*, Ch. Bubbling Oaks U.S. Mail. A beautiful example of the fact that show Samoyeds can also be capable sled Samoyeds. Bubbling Oaks owned by Jack and Amelia Price, Commack, New York.

1. Ch. Glokon's Cusona Blue Tornado, by Ch. Silver Storm of Kombo ex Bowlsam's Flamett of Glokon. Bred and handled by Mrs. Islay Aitchison. Owned by Cusona Samoyeds.

2. Eng., Can. and Am. Ch. Delmonte This Is It, English import who was the Samoyed Club of America's Top Winning Dog in 1976. The sire of the top winning top producer, Am. and Can. Ch. Moonlighter's Ima Bark Star. Owned by Moonlighter Samoyeds, Wayne and Jeanne Nonhof, Waldo, Wisconsin.

3. Ch. Kipperic Jasun, by Ch. Karalot's Hotshot of Windsong ex Ch. Gebaa Sun-Dee of Kipperic, in 1981 became the seventh Group-placing Samoyed at Kipperic, and in turn has sired a lovely Group-placing daughter bred by Lynn Massey. Jasun is bred, owned, and handled by Don and Dot Hodges, Kipperic Kennels, Poynette, Wisconsin.

4. Ch. Illusion's Mystic Traveller, by Ch. Totala's Wizard of Celter ex Ch. Luv N' Fun's Winter Illusion. This multiple Best of Breed winner and Group-placing champion is a homebred owned by Arlene Heffler, Illusion Samoyeds, Crystal Lake, Illnois.

5. Mithril's Chief of Caebryn at age seven months just before departure to his new owners in South Africa. By Silveracres Nachalnik ex Ch. Mithril's Star of Kheledzaram, bred in the United States by Mithril Samoyeds, Wisconsin Dells, Wisconsin. Owned by Irene Rowe of Zimbabwe.

6. Ch. Orion of Kipperic, the Hodgeses' first homebred champion, by Lulhaven's Snow Mist Ensign (Best in Show winner) ex Ch. Kipperic D'Lite of Frost River, C.D. Bred, owned and handled by Don and Dot Hodges. Sold to Cecilia de la Torre of Bogota following completion of title. "Rion" was also the first Kipperic-bred Group winner.

← **Overleaf:**

1. Ch. Sansaska's Mai Tai Too, by Sansaska's Mighty Michael ex Ch. Sansaska's Marzipan, at four and a half months of age. This Group-placer from the classes was bred by Derek and Marilyn Gitelson, Sansaska Samoyeds, Concord, California.

2. Aust. Ch. Crisam Charisma, by Aust. and N.Z. Ch. Kalina Imperial Ureka ex Aust. Ch. Snosheen Sadi Sally, is the foundation bitch at Crystalfern Samoyeds, owned by K. A. Carter, Eaglevale, New South Wales, Australia.

3. Eng. Ch. Novaskaya's Chandra Lafay, by Ch. Golway Mr. Chan ex Ch. Morgana Tisha Lafay of Novaskaya, was bred by Betty Moody and is owned by Peter Larcombe. In addition to her own good record, she is the dam of Eng. Ch. Moydessa Miss Terry, first Samoyed bitch to win Reserve in Group at Crufts.

4. Can. Ch. Wenricks Miss Jamie of White Spirits is owned and handled by Charlotte Baillie, Sault Ste. Marie, Ontario, Canada.

5. Ankraliak Arctic is an International Champion (Netherlands, Germany, Belgium, Luxembourg) and a Bundessieger 1983. One of the famous international-winning Samoyeds owned by J. A. C. Ouwerkerk, Rotterdam, Netherlands. By Samoya's Rooski ex Sedwa Aika.

6. Keftiu Arctic Legend, by Ch. Taz the Caliph ex Ch. Keftiu Rose Mellay, was bred and is owned by Miss R. C. Corr. "Ben" shows every promise of following in the paw-prints of his Best in Show winning parents. Miss Corr's kennels are at Annangrove, New South Wales, Australia.

1. Aladdin puppies owned by Joseph and Joyce Johnson, Kirkland, Washington.

2. Shada's Dancer of Tarahill who was pointed from the puppy class is by Ch. White Cliff's Sarmik Karu, C.D., ex Ch. Tarahill's Last Edition Shada, C.D.X. Owned by Tarahill Samoyeds, Cheryl A. Wagner, South Lyon, Michigan.

1

2

RIO GRANDE KC

WORKING

3

← **Overleaf:**

1. Barron's Sparkling Chablis, C.D., by Am. and Can. Ch. Nordika's Polar Barron, C.D., ex Lady Snowflake XIX, born August 1981. Bred by Angie and Dave Lucia. Owned by Barbara and Dan Cole, St. Charles, Missouri.

2. Ch. Rocinante Sundune Sandollar, by Jo Jo's Starbuck of Caribou ex Heritage Moriah Rocinante, finished in eight shows and won the breed over specials at 14 months. This multi-Best of Breed and Group-placer is owned and handled by Judy Lindsey, Canyon, Texas. Pictured winning the Working Group at Rio Grande K.C. under Lee Reasin. Photo courtesy of Mabel Dyer, Caribou Kennels.

3. Jubillie's Mystical Maverick and Mystical's Afternoon Delight, littermates sired by Jubillie's Moonlight Dancer ex Champion Risuko's Lit'l Bit O'Triskit, C.D., pictured at age six months. Maverick owned by Carol and Andy Hjort, Jubilee Samoyeds. Afternoon Delight owned by their breeders, Ron and Judi Schold, Mystical Samoyeds.

Overleaf: →

1. This is Heritage Matthew Star, foundation for Sunkist Samoyeds, Boynton Beach, Florida. Bred by Heritage, owned by Bill and Barbara McLane.

2. Danica's Russian Polar Kap, by Am. and Can. Ch. Nordika's Polar Barron, C.D., ex Ch. Danica's Russian Foxfire, bred by Dr. John and Judy Kovitch and owned by Robert and Jane Emmel.

3. These are Kandi and Rogue, two of the magnificent Silveracres Samoyeds owned by Harold and Doris McLaughlin, Morrison, Colorado.

1

2

3

WINNERS
BALD EAGLE
KENNEL CLUB
1985 DAVE ASHBEY

← **Overleaf:**

1. Windward's Sterling Legacy owned by Dr. Marion Jerszyk and Mary Ellen and Thomas Fydenkevez, taking the points at Taconic Hills in 1985. This Samoyed is by Sterling's Lord Chumley ex Sterling's Little Dickens.

2. Ahdoolo's Starmist Pearl, by Ch. Icemist's Silver Lightning ex Ch. Ahdoolo's Grotsia Tashi-Ling, owned by John and Marie Gemeinhardt, Cedar Grove, New Jersey.

3. Silverwood's Birch Mt. Tea at two years of age taking Best of Winners at Newton K.C. in 1985. Owned by Pamela and James Cropley.

4. A Frostyacres Samoyed puppy, from Frostyacres Kennels, Mrs. Karen S. McFarlane, Kearney, Missouri.

Overleaf: →

Sansaska's Panjandrum, by Sansaska's Mighty Michael ex Ch. Sansaska's Marzipan, at age three months. Bred by Derek and Marilyn Gitelson; owned by Marilyn Gitelson and Pam Pearman.

Chapter 7

Samoyeds in Other Areas

EIRE

We have received a most interesting note from an Irish fancier of the Samoyed, Jimmy Hyland, who with his wife Rita owns the Snowscape Samoyeds and Bichons Frises at Glen of Imaal, Co. Wicklow, Eire.

Jimmy remarks on the difficulty of making up a champion in his country, as Eire has a Point System which differs from that of the U.K. The requirement in Eire is that a dog gain 40 points at championship show level, which means that the dogs must have either two 10-Point Green Star Points awarded, or four times 5-point included in that total of 40. If only four dogs are actually present, then the winner could only receive a 3-Point Green Star. Say ten dogs are present, then an 8-Point Green Star. So one would, or perhaps we should say could if lucky, make up a dog after four Championship Shows. But this is rare, and it is quite possible to have the necessary 40 points but still the dog not become a champion due to the manner in which the points added up. In other words, 40 points alone is not sufficient; they must have been gained with the outlined Championship Show requisites fulfilled. This system, then, depends on a decent number of dogs actually being in competition, which sometimes just does not occur.

Considering all of this, Jimmy and Rita Hyland naturally take a very special pride in the fact that the first, second, fourth and fifth Samoyeds to have gained Eire Championship are from their kennel.

At the head of the list comes Eire Champion Arrakova of St. Nicholascript, a bitch by Champion Yanik of Arabis ex Zaza of St. Nicholascript. Breeder, J. P. Slatterly, England.

The second Samoyed on the list is Eire Champion Akim of Snowscape, a dog, by Ivan of Snowscape ex Eire Champion Arrakova of Nicholascroft, homebred by Jimmy Hyland.

The fourth Samoyed Eire Champion is Kristeena of Snowscape, a bitch, bred by Jimmy Hyland, by Ivan of Snowscape ex Eire Champion Arrakova of St. Nicholascript.

The fifth is Eire Champion Demitre of Snowscape, a son of the *third* Eire Champion Samoyed, Fairville White Opel ex the Green Star winner, Olga of Snowscape. Demitre, we understand, is the leading sire in Eire and gained his championship when only age 19 months. He, too, was bred by Jimmy Hyland.

Snowscape is the leading Samoyed kennel in Ireland, and is the only registered kennel of Samoyeds with the Irish Kennel Club.

Classes for Samoyeds at championship dog shows in Ireland are fairly recent, having only first been offered in 1973.

There has been a Specialty Club for Samoyeds in Ireland since that date, of which Mr. Hyland is Secretary-Treasurer. The organization holds an Annual Breed Championship Specialty each year, to which all the members look forward with keen anticipation. It is more like a Garden Fete than a dog show, a real get-together for Samoyed owners and their dogs. This is officially the Irish Samoyed Dog Club.

I am certain that all who read this book will enjoy and appreciate the story Mr. Hyland has shared with us about a Samoyed of his who, about 1982, was sold to a member of the Dublin-Wicklow Mountain Rescue Service. At the time no one thought that this bitch puppy would become a dog capable of great and heroic deeds! But she proved herself to be exactly that.

The Sam, Tars, was trained in Mountain Rescue by the Royal Air Force G.B. Mountain Rescue Team, and she accompanied the team wherever they might go.

A severe and terrible snow storm came to the Wicklow area, with snow drifting to a height of more than eight feet. A team of mountain climbers scaled Lugna Quilla, the second highest mountain in Ireland. Seventeen people from Union College in Dublin started out, and the Rescue Team was alerted when it was realized that none of them were returning from the mountain. The Rescue Team, of course with the Samoyed whose name is Tars, spent 12 hours searching for the missing people. Unknown to the searchers, 14 of these people had finally made it down, but three remained up there. Tars of Snowscape found one man who was dead, and continued searching until she had located the last two people, one girl and one man, both of them in terrible condition. The girl's feet were frostbitten, and the Team Leader carefully cut away her boots. Tars knew exactly what to do about *that*; he started licking her feet, bringing back the circulation. It was a joyous moment when the girl said, "O.K.—that's lovely," when she found the feeling returning to both feet. One more case of a Samoyed proving the breed's devotion to people!

BRAZIL

For a very long time there was only the most sparing Samoyed representation in Brazil—a pity, as this is a country of tremendous enthusiasm for breeding and showing excellent dogs, and one would expect so beautiful a breed as the Samoyed to be well represented there.

Fortunately in 1975 the picture changed for the better, due to the efforts of Mr. and Mrs. Werner Degenhardt, owners of the Bjelkiere Kennels; and now Samoyeds are enjoying success and admiration there, being very well represented by imports and homebred dogs from this now famous kennel.

The Degenhardts selected "Bjelkiers" as their kennel name, they tell us, owing to that having been the original name given to the breed by the native Russian Samoyed people. It was a Canadian-bred dog, Nanook Salton (by Ohmi's Polar Tosca ex Samko Khimo) and a Danish bitch, Jenisej's Laci (by Jenisej's Hebu ex Jenisej's Gitja) who started off their owners' project by becoming the foundation dog and bitch of their breeding program. And both earned the titles of Brazilian, Great Brazilian and International Champion in the show ring.

In due time these two were bred to one another, and in their first litter produced a son who became the first Samoyed to win

Best in Show in Brazil. This dog, Champion J. Yurak of Bjelkiers, owner-handled by Werner Degenhardt, gained the award at the A.B.C. Kennel Club of Sao Paulo in March 1983 at the age of five years. That same year he also earned the distinction of becoming #9 *all breeds* among outstanding Brazilian-bred show dogs of the year.

In 1978 Mr. and Mrs. Degenhardt purchased and brought to Brazil the American Champion Silverseas Ivan of Arandale, by Champion Halee's Wee Willie Winkie ex Champion Angelique of Arandale followed later by American Champion Pooka's Centurian of the Pines, called "Blu" at home, by Champion Silveracres Chief Polar Bear ex Champion Pooka's Surprise O'Frostymorn, C.D. These two helped to maintain the already good quality in their kennel, and to come nearer to the original working Samoyed with their lovely smiling faces. In the shows, both were mainly placed among the four Group best.

Ivan was the first Samoyed male and Brazilian, Great Brazilian and International Champion J. Kirova of Bjelkiers (litter sister to Yurak) the first Samoyed bitch to receive the title of South American Champion. Both accomplished this at the II SICASUD-SHOW in Montevideo, Uruguay, the yearly International Show which each time is held in a different South American country. The judge was John Connolly from the United States.

Ivan became American, Brazilian, International (FCI), and South American Champion, thereby winning the *Dog World* Award For Canine Distinction. This was published in the December 1980 issue of *Dog World* magazine.

Blu became American, Brazilian, Great Brazilian, International, and also South American Champion. Both of these dogs were highly successful sires with many outstanding offspring to their credit.

In 1982 the bitch, Co-Lee's Chrystal of Bjelkiers, by American and Canadian Champion Co-Lee's Calipso ex American and Canadian Champion Kalmarli'd Aloja Tehani joined the Degenhardts in Brazil, in short becoming a Brazilian, Great Brazilian, and International Champion.

Two years later, Brazilian, Great Brazilian, International, and South American Champion J. Rebecca of Bjelkiers, who is the last edition of their two original foundation dogs, was taken to California for breeding to American, Canadian, and Mexican Champion

The Danish-bred bitch, Jenisej's Laci, (Freya) has earned the titles Brazilian, Great-Brazilian, International Champion. She is the foundation bitch of Bjelkiers Kennels.

The Hoof'n Paw White Knight (by Champion Kiskas Karaholme Cherokee ex Ice Way's Angel). The results of this effort, to combine the old heritage of the same English ancestors, was a complete success.

One of these puppies remained with the Degenhardts. His name, Rebecca's Orion of Bjelkiers, and he is already a Brazilian Champion. His sister, Rebecca's Olinda of Bjelkiers, went to Denmark where she is making all concerned extremely proud, having in June 1985, at only 13½ months of age, become Youth World Champion over 66 dogs during the World Show at Amsterdam. As Olinda is always breeder-shown, Werner Degenhardt flew especially from Brazil to Holland to handle her there. It was well worthwhile to him, I am sure, as later that same day she was winner of 4th place among 143 bitches between the ages of nine and 14 months with 64 breeds in competition. Later in the year, during October 1985, she earned the title Bundessieger '85 in Dortmund, Germany, during the interim having also won Groups in Denmark and having started nicely on her way to Danish, German, and International Champion titles. In the Danish annual final ratings, she was ranked #2 Bitch.

197

Some of the Samoyeds owned by Werner and Ingrid Degenhardt: (*Left to right*) Ch. Kirova (daughter, seven years old), Ch. Freya (mother, nine years old) and Ch. Rebecca (daughter, three years old).

Needless to say, Rebecca is coming to the United States to be bred again, hoping to get the same or perhaps even better results from again using the same bloodlines.

1986 has started out well for Bjelkiers Kennel in that their Brazilian, Great Brazilian, Uruguay, Paraguay, International, and South American Champion Kenosha's Amik of Silver Tip, by Champion Sabarka's Kenosha of Silver Tip ex J. Sashe of Bjelkiers, won his 12th Best in Show during January.

OTHER COUNTRIES

We are duly impressed with the fact that some truly splendid examples of the Samoyed breed are being raised and shown on the European Continent, gaining exciting records there. A friend from Brazil was recently on a judging assignment in Belgium, at the Flanders Dog Show, where he judged all Nordic breeds. This gentleman is Mr. Werner Degenhardt from Sao Paulo, Brazil, a Samoyed breeder of note.

We understand that there are some especially outstanding Samoyeds, as well, owned by Mr. Uyttersprot in Belgium, and that some lovely type and quality are also to be seen in Germany.

Mr. Degenhardt flew from Brazil especially to attend the World Championship Dog Show at Amsterdam in 1985, and has done so on other occasions as well. From him we know that these shows in Europe draw sizeable entries, reflecting the activities of the breeders.

Mr. J.A.C. Ouwerkerk's Samoyed Kennels are at Rotterdam in the Netherlands. He is the owner of such dogs as Dutch, German, Belgium, Luxembourg, and International Champion Akraliak Arctic, Bundessieger 1983, who represents English bloodlines on his sire's side, as he is a grandson of the English importations, Damon Samoye of Snowcryst and Snowcryst Susette.

Then there is Dutch, German, International, Belgium, and VHD Champion Nikara's Kareena, a Junior Warrant winner in 1983, Bundessieger in 1984.

A magnificent younger dog, born in 1984, is Special Encounter, who represents an almost solid Fairvilla background, going back into Kobe. He is a dog with a bright future, already a proven sire of quality, who should bring further laurels to his family in the Netherlands.

Nikara Kareena (Ch. Kafka Kes–Ch. Kamelia of Fairville) on left. Special Encounter (Ch. Zoox Katodzki–Nenetsky Stargazer) on right. Between them, in background, six-week-old Sam puppy. All owned by J. A. C. Ouwerkerk, Rotterdam, Netherlands. Outstanding examples of the type and quality of Samoyed found in this kennel.

Chapter 8

The Breed Standard

The standard of the breed, to which one sees and hears such frequent reference wherever purebred dogs are written of or discussed, is the word picture of what is considered to be the ideal specimen of the breed in question. It outlines, in minute detail, each and every feature of this breed, both in physical characteristics and in temperament, accurately describing the dog from whisker to tail, creating a clear impression of what is to be considered correct or incorrect, the features comprising "breed type," and the probable temperament and behavior pattern of typical members of that breed.

The standard is the guide for breeders endeavoring to produce quality dogs and for fanciers wishing to learn what is considered beautiful in the breed, and it is the tool with which judges evaluate and make their decisions in the ring. The dog it describes is the one which we seek and to which we compare in making our evaluations. It is the result of endless hours spent in dedicated work by knowledgeable members of each parent Specialty club, resulting from the combined efforts of the club itself, its individual members, and finally the American Kennel Club, by whom official approval must be granted prior to each standard's acceptance, or that of any amendments or changes to it, in the United States. In Great Britain, the governing body for all purebred dogs

Facing page:
Top: The famous Best in Show winning Samoyed Ch. Karasea's Silver Kim in June 1966 taking Best in Show at the Green Mountain Kennel Club Dog Show. Robert S. Forsyth is handling this very excellent dog for Alexandra and Louis Bishop, New York City. *Bottom:* The magnificent Am. and Can. Ch. Danica's Russian Roulette, multiple Group winner and placer, was among the 15 top Samoyeds in the United States for three years. An outstanding stud dog, his death at only seven and a half years old was a sad loss to his breed and his owners, Dr. John and Judy Kovitch and Sue Grasley.

is the Kennel Club. Breed standards are based on intensive study of breed history, earlier standards in the United States, and the purposes for which the breed was originally created and developed. All such factors have played their part in the drawing up of our present standards. Below is the current AKC Standard for Samoyeds.

GENERAL CONFORMATION

(a) *General Appearance*—The Samoyed, being essentially a working dog, should present a picture of beauty, alertness and strength, with agility, dignity and grace. As his work lies in cold climates, his coat should be heavy and weather-resistant, well groomed, and of good quality rather than quantity. The male carries more of a "ruff" than the female. He should not be long in the back as a weak back would make him practically useless for his legitimate work, but at the same time, a close-coupled body would also place him at a great disadvantage as draft dog. Breeders should aim for the happy medium, a body not long but muscular, allowing liberty, with a deep chest and well-sprung ribs, strong neck, straight front, and especially strong loins. Males should be masculine in appearance and deportment without unwarranted aggressiveness; bitches feminine without weakness of structure or apparent softness of temperament. Bitches may be slightly longer in back than males. They should both give the appearance of being capable of great endurance but be free from coarseness. Because of the depth of chest required, the legs should be moderately long. A very short-legged dog is to be deprecated. Hindquarters should be particularly well developed, stifles well bent and any suggestion of unsound stifles or cowhocks severely penalized. General appearance should include movement and general conformation, indicating balance and good substance.

(b) *Substance*—Substance is that sufficiency of bone and muscle which rounds out a balance with the frame. The bone is heavier than would be expected in a dog of this size, but not so massive as to prevent the speed and agility most desirable in a Samoyed. In all builds, bone should be in proportion to body size. The Samoyed should never be so heavy as to appear clumsy nor so light as to appear racy. The weight should be in proportion to the height.

(c) *Height*—Males, 21-23½ inches; females, 19-21 inches at the withers. An oversized or undersized Samoyed is to be penalized according to the extent of the deviation.

(d) *Coat* (texture and condition)—The Samoyed is a double-coated dog. The body should be well covered with an undercoat of soft, short, thick, close wool with longer and harsh hair growing through it to form the outer coat, which stands straight out from the body and should be free from curl. The coat should form a ruff around the neck and shoulders, framing the head (more on males than on females). Quality of coat should be weather resistant and considered more than quantity. A droopy coat is undesirable. The coat should glisten with a silver sheen. The female does not usually carry as long a coat as most males and it is softer in texture.

(e) *Color*—Samoyeds should be pure white, white and biscuit, cream, or all biscuit. Any other colors disqualify.

MOVEMENT

(a) *Gait*—The Samoyed should trot, not pace. He should move with a quick agile stride that is well timed. The gait should be free, balanced and vigorous, with good reach in the forequarters and good driving power in the hindquarters. When trotting, there should be a strong rear action drive. Moving at a slow walk or trot, they will not single-track, but as speed increases the legs gradually angle inward until the pads are finally falling on a line directly under the longitudinal center of the body. As the pad marks converge, the forelegs and hind legs are carried straight forward in travelling, the stifles not turned in nor out. The back should remain strong, firm and level. A choppy or stilted gait should be penalized.

(b) *Rear End*—Upper thighs should be well developed. Stifles well bent—approximately 45 degrees to the ground. Hocks should be well developed, sharply defined, and set at approximately 30 per cent of hip height. The hind legs should be parallel when viewed from the rear in a natural stance, strong, well developed, turning neither in nor out. Straight stifles are objectionable. Double-jointedness or cowhocks are a fault. Cowhocks should only be determined if the dog has had an opportunity to move properly.

(c) *Front End*—Legs should be parallel and straight to the pasterns. The pasterns should be strong, sturdy and straight, but flexible with some spring for proper let-down of feet. Because of depth of chest, legs should be moderately long. Length of leg from the ground to the elbow should be approximately 55 per cent of the total height at the withers—a very short-legged dog is to be deprecated. Shoulders should be long and sloping, with a layback of 45 degrees, and be firmly set. Out at the shoulders or out at the elbows should be penalized. The withers separation should be approximately 1-1½ inches.

(d) *Feet*—Large, long, flattish—a hare-foot, slightly spread but not splayed; toes arched; pads thick and tough, with protective growth of hair between the toes. Feet should turn neither in nor out in a natural stance but may turn in slightly in the act of pulling. Turning out, pigeon-toed, round or cat-footed or splayed are faults. Feathers on feet are not too essential but are more profuse on females than on males.

HEAD

(a) *Conformation*—Skull is wedge-shaped, broad, slightly crowned, not round or apple-headed, and should form an equilateral triangle on lines between the inner base of the ears and the central point of the stop. **Muzzle**—Muzzle of medium length and medium width, neither coarse nor snipy; should taper toward the nose and be in proportion to the size of the dog and the width of the skull. The muzzle must have depth. **Stop**—Not too abrupt, nevertheless well defined. **Lips**—Should be black for preference and slightly curved up at the corners of the mouth, giving the "Samoyed smile." Lip lines should not have the appearance of being coarse, nor should the flews drop predominantly at corners of the mouth.

Ears—Strong and thick, erect, triangular and slightly rounded at the tips; should not be large or pointed, nor should they be small and "bear-eared." Ears should conform to head size and the size of the dog; they should be set well apart but be within the border of the outer edge of the head; they should be mobile and well covered inside with hair; hair full and stand-off before the ears. Length of ear should be the same measurement as the distance from inner base of ear to outer corner of eye.

Eyes—Should be dark for preference; should be placed well apart and deep-set; almond-shaped with lower lid slanting toward an imaginary point approximately the base of the ears. Dark eye rims for preference. Round or protruding eyes penalized. Blue

Best in Show (all-breed and Specialty) winning Ch. Me Too of Bubbling Oaks illustrates Samoyed movement at its best. Owned by Jack and Amelia Price, Bubbling Oaks, Commack, New York.

eyes disqualifying.

Nose—Black for preference but brown, liver, or Dudley nose not penalized. Color of nose sometimes changes with age and weather.

Jaws and Teeth—Strong, well-set teeth, snugly overlapping with scissors bite. Undershot or overshot should be penalized.

(b) *Expression*—The expression, referred to as "Samoyed expression," is very important and is indicated by sparkle of the eyes, animation, and lighting up of the face when alert or intent on anything. Expression is made up of a combination of eyes, ears and mouth. The ears should be erect when alert; the mouth should be slightly curved up at the corners to form the "Samoyed smile."

Ch. Mauyak's English Star of My Way, an informal headstudy. Owned and bred by Kathy and Randy Lensen, My Way Samoyeds, Cascade, Wisconsin.

TORSO

(a) *Neck*—Strong, well muscled, carried proudly erect, set on sloping shoulders to carry head with dignity when at attention. Neck should blend into shoulders with a graceful arch.

(b) *Chest*—Should be deep, with ribs well sprung out from the spine and flattened at the sides to allow proper movement of the shoulders and freedom for the front legs. Should not be barrel-chested. Perfect depth of chest approximates the point of elbows, and the deepest part of the chest should be back of the forelegs—near the ninth rib. Heart and lung room are secured more by body depth than by width.

(c) *Loin and Back*—The withers form the highest part of the back. Loins strong and slightly arched. The back should be straight to the loin, medium in length, very muscular and neither long nor short-coupled. The dog should be "just off square"—the length being approximately 5 percent more than the height. Females allowed to be slightly longer than males. The belly should be well shaped and tightly muscled and, with the rear of the thorax, should swing up in a pleasing curve (tuck-up). Croup must be full, slightly sloping, and must continue imperceptibly to the tail root.

TAIL

The tail should be moderately long with the tail bone terminating approximately at the hock when down. It should be profusely covered with long hair and carried forward over the back or side when alert, but sometimes dropped when at rest. It should not be high or low set and should be mobile and loose—not tight over the back. A double hook is a fault. A judge should see the tail over the back once when judging.

DISPOSITION

Intelligent, gentle, loyal, adaptable, alert, full of action, eager to serve, friendly but conservative, not distrustful or shy, not overly aggressive. Unprovoked aggressiveness to be severely penalized.

Disqualifications

Any color other than pure white, cream, biscuit, or white and biscuit. Blue eyes.

Approved April 9, 1963

KENNEL CLUB OF GREAT BRITAIN VARIATION TO THE AKC STANDARD

The Kennel Club of Great Britain Standard for Samoyeds is almost identical to the American Kennel Club (AKC) Standard, except for the following:

With regard to *feet*, the British consider a round cat foot to be highly undesirable. In the United States, however, not only the round cat foot is to be faulted, but the following, as well: feet that turn out, feet that are pigeon-toed, and feet that are splayed.

With regard to the *tail*, in the United States a double hook (kink at the end of the tail) is considered a fault, whereas there is no mention of this in the British Standard.

With regard to *eyes*, in Britain the Standard calls for medium to dark brown; light or black eyes are undesirable. In the United States, dark eyes are preferred; blue eyes are a disqualification.

With regard to *coat color*, in Britain mention is made of pure white, white and biscuit, and cream—no mention of "all biscuit" as a color. In the United States, pure white, white and biscuit, cream, and all biscuit are recognized; any other colors disqualify.

Height requirements vary from Britain to the United States: in Britain, male Samoyeds should measure 51 to 56 cms (20 to 22 inches) and females should measure 46 to 51 cms (18 to 20 inches); in the United States, males should measure 21 to 23½ inches and females should measure 19 to 21 inches.

Chapter 9

Judging the Samoyed
by Elizabeth Lockman Hooyman

The Samoyed is a beautiful, natural breed. What confuses many judges, and infuriates the true breeder, is the inconsistency in the true identity of this breed. Many people do not understand that this handsome dog is an intelligent, tough-working animal. In judging the Samoyed never forget that a naturally beautiful dog can in fact be a strong, utilitarian animal underneath the beauty. These dogs went with Amundsen to the South Pole. They were, prior to the Expeditions, herding dogs for the Sammi people who were nomads following reindeer; and yet have such outstanding beauty they are in themselves breathtaking. Please do not expect anything less of this breed than you would of any arctic, for if you do the breed will be suffering a great disservice. Everyone has their own style of judging, and I do not want to presume to judge for anyone else. Thus the following text is merely a guideline to help others to interpret the standard and give some finer tips to those who judge the breed but who are not breeders of it.

HANDS–OFF OBSERVATION
When judging the Samoyed, take a few moments to look at your entry, before you have them gait or before you examine them, and consider the following points. I like to start from the ground up

Facing page:
Am. and Can. Ch. Bubbles La Rue of Oakwood baiting nicely for her handler, Joy Brewster, as she awaits the attention of the judge. On this occasion she went Group 2nd, the highest win ever made by a Samoyed at Westminster. Jack and Amelia Price, owners, Bubbling Oaks Samoyeds, Commack, New York.

and look for overall balance. I like to see good feet, proper bone, nice angles, a good eye placement, proper coat, and, most importantly, the proper length of leg. One of the big problems in the breed is lack of leg length. The length of the leg from the ground to elbow should be 55% of the total height at the withers. The Samoyed must have this length of leg or else the whole picture is ruined. Unlike the other arctics, our breed has sometimes been allowed to win in the show ring looking more like Chow Chows or Keeshonden than like Samoyeds. Some judges have a mistaken impression of what the Samoyed should look like, never demanding the top condition a true arctic must have. The Siberian Husky has not been burdened with this problem due to a height disqualification and a shorter coat required on that breed. The Alaskan Malamute similarly has kept much of its integrity because as a breed they are so much larger than a Samoyed.

As well as proper leg length, a good specimen will *not* be square, but rather about 55% off square and a little longer for bitches. With proper leg length, you will be able to evaluate the chest and shape of bodies easily from the center of the ring. The chest is deep, comes down to the elbows, and is clearly defined. When you have proper balance in leg length and body length the chest, ribs and loin of the dog stand out remarkably well and form, from the chest backwards, a nice oval thinning out to the rear quarters of the dog. So often in the ring we see specimens without daylight under them, or with so little that their bodies cannot be seen, and the overall effect is a nightmare to the true believer of the breed. Never fail to remember that a Samoyed cannot be agile functioning on short legs and square bodies, nor on short legs and long bodies.

After you have considered the leg and body proportions, start looking for good length of neck and a proper amount of forechest on the dog. Visually draw a parallel line from the withers down to the ground and block out the rest of the dog. Even through all that coat, a good forechest can easily be seen. The standard requires a 45-degree layback of the shoulder and a deep set chest, not a wide chest. Be careful of the barrel-chested dogs, as often they lack forechest and can be short legged; or the slabsided dogs that may have longer legs but the chest does not reach to the elbow. If this is the case, you may suspect age, as often the Samoyed will gain height and look mature many years before the chest can develop and the dog become actually mature. A proper Samoyed will have a lovely, developed sternum with a depth of chest clearly defined and good length of leg underneath with a well-developed 45 degree stifle.

As you move back from withers to croup, balance is again the key Nice angles up front deserve the same treatment behind. Often times with the tail lying over the croup and to the side, the topline seems higher in the rear than it should. The reason for this can be due to a puppy coat or to poor grooming, and it is best to check manually on the croup during examination.

At this point, instead of gaiting them immediately, I like to go over to each entry, approaching from the front of the line and working to the rear, checking on eye-set and shape, eye color, Sammy smile, head shape, and ears. When the standard calls for a Sammy smile, we are very sincere. Whenever a photo is taken, we *want* the mouth open to show this smile, for the upturned clean mouth is essential to the breed. Loose flews or a droopy mouth distort this image. As you approach, we want you to see a dark brown eye and an eye slant towards the base of the ears. This expression is quite literally alert and sparkling, as the dogs are happy to see you. A poor eye-set, rounded eyes, light or yellow eyes, give the Samoyed a mean or hopeless look. The ears should fit the head of the dog on the border of the edge of the head. If you are in doubt as to the size of the ears, being too small (i.e. Teddy-bear ears) or too large, bend the ear over and correctly it should reach the inner corner of the eye.

Be wary of jet black noses, for many have been treated or colored. Often Samoyeds as they age lose the dark pigment on the nose they once had as puppies. Some fade to a Dudley color; others to a greyish black; some to a pink, showing poor pigment. The problem for the judge not too familiar with the breed, on seeing a natural nose next to the many treated noses, is which is natural. To be fair, check the pigment on lip rims and the inside of the mouth on each of the dogs in the class. A dog with truly superior pigment always has jet black mouth rims and a jet black mouth down to the tonsils.

The head of the Samoyed should be wedge-shaped, with, therefore, everything fitting in balance on the wedge. The topskull should not be round or apple-headed, nor should it be flat. It should rise gently, crowning at the topskull. Often an apple-headed Samoyed (one with too rounded a topskull) will also have too rounded an eye, giving a mean look. The Sammy should *never* have round eyes.

The muzzle should be medium length and depth and should be in proportion to the size of the dog and the width of the skull, but remember that the overall head must be a wedge shape. We prefer whiskers on the Samoyed, once again opting for as natural a look as possible.

PROFILE GAIT

When observed gaiting from the side, the Samoyed should have excellent extension front and rear, not over-reaching, and with a firm, level topline. I personally like to see a smooth, flowing, easy gait with the front leg reaching just past or up to under the chin. Stride here is more important than speed, with the rear driving almost with a kick, moving in balance with the front. A choppy or stilted gait will show up easier here on profile and must be considered undesirable. Also at this time you may check on a tail that has not gone over the back while standing. Generally during gaiting a reluctant tail will come over the back and you need only to see it once over the back during judging.

HANDS-ON REALITY

When individually examining the Samoyed, once again check eye shape, eye color, lip and mouth pigment. Check length of muzzle, and feel the shape of the topskull. Prior to checking the bite, hold the dog's head and make sure that the head is wedge-shaped and the ears are in balance with the head.

Lack of full dentition generally is not a problem in the Samoyed, and very rarely will you see an overshot or undershot mouth. A scissors bite is required.

The neck should be strong, set on sloping shoulders with a layback of 45 degrees, and a deep, not wide, chest should extend down to the elbows. Please expect good muscle tone and development, for these dogs are arctics. The Samoyed's essential structure is formed for top performance in harsh conditions, so they must be strong dogs. Expect, under that lovely coat, to feel good muscle development covering the shoulders, forechest, ribs, loin, croup, upper thighs, all the way down to the muscle between the toes. I like to feel the development of muscle on the shoulder right up and over the withers. Moving your hands down the topline, a Samoyed should feel strong with muscle firm along the back. You should *not* be able to pick up a handful of flesh and rotate it over the spine. Remember that these dogs are *not* square, and that the loin should be strong and firm. The croup is full, slightly sloping to the tail root. Do not hesitate at this time to pick up the tail, put your hands on the croup, and then check the tail for length and set.

The upper thigh is well developed, with the stifle well bent, about 45 degrees, to the ground. The front and rear legs are parallel, and the feet point straight forward with a hare-foot required along with strong, thick pads and toes. The substance of bone is heavier than expected for a dog of this size, and should balance out the whole dog. I often find both extremes, too much bone and too little; but what we want is a balance to fit the frame, including the feet. If you see a cat foot or a splayed foot, often the bone or substance of the dog is too little to fit the frame, or too much dog.

COAT

This breed is sometimes difficult to judge because of the beautiful coat the Samoyed carries. On the one hand I have been stressing the importance of correct structure and conditioning of this true arctic, and now I would like you to understand how very important the coat is to the breed, and how poor judging regarding the coat could actually be harmful to the breed.

This coat must repel snow and ice, not being so long and soft as to ice up or ball up with snow during winter conditions. A long or a soft coat is not correct for this reason. The coat is a double coat, with harsh guard hairs and soft undercoat. Therefore in winter, the dog can shake off snow, keeping it from collecting. In summer, the soft undercoat will molt off the dog, allowing a cool insulation effect with the guard hairs left on the body. We want a short stand-off coat on the torso and longer coat on the mane, chest and britches. A curly coat is very undesirable. Texture of the guard hairs should be harsh, although not as harsh in bitches as in dogs, nor as long.

Please do not deprecate those dogs with biscuit or cream in their coats, legs or faces. There are many varieties of white, and biscuit or cream can be in patches, freckles, splotches, or over the entire dog. This is the way nature has provided for these dogs. By ignoring the dogs with the biscuit or cream, you are disturbing the laws of nature.

The coat of the Samoyed should be a *pleasure* to go through with your fingers. Gone are the days of poor grooming. The Samoyed exhibitors and breeders are extremely sophisticated in the world of grooming. Unlike other breeds, when you go over a Samoyed your hands will be clean. Many, many hours are spent bathing and grooming these dogs prior to the show. Only rarely will you find a dirty Samoyed, or one with chalk or powder in the coat. The leaders and top winners in the breed are very competitive in grooming and handling, so it is a pleasure to judge this breed. Staying with the natural look, we like to see whiskers, and abhor a scissored or sculpted coat. The only scissoring should be on the feet and hocks. Beware of sculpted or scissored manes, ears, torsos, and britches, for it implies a problem either of too long a coat or trying to change a structural problem by visual deception.

The Specialty-winning Ch. Blue Sky's Piece of Cake showing off excellent reach and drive in action. Owned by Dr. P. J. and Elizabeth Lockman Hooyman, Blue Sky Samoyeds, Pine, Colorado.

Randy and Sparkle, "the team"! Ch. Moonlighter's Ima Spark O'Bark was owner-handled throughout her show career by Randy Lensen (My Way Samoyeds, Cascade, Wisconsin) who co-owns this magnificent bitch with Kathie Lensen.

INDIVIDUAL GAITING

The Samoyed should have a well-timed, vigorous gait, driving in the rear and reaching in the front. Moving at proper speed, the dog should single track with the legs angling inward, with the pads falling in line directly under the longitudinal center of the body. As the pads converge, the front and rear legs go straight forward. I like to see a loose lead at all times with the Samoyed. Remember, these dogs must have a smooth stride, not a choppy or stilted gait. The motion should be going forward, not up and down, thus instead of taking many steps, the dog takes fewer with a longer stride. In other words, the Samoyed should be clean coming and going, single tracking and not taking mincing steps going down and back.

216

Chapter 10

The Samoyed as a Family Dog

The Samoyed makes a truly ideal family dog. His intelligence, his versatility, his willingness to please, and his sunny disposition all add up to make him truly a pleasure to have around. Not to mention the beauty that his appearance brings to your home.

Even in writing of the breed from its early days, as sledge dogs on the Samoyede Peninsula, have come references to the companionship as well as service provided by the dogs. Alfred H. Seeley, writing of the breed in the American Kennel *Gazette* in 1925, spoke of them as "biteless dogs with an almost human brain."

Thus their heritage is of an intelligent, amiable, people-loving breed, and they have been true to it every step of the way! One has but to look at the smiling and friendly expression of a Samoyed's face to realize that he is a kind, gentle dog.

There is a very close affinity between Samoyeds and children. These dogs truly love kids, can be trusted with them, and will guard them well.

In the same article we have quoted above, Mr. Seeley tells a very touching and revealing incident about his great importation of the 1920's, Champion Donerna's Barin. It seems that as a family pet in Yorkshire prior to his discovery by the dog show world,

Facing page:
Top: Great photo of Am. and Can. Ch. Kristik's English Autumn, *left*, with dam Can. Ch. Kristik's Snow Panda, *right*. Photo courtesy of Linda Zaraza, Autumn Samoyeds, Southbury, Connecticut. Just a bit of socializing between rounds at the dog show! *Bottom*: Sterling Nathan Hail with a friend. Samoyeds get on well with other dogs! Nathan Hail is by Ch. Aladdin's Dominator ex Ch. Nentsi's Nordic Mia-Kis. Bred and owned by Dr. Marion Jerszyk, Sterling Samoyeds, Mendham, New Jersey.

Barin had been accustomed to taking his owners' three-year-old daughter for a daily walk, strolling through the village, always with her tiny hand held gently in his mouth, much as a mother would keep hold of her three-year-old's hand. Several years later, after Barin had been sold to the Seeleys and had taken up life and a show career in America, his former Yorkshire family paid a visit to the United States. The youngster he had loved so dearly wanted most of all to take a trip to again see Barin, finally persuading her parents to make arrangements for her to do so. To quote Mr. Seeley, "recognition between the two was instantaneous . . . and it was a sight to warm the heart to see the mutual display of affection throughout the week's visit. Although the surroundings were quite different, neither side had forgotten the daily rambles, which were immediately renewed." It seems that after his former friend had departed for home, Barin refused all food for several days, and it was only through great effort on the part of some of his new young playmates that he finally returned to his usual cheerful self.

Just think how pleasant it is to have a dog who seems to almost perpetually smile with you day after day! It is difficult, indeed, for one to feel bad-tempered or out of sorts or mad at the world as one looks at that cheerful and beautiful expression! That, alone, should "sell" the breed to many people wishing a dog for companionship. Plus the great beauty of the breed with its handsome, well-balanced conformation; and that gorgeous shining coat.

The Samoyed is a strong and capable working dog. Right through from simple household obedience to the most complicated obedience routines, he is a winner. His intelligence and brains make it a cinch for him. He is a dog who was raised originally for sledge work under most difficult circumstances; thus pulling a cart or a sled is second nature to him even now.

If you enjoy backpacking, here again the Samoyed is the dog for you, strong and willing and seemingly tireless.

Although not generally thought of as such, the Samoyed is an expert and efficient herding dog. After all, those early Arctic duties included the herding of reindeer as the Samoyede people moved with them from place to place, as food supplies demanded.

The Samoyed is an alert and efficient watchdog, although not, by any means, an attack dog. He will give the warning of danger, which he is quick to sense when it is near; and he can look quite

218

formidable under those circumstances to someone bent on mischief. The dogs of this breed are not "nuisance barkers" who just seem to yap on general principles. When one of them sounds the alarm, there is almost invariably a reason.

The Samoyed's size, too, is in the breed's favor, since he is neither a small nor a huge dog. His medium size makes him a pleasant, manageable house dog. He is tidy and well mannered, as well, along with being companionable. If your Samoyed makes it clear that he would love to share your bed, remember that his long ago ancestors did exactly that, as one of their uses was to provide warmth through the bitter cold nights in the Arctic by sharing sleeping quarters with their owners.

His medium size is another attribute to be considered when you select a dog as a companion for your children. Too small a breed can often be injured by rough romping and play with children who sometimes do not stop to think that harm can thus be done by accident. On the other hand, too huge a dog (or a dog of a less friendly and loving disposition) may injure a small child just by sheer size, or lose patience if the game becomes unpleasant for it. You could hardly find a more reliable dog for children than a Samoyed! Which does *not* mean that the kids should be encouraged to take advantage of this fact, as they should be taught the same "basic rules" for kindness to their pet with this and with all breeds; but you can enjoy the feeling that the dog is of a reliable, patient disposition and of sufficient size, with the added protection of his thick coat, not to suffer harm except in extreme circumstances.

Samoyed are "good doers," thus easy dogs to keep in proper shape and condition. They require a minimum of care despite their heavy and beautiful coat; do not suffer excessively from weather conditions of heat or cold; and they get on well with dogs, cats, and whatever you may have in the way of other pets. They can adjust to your life-style whatever it may be; but they should be allowed to share in it, as they are companionable dogs who like to share, not be stuck off by themselves, nor constantly kenneled. In other words, if you select a Samoyed as a family dog, permit it to be a family dog, participating in your activities and living in your home with you and your family.

Probably one of the nicest things about Samoyeds is their long lifespan (with proper care) and how slowly they seem to age. To me it is heartbreaking to lose a dog at eight or nine years, which is so usual in many breeds. By then a dog should be at his best with a goodly number of years ahead for you both to enjoy. Thus may I point out to you the number of "senior citizen" dogs of this breed who go into the show ring and win at 10 or 11 years of age or even older, and the number we hear of with a lifespan well beyond their middle teens.

Chapter 11

The Purchase of Your Samoyed

Careful consideration should be given to what breed of dog you wish to own prior to your purchase of one. If several breeds are attractive to you, and you are undecided as to which you prefer, learn all you can about the characteristics of each before making your decision. As you do so, you are thus preparing yourself to make an intelligent choice; and this is very important when buying a dog who will be, with reasonable luck, a member of your household for at least a dozen years or more. Obviously, since you are reading this book, you have decided on the breed—so now all that remains is to make a good choice.

It is never wise to just rush out and buy the first cute puppy who catches your eye. Whether you wish a dog to show, one with whom to compete in obedience, or one as a family dog purely for his (or her) companionship, the more time and thought you invest as you plan the purchase, the more likely you are to meet with

Facing page: Ch. My Way's Lil Bit O'Frosty Acres, a beautiful example of correct head and expression, owned by Kathie and Randy Lensen, My Way Samoyeds, Cascade, Wisconsin.

complete satisfaction. The background and early care behind your pet will reflect in the dog's future health and temperament. Even if you are planning the purchase purely as a pet, with no thoughts of showing or breeding in the dog's or puppy's future, it is essential that, if the dog is to enjoy a trouble-free future, you assure yourself of a healthy, properly raised puppy or adult from sturdy, well-bred stock.

Throughout the pages of this book you will find the names and locations of many well-known and well-established kennels in various areas. Another source of information is the American Kennel Club (51 Madison Avenue, New York, New York 10010), from whom you can obtain a list of recognized breeders in the vicinity of your home. If you plan to have your dog campaigned by a professional handler, by all means let the handler help you locate and select a good dog. Through their numerous clients, handlers have access to a variety of interesting show prospects; and the usual arrangement is that the handler re-sells the dog to you for what his cost has been, with the agreement that the dog be campaigned for you by him throughout the dog's career. It is most strongly recommended that prospective purchasers follow these suggestions, as you thus will be better able to locate and select a satisfactory puppy or dog.

Your first step in searching for your puppy is to make appointments at kennels specializing in your breed, where you can visit and inspect the dogs, both those available for sale and the kennel's basic breeding stock. You are looking for an active, sturdy puppy with bright eyes and intelligent expression and who is friendly and alert; avoid puppies who are hyperactive, dull, or listless. The coat should be clean and thick, with no sign of parasites. The premises on which he was raised should look (and smell) clean and be tidy, making it obvious that the puppies and their surroundings are in capable hands. Should the kennels featuring the breed you intend to own be sparse in your area or not have what you consider attractive, do not hesitate to contact others at a distance and purchase from them if they seem better able to supply a puppy or dog who will please you—*so long as it is a recognized breeding kennel of that breed*. Shipping dogs is a regular practice nowadays, with comparatively few problems when one considers the number of dogs shipped each year. A reputable, well-known breeder wants the customer to be satisfied; thus, he will represent the puppy fairly. Should you not be pleased with the puppy upon arrival, a breeder, such as described, will almost certainly permit its return. A conscientious breeder takes real interest and concern in the welfare of the dogs he or she causes to be brought into the world. Such a breeder also is proud of a reputation for integrity. Thus on two counts, for the sake of the dog's future and the breeder's reputation, to such a person a *satisfied* customer takes precedence over a sale at any cost.

If your puppy is to be a pet or "family dog," the earlier the age at which it joins your household the better. Puppies are weaned and ready to start out on their own, under the care of a sensible new owner, at about six weeks old; and if you take a young one, it is often easier to train it to the routine of your household and to your requirements of it than is the case with an older dog which, even though still technically a puppy, may have already started habits you will find difficult to change. The younger puppy is usually less costly, too, as it stands to reason the breeder will not have as much expense invested in it. Obviously, a puppy that has been raised to five or six months old represents more in care and cash expenditure on the breeder's part than one sold earlier; therefore he should be, and generally is, priced accordingly.

There is an enormous amount of truth in the statement that "bargain" puppies seldom turn out to be that. A "cheap" puppy, raised purely for sale and profit, can and often does lead to great heartbreak, including problems and veterinarian's bills which can add up to many times the initial cost of a properly reared dog. On the other hand, just because a puppy is expensive does not assure one that is healthy and well reared. There have been numerous cases where unscrupulous dealers have sold, for several hundred dollars, puppies that were sickly, in poor condition, and such poor specimens that the breed of which they were supposedly members was barely recognizable. So one cannot always judge a puppy by price alone. Common sense must guide a prospective purchaser, plus the selection of a *reliable*, well-recommended dealer whom you know to have well-satisfied customers or, best of all, a specialized breeder. You will probably find the fairest pricing at the kennel of a breeder. Such a person, experienced with the breed in general and with his or her own stock in particular, through extensive association with these dogs, has watched enough of them mature to have obviously learned to assess quite accurately each puppy's potential—something impossible where such background is non-existent.

One more word on the subject of pets. Bitches make a fine choice for this purpose as they are usually quieter and more gentle than the males, easier to house train, more affectionate, and less inclined to roam. If you do select a bitch and have no intention of breeding or showing her, by all means have her spayed, for your sake and for hers. The advantages to the owner of a spayed bitch include avoiding the nuisance of "in season" periods which normally occur twice yearly—with the accompanying eager canine swains haunting your premises in an effort to get close to your female—plus the unavoidable messiness and spotting of furniture and rugs at this time, which can be annoying if she is a household companion in the habit of sharing your sofa or bed. As for the spayed bitch, she benefits as she grows older because this simple operation almost entirely eliminates the possibility of breast cancer ever occurring. It is recommended that all bitches eventually be spayed—even those used for show or breeding when their careers have ended—in order that they may enjoy a happier, healthier old age. Please take note, however, that a bitch who has been spayed (or an altered dog) *cannot be shown at American Kennel Club dog shows once this operation has been performed*. Be certain that you are *not* interested in showing her before taking this step.

Also, in selecting a pet, never underestimate the advantages of an older dog, perhaps a retired show dog or a bitch no longer needed for breeding, who may be available and quite reasonably priced by a breeder anxious to place such a dog in a loving home. These dogs are settled and can be a delight to own, as they make wonderful companions, especially in a household of adults where raising a puppy can sometimes be a trial.

Everything that has been said about careful selection of your pet puppy and its place of purchase applies, but with many further considerations, when you plan to buy a show dog or foundation stock for a future breeding program. Now is the time for an in-depth study of the breed, starting with every word and every illustration in this book and all others you can find written on the subject. The Standard of the breed has now become your guide, and you must learn not only the words but also how to interpret them and how to apply them to actual dogs before you are ready to make an intelligent selection of a show dog.

If you are thinking in terms of a dog to show, obviously you must have learned about dog shows and must be in the habit of attending them. This is fine, but now your activity in this direction should be increased, with your attending every single dog show within a reasonable distance from your home. Much can be learned about a breed at ringside at these events. Talk with the breeders who are exhibiting. Study the dogs they are showing. Watch the judging with concentration, noting each decision made, and attempt to follow the reasoning by which the judge has reached it. Note carefully the attributes of the dogs who win and, for your later use, the manner in which each is presented. Close your ears to the ringside know-it-alls, usually novice owners of a dog or two and very new to the Fancy, who have only derogatory remarks to make about all that is taking place unless they happen to win. This is the type of exhibitor who "comes and goes" through the Fancy and whose interest is usually of very short duration, owing to lack of knowledge and dissatisfaction caused by the failure to recognize the need to learn. You, as a fancier whom we hope will last and enjoy our sport over many future years, should develop independent thinking at this stage; you should learn to draw your own conclusions about the merits, or lack of them, seen before you in the ring and, thus, sharpen your own judgement in preparation for choosing wisely and well.

Note carefully which breeders campaign winning dogs—not just an occasional isolated good one, but consistent, homebred winners. It is from one of these people that you should select your own future "star."

If you are located in an area where dog shows take place only occasionally or where there are long travel distances involved, you will need to find another testing ground for your ability to select a worthy show dog. Possibly, there are some representative kennels raising this breed within a reasonable distance. If so, by all means ask permission of the owners to visit the kennels and do so when permission is granted. You may not necessarily buy then and there, as they may not have available what you are seeking that

225

very day, but you will be able to see the type of dog being raised there and to discuss the dogs with the breeder. Every time you do this, you add to your knowledge. Should one of these kennels have dogs which especially appeal to you, perhaps you could reserve a show-prospect puppy from a coming litter. This is frequently done, and it is often worth waiting for a puppy, unless you have seen a dog with which you truly are greatly impressed and which is immediately available.

The purchase of a puppy has already been discussed. Obviously this same approach applies in a far greater degree when the purchase involved is a future show dog. The only place from which to purchase a show prospect is a breeder who raises show-type stock; otherwise, you are almost certainly doomed to disappointment as the puppy matures. Show and breeding kennels obviously cannot keep all of their fine young stock. An active breeder-exhibitor is, therefore, happy to place promising youngsters in the hands of people also interested in showing and winning with them, doing so at a fair price according to the quality and prospects of the dog involved. Here again, if no kennel in your immediate area has what you are seeking, do not hesitate to contact top breeders in other areas and to buy at long distance. Ask for pictures, pedigrees, and a complete description. Heed the breeder's advice and recommendations, after truthfully telling exactly what your expectations are for the dog you purchase. Do you want something with which to win just a few ribbons now and then? Do you want a dog who can complete his championship? Are you thinking of the real "big time" (*i.e.*, seriously campaigning with Best of Breed, Group wins, and possibly even Best in Show as your eventual goal)? Consider it all carefully in advance; then honestly discuss your plans with the breeder. You will be better satisfied with the results if you do this, as the breeder is then in the best position to help you choose the dog who is most likely to come through for you. A breeder selling a show dog is just as anxious as the buyer for the dog to succeed, and the breeder will represent the dog to you with truth and honesty. Also, this type of breeder does not lose interest the moment the sale has been made but, when necessary, will be right there to assist you with beneficial advice and suggestions based on years of experience.

As you make inquiries of at least several kennels, keep in mind

226

that show-prospect puppies are less expensive than mature show dogs, the latter often costing close to four figures, and sometimes more. The reason for this is that, with a puppy, there is always an element of chance, the possibility of it's developing unexpected faults as it matures or failing to develop the excellence and quality that earlier had seemed probable. There definitely is a risk factor in buying a show-prospect puppy. Sometimes all goes well, but occasionally the swan becomes an ugly duckling. Reflect on this as you consider available puppies and young adults. It just might be a good idea to go with a more mature, though more costly, dog if one you like is available.

When you buy a mature show dog, "what you see is what you get," and it is not likely to change beyond coat and condition, which are dependent on your care. Also advantageous for a novice owner is the fact that a mature dog of show quality almost certainly will have received show-ring training and probably match-show experience, which will make your earliest handling ventures much easier.

Frequently it is possible to purchase a beautiful dog who has completed championship but who, owing to similarity in bloodlines, is not needed for the breeder's future program. Here you have the opportunity of owning a champion, usually in the two-to-five-year-old range, which you can enjoy campaigning as a special (for Best of Breed competition) and which will be a settled, handsome dog for you and your family to enjoy with pride.

If you are planning foundation for a future kennel, concentrate on acquiring one or two really superior bitches. These need not be top show-quality, but they should represent your breed's finest producing bloodlines from a strain noted for producing quality, generation after generation. A proven matron who is already the dam of show-type puppies is, of course, the ideal selection; but these are usually difficult to obtain, no one being anxious to part with so valuable an asset. You just might strike it lucky, though, in which case you are off to a flying start. If you cannot find such a matron available, select a young bitch of finest background from top-producing lines who is herself of decent type, free of obvious faults, and of good quality.

Great attention should be paid to the pedigree of the bitch from whom you intend to breed. If not already known to you, try to see the sire and dam. It is generally agreed that someone starting with a breed should concentrate on a fine collection of topflight bitches and raise a few litters from these before considering keeping one's own stud dog. The practice of buying a stud and then breeding everything you own or acquire to that dog does not always work out well. It is better to take advantage of the many noted sires who are available to be used at stud, who represent all of the leading strains, and, in each case, to carefully select the one who in type and pedigree seems most compatible to each of your bitches, at least for your first several litters.

To summarize, if you want a "family dog" as a companion, it is best to buy it young and raise it according to the habits of your household. If you are buying a show dog, the more mature it is, the more certain you can be of its future beauty. If you are buying foundation stock for a kennel, then bitches are better, but they

Eng. Ch. Zamotski Lucky Star at Ostyak, by Eng. Ch. Hurkur Jingles (Top Winning Samoyed in England) ex Fairville Silver Jewel. Breeders, Mr. and Mrs. Hamilton. Owner, Carol Fox. Photo courtesy of Mrs. Betty Moody, Novaskaya Samoyeds.

N.Z. Ch. Novaskaya Georgia Mist (U.K. import) at 16 months following her fifth Challenge Certificate win. By Novaskaya Silva Starsun ex Novaskaya Georgia Peach. Owned by Mr. and Mrs. T. Blewitt. Photo courtesy of Mrs. Betty Moody.

must be from the finest *producing* bloodlines.

When you buy a pure-bred dog that you are told is eligible for registration with the American Kennel Club, you are entitled to receive from the seller an application form which will enable you to register your dog. If the seller cannot give you the application form, you should demand and receive an identification of your dog, consisting of the name of the breed, the registered names and numbers of the sire and dam, the name of the breeder, and your dog's date of birth. If the litter of which your dog is a part is already recorded with the American Kennel Club, then the litter number is sufficient identification.

Do not be misled by promises of papers at some later date. Demand a registration application form or proper identification as described above. If neither is supplied, do not buy the dog. So warns the American Kennel Club, and this is especially important in the purchase of show or breeding stock.

Chapter 12

The Care of Your Samoyed Puppy

The moment you decide to be the new owner of a puppy is not one second too soon to start planning for the puppy's arrival in your home. Both the new family member and you will find the transition period easier if your home is geared in advance of the arrival.

The first things to be prepared are a bed for the puppy and a place where you can pen him up for rest periods. Every dog should have a crate of its own from the very beginning, so that he will come to know and love it as his special place where he is safe and happy. It is an ideal arrangement, for when you want him to be free, the crate stays open. At other times you can securely latch it and know that the pup is safely out of mischief. If you travel with him, his crate comes along in the car; and, of course, in traveling by plane there is no alternative but to have a carrier for the dog. If you show your dog, you will want him upon occasion to be in a crate a good deal of the day. So from every consideration, a crate is a very sensible and sound investment in your puppy's future safety and happiness and for your own peace of mind.

The crates most desirable are the wooden ones with removable side panels, which are ideal for cold weather (with the panels in

Facing page:
Nordic's Quicksilver Kodiac, C.D., by Ch. Tsiulikagta's Skagit ex Ch. Nordic's Kristi of Cool Hill. Bred by Gail and Dick Mathews. Owned by Dr. Marion M. Jerszyk, Sterling Samoyeds, Mendham, N.J.

231

place to keep out drafts) and in hot weather (with the panels removed to allow better air circulation). Wire crates are all right in the summer, but they give no protection from cold or drafts. Aluminum crates, due to the manner in which the metal reflects surrounding temperatures, are not recommended. If it is cold, so is the metal of the crate; if it is hot, the crate becomes burning hot.

When you choose the puppy's crate, be certain that it is roomy enough not to become outgrown. The crate should have sufficient height so the dog can stand up in it as a mature dog and sufficient area so that he can stretch out full length when relaxed. When the puppy is young, first give him shredded newspaper as a bed; the papers can be replaced with a mat or turkish towels when the dog is older. Carpet remnants are great for the bottom of the crate, as they are inexpensive and in case of accidents can be quite easily replaced. As the dog matures and is past the chewing age, a pillow or blanket in the crate is an appreciated comfort.

Sharing importance with the crate is a safe area in which the puppy can exercise and play. If you are an apartment dweller, a baby's playpen works out well for a young dog; for an older puppy use a portable exercise pen which you can use later when travelling with your dog or for dog shows. If you have a yard, an area where he can be outside in safety should be fenced in prior to the dog's arrival at your home. This area does not need to be huge, but it does need to be made safe and secure. If you are in a suburban area where there are close neighbors, stockade fencing works out best, as then the neighbors are less aware of the dog and the dog cannot see and bark at everything passing by. If you are out in the country where no problems with neighbors are likely to occur, then regular chain-link fencing is fine. For added precaution in both cases, use a row of concrete blocks or railroad ties inside against the entire bottom of the fence; this precludes or at least considerably lessens the chances of your dog digging his way out.

Be advised that if yours is a single dog, it is very unlikely that it will get sufficient exercise just sitting in the fenced area, which is what most of them do when they are there alone. Two or more dogs will play and move themselves around, but one by itself does little more than make a leisurely tour once around the area to check things over and then lie down. You must include a daily walk or two in your plans if your puppy is to be rugged and well.

Exercise is extremely important to a puppy's muscular development and to keep a mature dog fit and trim. So make sure that those exercise periods, or walks, a game of ball, and other such activities, are part of your daily program as a dog owner.

If your fenced area has an outside gate, provide a padlock and key and a strong fastening for it, and use them, so that the gate cannot be opened by others and the dog taken or turned free. The ultimate convenience in this regard is, of course, a door (unused for other purposes) from the house around which the fenced area can be enclosed, so that all you have to do is open the door and out into his area he goes. This arrangement is safest of all, as then you need not be using a gate, and it is easier in bad weather since then you can send the dog out without taking him and becoming soaked yourself at the same time. This is not always possible to manage, but if your house is arranged so that you could do it this way, you would never regret it due to the convenience and added safety thus provided. Fencing in the entire yard, with gates to be opened and closed whenever a caller, deliveryman, postman, or some other person comes on your property, really is not safe at all because people not used to gates are frequently careless about closing and latching them *securely*. Many heartbreaking incidents have been brought about by someone carelessly half closing a gate (which the owner had thought to be firmly latched) and the dog wandering out. For greatest security a fenced *area* definitely takes precedence over a fenced *yard*.

The puppy will need a collar (one that fits now, not one to be grown into) and a lead from the moment you bring him home. Both should be an appropriate weight and type for his size. Also needed are a feeding dish and a water dish, both made preferably of unbreakable material. Your pet supply shop should have an interesting assortment of these and other accessories from which you can choose. Then you will need grooming tools of the type the breeder recommends and some toys. Equally satisfactory is Nylabone®, a nylon bone that does not chip or splinter and that "frizzles" as the puppy chews, providing healthful gum massage. Avoid plastics and any sort of rubber toys, *particularly those with squeakers* which the puppy may remove and swallow. If you want a ball for the puppy to use when playing with him, select one of very hard construction made for this purpose and do not leave it alone with him because he may chew off and swallow bits of the rubber. Take the ball with you when the game is over. This also applies to some of those "tug of war" type rubber toys which are fun when used with the two of you for that purpose but again should *not* be left behind for the dog to work on with his teeth. Bits of swallowed rubber, squeakers, and other such foreign articles can wreak great havoc in the intestinal tract—do all you can to guard against them.

Too many changes all at once can be difficult for a puppy. For at least the first few days he is with you, keep him on the food and feeding schedule to which he is accustomed. Find out ahead of time from the breeder what he feeds his puppies, how frequently, and at what times of the day. Also find out what, if any, food supplements the breeder has been using and recommends. Then be prepared by getting in a supply of the same food so that you will have it there when you bring the puppy home. Once the puppy is accustomed to his new surroundings, then you can switch the type of food and schedule to fit your convenience, but

To satisfy the chewing instincts of your Samoyed, give him a Nylabone®. Nylabones are available in several sizes and flavors. They are safe and enjoyed by dogs of all sizes and ages.

A Gumabone Frisbee® Flying Disc is a most appropriate device for exercising and training an active dog, such as a Samoyed. Made of a pliable but very tough non-toxic polyurethane, it can withstand extended use and abuse by even the largest of dog breeds.

for the first several days do it as the puppy expects.

Your selection of a veterinarian should also be attended to before the puppy comes home, because you should stop at the vet's office for the puppy to be checked over as soon as you leave the breeder's premises. If the breeder is from your area, ask him for recommendations. Ask you dog-owning friends for their opinions of the local veterinarians, and see what their experiences with those available have been. Choose someone whom several of your friends recommend highly, then contact him about your puppy, perhaps making an appointment to stop in at his office. If the premises are clean, modern, and well equipped, and if you like the veterinarian, make an appointment to bring the puppy in on the day of purchase. Be sure to obtain the puppy's health record from the breeder, including information on such things as shots and worming that the puppy has had.

JOINING THE FAMILY

Remember that, exciting and happy an occasion as it is for you, the puppy's move from his place of birth to your home can be, for him, a traumatic experience. His mother and littermates will be missed. He quite likely will be awed or frightened by the change of surroundings. The person on whom he depended will be gone. Everything should be planned to make his arrival at your home pleasant—to give him confidence and to help him realize that yours is a pretty nice place to be after all.

Never bring a puppy home on a holiday. There is just too much going on with people and gifts and excitement. If he is in honor of an "occasion," work it out so that his arrival will be a few days earlier, or perhaps even better, a few days later than the "occasion." Then your home will be back to its normal routine and the puppy can enjoy your undivided attention. Try not to bring the puppy home in the evening. Early morning is the ideal time, as then he has the opportunity of getting acquainted and the initial strangeness should wear off before bedtime. You will find it a more peaceful night that way. Allow the puppy to investigate as he likes, under your watchful eye. If you already have a pet in the household, keep a careful watch that the relationship between the two gets off to a friendly start or you may quickly find yourself with a lasting problem. Much of the future attitude of each toward the other will depend on what takes place that first day, so keep your mind on what they are doing and let your other activities slide for the moment. Be careful not to let your older pet become jealous by paying more attention to the puppy than to him, as that will start a bad situation immediately.

If you have a child, here again it is important that the relationship start out well. Before the puppy is brought home, you should have a talk with the youngster. He must clearly understand that puppies are fragile and can easily be injured; therefore, they should not be teased, hurt, mauled, or overly rough-housed. A puppy is not an inanimate toy; it is a living thing with a right to be loved and handled respectfully, treatment which will reflect in the dog's attitude toward your child as both mature together. Never permit your children's playmates to mishandle the puppy, tormenting the puppy until it turns on the children in self-defense. Children often do not realize how rough is too rough. You, as a responsible adult, are obligated to assure that your puppy's relationship with children is a pleasant one.

Do not start out by spoiling your puppy. A puppy is usually pretty smart and can be quite demanding. What you had considered to be "just for tonight" may be accepted by the puppy as "for keeps." Be firm with him, strike a routine, and stick to it.

The puppy will learn more quickly this way, and everyone will be happier as a result. A radio playing softly or a dim night light are often comforting to a puppy as it gets accustomed to new surroundings and should be provided in preference to bringing the puppy to bed with you—unless, of course, you intend him to share the bed as a permanent arrangement.

SOCIALIZING AND TRAINING

Socialization and training of your puppy should start the very day of his arrival in your home. Never address him without calling him by name. A short, simple name is the easiest to teach as it catches the dog's attention quickly; avoid elaborate call names. Always address the dog by the same name, not a whole series of pet names; the latter will only confuse the puppy.

Use his name clearly, and call the puppy over to you when you see him awake and wandering about. When he comes, make a big fuss over him for being such a good dog. He thus will quickly associate the sound of his name with coming to you and a pleasant happening.

Several hours after the puppy's arrival is not too soon to start accustoming him to the feel of a light collar. He may hardly notice it; or he may struggle, roll over, and try to rub it off his neck with his paws. Divert his attention when this occurs by offering a tasty snack or a toy (starting a game with him) or by petting him. Before long he will have accepted the strange feeling around his neck and no longer appear aware of it. Next comes the lead. Attach it and then immediately take the puppy outside or otherwise try to divert his attention with things to see and sniff. He may struggle against the lead at first, biting at it and trying to free himself. Do not pull him with it at this point; just hold the end loosely and try to follow him if he starts off in any direction. Normally his attention will soon turn to investigating his surroundings if he is outside or you have taken him into an unfamiliar room in your house; curiosity will take over and he will become interested in sniffing around the surroundings. Follow him with the lead slackly held until he seems to have completely forgotten about it; then try with gentle urging to get him to follow you. Don't be rough or jerk at him; just tug gently on the lead in short quick motions (steady pulling can become a battle of wills), repeating his name or trying to get him to follow your hand which is holding a bite of food or

237

an interesting toy. If you have an older lead-trained dog, then it should be a cinch to get the puppy to follow along after *him*. In any event the average puppy learns quite quickly and will soon be trotting along nicely on the lead. Once that point has been reached, the next step is to teach him to follow on your left side, or heel. This will not likely be accomplished all in one day; it should be done with short training periods over the course of several days until you are satisfied with the result.

During the course of house training your puppy, you will need to take him out frequently and at regular intervals: first thing in the morning directly from the crate, immediately after meals, after the puppy has been napping, or when you notice that the puppy is looking for a spot. Choose more or less the same place to take the puppy each time so that a pattern will be established. If he does not go immediately, do not return him to the house as he will probably relieve himself the moment he is inside. Stay out with him until he has finished; then be lavish with your praise for his good behavior. If you catch the puppy having an accident indoors, grab him firmly and rush him outside, sharply saying "No!" as you pick him up. If you do not see the accident occur, there is little point in doing anything except cleaning it up, as once it has happened and been forgotten, the puppy will most likely not even realize why you are scolding him.

If you live in a big city or are away many hours at a time, having a dog that is trained to go on paper has some very definite advantages. To do this, one proceeds pretty much the same way as taking the puppy outdoors, except now you place the puppy on the newspaper at the proper time. The paper should always be kept in the same spot. An easy way to paper train a puppy if you have a playpen for it or an exercise pen is to line the area with newspapers; then gradually, every day or so, remove a section of newspaper until you are down to just one or two. The puppy acquires the habit of using the paper; and as the prepared area grows smaller, in the majority of cases the dog will continue to use whatever paper is still available. It is pleasant, if the dog is alone for an excessive length of time, to be able to feel that if he needs it the paper is there and will be used.

The puppy should form the habit of spending a certain amount of time in his crate, even when you are home. Sometimes the puppy will do this voluntarily, but if not, he should be taught to do so, which is accomplished by leading the puppy over by his collar, gently pushing him inside, and saying firmly, "Down" or "Stay." Whatever expression you use to give a command, stick to the very same one each time for each act. Repetition is the big thing in training—and so is association with what the dog is expected to do. When you mean "Sit," always say exactly that. "Stay" should mean *only* that the dog should remain where he receives the command. "Down" means something else again. Do not confuse the dog by shuffling the commands, as this will create training problems for you.

As soon as he had had his immunization shots, take your puppy with you whenever and wherever possible. There is nothing that will build a self-confident, stable dog like socialization, and it is extremely important that you plan and give the time and energy necessary for this, whether your dog is to be a show dog or a pleasant, well-adjusted family member. Take your puppy in the car so that he will learn to enjoy riding and not become carsick, as dogs may do if they are infrequent travelers. Take him anywhere you are going where you are certain he will be welcome: visiting friends and relatives (if they do not have housepets who may resent the visit), busy shopping centers (keeping him always on lead), or just walking around the streets of your town. If someone admires him (as always seems to happen when one is out with puppies), encourage the stranger to pet and talk with him. Socialization of this type brings out the best in your puppy and helps him to grow up with a friendly outlook, liking the world and its inhabitants. The worst thing that can be done to a puppy's personality is to shelter him. By always keeping him at home away from things and people unfamiliar to him, you may be creating a personality problem for the mature dog that will be a cross for you to bear later on.

FEEDING YOUR DOG

Time was when providing nourishing food for dogs involved a far more complicated procedure than people now feel is necessary. The old school of thought was that the daily ration must consist of fresh beef, vegetables, cereal, egg yolks, and cottage cheese as basics with such additions as brewer's yeast and vitamin tablets on a daily basis.

During recent years, however, many minds have changed regarding this procedure. Eggs, cottage cheese, and supplements to the diet are still given, but the basic method of feeding dogs has changed; and the change has been, in the opinion of many authorities, definitely for the better. The school of thought now is that you are doing your dogs a favor when you feed them some of the fine commercially prepared dog foods in preference to your own home-cooked concoctions.

The reason behind this new outlook is easily understandable. The dog food industry has grown to be a major one, participated in by some of the best known and most respected names in America. These trusted firms, it is agreed, turn out excellent products, so people are feeding their dog food preparations with confidence and the dogs are thriving, living longer, happier, and healthier lives than ever before. What more could one want?

There are at least half a dozen absolutely top-grade dry foods to be mixed with broth or water and served to your dog according to directions. There are all sorts of canned meats, and there are several kinds of "convenience foods," those in a packet which you open and dump out into the dog's dish. It is just that simple. The convenience foods are neat and easy to use when you are away from home, but generally speaking a dry food mixed with hot water (or soup) and meat is preferred. It is the opinion of many that the canned meat, with its added fortifiers, is more beneficial to the dogs than the fresh meat. However, the two can be alternated or, if you prefer and your dog does well on it, by all means use fresh ground beef. A dog enjoys changes in the meat part of his diet, which is easy with the canned food since all sorts of beef are available (chunk, ground, stewed, and so on), plus lamb, chicken, and even such concoctions as liver and egg, plain liver flavor, and a blend of five meats.

There is also prepared food geared to every age bracket of your dog's life, from puppyhood on through old age, with special additions or modifications to make it particularly nourishing and beneficial. Previous generations never had it so good where the canine dinner is concerned, because these commercially prepared foods are tasty and geared to meeting the dog's gastronomic approval.

Additionally, contents and nutrients are clearly listed on the labels, as are careful instructions for feeding just the right amount for the size, weight, and age of each dog.

With these foods the addition of extra vitamins is not necessary, but if you prefer there are several kinds of those, too, that serve as taste treats as well as being beneficial. Your pet supplier has a full array of them.

Of course there is no reason not to cook up something for your dog if you would feel happier doing so. But it seems unnecessary when such truly satisfactory rations are available with so much less trouble and expense.

How often you feed your dog is a matter of how it works out best for you. Many owners prefer to do it once a day. It is generally agreed that two meals, each of smaller quantity, are better for the digestion and more satisfying to the dog, particularly if yours is a household member who stands around and watches preparations for the family meals. Do not overfeed. This is the shortest route to all sorts of problems. Follow directions and note carefully how your dog is looking. If your dog is overweight, cut back the quantity of food a bit. If the dog looks thin, then increase the amount. Each dog is an individual and the food intake should be adjusted to his requirements to keep him feeling and looking trim and in top condition.

From the time puppies are fully weaned until they are about twelve weeks old, they should be fed four times daily. From three months to six months of age, three meals should suffice. At six months of age the puppies can be fed two meals, and the twice daily feedings can be continued until the puppies are close to one year old, at which time feeding can be changed to once daily if desired. If you do feed just once a day, do so by early afternoon at the latest and give the dog a snack, a biscuit or two, at bedtime.

Remember that plenty of fresh water should always be available to your puppy or dog for drinking. This is of utmost importance to his health.

Chapter 13

The Making of a Show Dog

If you have decided to become a show dog exhibitor, you have accepted a very real and very exciting challenge. The groundwork has been accomplished with the selection of your future show prospect. If you have purchased a puppy, it is assumed that you have gone through all the proper preliminaries concerning good care, which should be the same if the puppy is a pet or future show dog, with a few added precautions for the latter.

GENERAL CONSIDERATIONS

Remember the importance of keeping your future winner in trim, top condition. Since you want him neither too fat nor too thin, his appetite for his proper diet should be guarded, and children and guests should not be permitted to constantly feed him "goodies." The best treat of all is a small wad of raw ground beef or a packaged dog treat. To be avoided are ice cream, cake, cookies, potato chips, and other fattening items which will cause the dog to put on weight and may additionally spoil his appetite for the proper, nourishing, well-balanced diet so essential to good health and condition.

The importance of temperament and showmanship cannot possibly be overestimated. They have put many a mediocre dog

Facing page:
This lovely headstudy is of Am. and Can. Ch. Danica's Russian Roulette. Courtesy of Dr. John and Judy Kovitch, Danica Samoyeds, Bloomsburg, Pennsylvania.

across, while lack of them can ruin the career of an otherwise outstanding specimen. From the day your dog joins your family, socialize him. Keep him accustomed to being with people and to being handled by people. Encourage your friends and relatives to "go over" him as the judges will in the ring so this will not seem a strange and upsetting experience. Practice showing his "bite" (the manner in which his teeth meet) quickly and deftly. It is quite simple to slip the lips apart with your fingers, and the puppy should be willing to accept this from you or the judge without struggle.

Some judges prefer that the exhibitors display the dog's bite and other mouth features themselves. These are the considerate ones, who do not wish to chance the spreading of possible infection from dog to dog with their hands on each one's mouth—a courtesy particularly appreciated in these days of virus epidemics. But the old-fashioned judges still persist in doing it themselves, so the dog should be ready for either possibility.

Take your future show dog with you in the car, thus accustoming him to riding so that he will not become carsick on the day of a dog show. He should associate pleasure and attention with going in the car, van, or motor home. Take him where it is crowded: downtown, to the shops, everywhere you go that dogs are permitted. Make the expeditions fun for him by frequent petting and words of praise; do not just ignore him as you go about your errands.

Do not overly shelter your future show dog. Instinctively you may want to keep him at home where he is safe from germs or danger. This can be foolish on two counts. The first reason is that a puppy kept away from other dogs builds up no natural immunity against all the things with which he will come in contact at dog shows, so it is wiser to keep him up-to-date on all protective shots and then let him become accustomed to being among dogs and dog owners. Also, a dog who is never among strange people, in strange places, or among strange dogs may grow up with a shyness or timidity of spirit that will cause you real problems as his show career draws near.

Keep your show prospect's coat in immaculate condition with frequent grooming and daily brushing. When bathing is necessary, use a mild dog shampoo or whatever the breeder of your puppy may suggest. Several of the brand-name products do an excellent job. Be sure to rinse thoroughly so as not to risk skin irritation by traces of soap left behind, and protect against soap entering the eyes by a drop of castor oil in each before you lather up. Use warm water (be sure it is not uncomfortably hot or chillingly cold) and a good spray. Make certain you allow your dog to dry thoroughly in a warm, draft-free area (or outdoors, if it is warm and sunny) so that he doesn't catch cold. Then proceed to groom him to perfection.

A show dog's teeth must be kept clean and free of tartar. Hard dog biscuits can help toward this, but if tartar accumulates, see that it is removed promptly by your veterinarian. Bones for chewing are not suitable for show dogs as they tend to damage and wear down the tooth enamel.

Assuming that you will be handling the dog yourself, or even if he will be professionally handled, a few moments each day of dog show routine is important. Practice setting him up as you have seen the exhibitors do at the shows you've attended, and teach him to hold this position once you have him stacked to your satisfaction. Make the learning period pleasant by being firm but lavish in your praise when he responds correctly. Teach him to gait at your side at a moderate rate on a loose lead. When you have mastered the basic essentials at home, then hunt out and join a training class for future work. Training classes are sponsored by show-giving clubs in many areas, and their popularity is steadily increasing. If you have no other way of locating one, perhaps your veterinarian would know of one through some of his other clients; but if you are sufficiently aware of the dog show world to want a show dog, you will probably be personally acquainted with other people who will share information of this type with you.

Accustom your show dog to being in a crate (which you should be doing with a pet dog as well). He should relax in his crate at the shows "between times" for his own well being and safety.

MATCH SHOWS

Your show dog's initial experience in the ring should be in match show competition. This type of event is intended as a learning experience for both the dog and the exhibitor. You will not feel embarrassed or out of place no matter how poorly your puppy may behave or how inept your attempts at handling may be, as you will find others there with the same type of problems. The important thing is that you get the puppy out and into a show ring where the two of you can practice together and learn the ropes.

Only on rare occasions is it necessary to make match show entries in advance, and even those with a pre-entry policy will usually accept entries at the door as well. Thus you need not plan several weeks ahead, as is the case with point shows, but can go when the mood strikes you. Also there is a vast difference in the cost, as match show entries only cost a few dollars while entry fees for the point shows may be over ten dollars, an amount none of us needs to waste until we have some idea of how the puppy will behave or how much more pre-show training is needed.

Match shows are frequently judged by professional handlers who, in addition to making the awards, are happy to help new exhibitors with comments and advice on their puppies and their presentation of them. Avail yourself of all these opportunities before heading out to the sophisticated world of the point shows.

POINT SHOWS

As previously mentioned, entries for American Kennel Club point shows must be made in advance. This must be done on an official entry blank of the show-giving club. The entry must then be filed either personally or by mail with the show superintendent or the show secretary (if the event is being run by the club members alone and a superintendent has not been hired, this information will appear on the premium list) in time to reach its destination prior to the published closing date or filling of the quota. These entries must be made carefully, must be signed by the owner of the dog or the owner's agent (your professional handler), and must be accompanied by the entry fee; otherwise they will not be accepted. Remember that it is not when the entry leaves your hands that counts, but the date of arrival at its destination. If you are relying on the mails, which are not always dependable, get the entry off well before the deadline to avoid disappointment.

A dog must be entered at a dog show in the name of the actual owner at the time of the entry closing date of that specific show. If a registered dog has been acquired by a new owner, it must be entered in the name of the new owner in any show for which entries close after the date of acquirement, regardless of whether the new owner has or has not actually received the registration certificate indicating that the dog is recorded in his name. State on the entry form whether or not transfer application has been mailed to the American Kennel Club, and it goes without saying that the latter should be attended to promptly when you purchase a registered dog.

In filling out your entry blank, type, print, or write clearly, paying particular attention to the spelling of names, correct registration numbers, and so on. Also, if there is more than one variety in your breed, be sure to indicate into which category your dog is being entered.

The **Puppy Class** is for dogs or bitches who are six months of age and under twelve months and who are not champions. The age of a dog shall be calculated up to and inclusive of the first day of a show. For example, the first day a dog whelped on January 1st is eligible to compete in a Puppy Class at a show is July 1st of the same year; and he may continue to compete in Puppy Classes up to and including a show on December 31 of the same year, but he is *not* eligible to compete in a Puppy Class at a show held on or after January 1 of the following year.

The Puppy Class is the first one in which you should enter your puppy. In it a certain allowance will be made for the fact that they *are* puppies, thus an immature dog or one displaying less than perfect showmanship will be less severely penalized than, for instance, would be the case in Open. It is also quite likely that others in the class will be suffering from these problems, too. When you enter a puppy, be sure to check the classification with care, as some shows divide their Puppy Class into a 6-9 months old section and a 9-12 months old section.

The **Novice Class** is for dogs six months of age and over, whelped in the United States or Canada, who *prior to the official closing date for entries* have *not* won three first prizes in the Novice Class, any first prize at all in the Bred-by-Exhibitor, American-bred, or Open Classes, or one or more points toward championship. The provisions for this class are confusing to many people, which is probably the reason exhibitors do not enter in it more frequently. A dog may win any number of first prizes in the Puppy Class and still retain his eligibility for Novice. He may place second, third, or fourth not only in Novice on an unlimited number of occasions, but also in Bred-by-Exhibitor, American-bred and Open and still remain eligible for Novice. But he may

Annecy's Chase the Wind, by Ch. The Kingmaker of Annecy ex Ch. Snowheron Serena of Sworddale and Annecy, with Mrs. M. J. Wilcock and Mr. K. Robin Newhouse, winner of two Reserve Challenge Certificates prior to reaching nine months' age. The only Samoyed to qualify for Spillers' Pup of the Year Award in 1985.

Pure-Bred Dogs/American Kennel Gazette, the official publication of the American Kennel Club.

The scale of championship points for each breed is worked out by the American Kennel Club and reviewed annually, at which time the number required in competition may be either changed (raised or lowered) or remain the same. The scale of championship points for all breeds is published annually in the May issue of the *Gazette*, and the current ratings for each breed within that area are published in every show catalog.

When a dog or bitch is adjudged Best of Winners, its championship points are, for that show, compiled on the basis of which sex had the greater number of points. If there are two points in dogs and four in bitches and the dog goes Best of Winners, then *both* the dog and the bitch are awarded an equal number of points, in this case four. Should the Winners Dog or the Winners Bitch go on to win Best of Breed or Best of Variety, additional points are accorded for the additional dogs and bitches defeated by so doing, provided, of course, that there were entries specifically for Best of Breed competition or Specials, as these specific entries are generally called.

If your dog or bitch takes Best of Opposite Sex after going Winners, points are credited according to the number of the same sex defeated in both the regular classes and Specials competition. If Best of Winners is also won, then whatever additional points for each of these awards are available will be credited. Many a one- or two-point win has grown into a major in this manner.

Moving further along, should your dog win its **Variety Group** from the classes (in other words, if it has taken either Winners Dog or Winners Bitch), you then receive points based on the greatest number of points awarded to any member of any breed included within that Group during that show's competition. Should the day's winning also include Best in Show, the same rule of thumb applies, and your dog or bitch receives the highest number of points awarded to any other dog of any breed at that event.

Best of Breed competition consists of the Winners Dog and the Winners Bitch, who automatically compete on the strength of those awards, in addition to whatever dogs and bitches have been entered specifically for this class for which champions of record are eligible. Since July 1980, dogs who, according to their owner's

Gt. Ch., Intl. Ch. J. Yurok of Bjelkiers is the first Samoyed to have become a Best in Show winner in Brazil, owner-handled, at the ABC Kennel Club in São Paulo in March 1983 at five years old. The same year he was ranked 9th Top Winner, All Breeds among Brazilian-bred dogs. Owned by Mr. and Mrs. Werner Degenhardt, Bjelkiers Kennel, São Paulo, Brazil.

no longer be shown in Novice when he has won three blue ribbons in that class, when he has won even one blue ribbon in either Bred-by-Exhibitor, American-bred, or Open, or when he has won a single championship point.

In determining whether or not a dog is eligible for the Novice Class, keep in mind the fact that previous wins are calculated according to the official published date for closing of entries, not by the date on which you may actually have made the entry. So if in the interim, between the time you made the entry and the official closing date, your dog makes a win causing him to become ineligible for Novice, change your class *immediately* to another for which he will be eligible, preferably either Bred-by-Exhibitor or American-bred. To do this, you must contact the show's superintendent or secretary, at first by telephone to save time and then in writing to confirm it. The Novice Class always seems to have the fewest entries of any class, and therefore it is a splendid "practice ground" for you and your young dog while you are getting the "feel" of being in the ring.

Bred-by-Exhibitor Class is for dogs whelped in the United States or, if individually registered in the American Kennel Club Stud Book, for dogs whelped in Canada who are six months of age or older, are not champions, and are owned wholly or in part by the person or by the spouse of the person who was the breeder or one of the breeders of record. Dogs entered in this class must be handled in the class by an owner or by a member of the immediate family of the owner. Members of an immediate family for this purpose are husband, wife, father, mother, son, daughter, brother, or sister. This is the class which is really the "breeders' showcase," and the one which breeders should enter with particular pride to show off their achievements.

The **American-bred Class** is for all dogs excepting champions, six months of age or older, who were whelped in the United States by reason of a mating which took place in the United States.

The **Open Class** is for any dog six months of age or older (this is the only restriction for this class). Dogs with championship points compete in it, dogs who are already champions are eligible to do so, dogs who are imported can be entered, and, of course, American-bred dogs compete in it. This class is, for some strange reason, the favorite of exhibitors who are "out to win." They rush

Kids and Sammys are a "natural"! Ch. Weathervane's Trouble Maker resides with Dr. John and Judy Kovitch in Bloomsburg, Pennsylvania.

Ch. Oakhurst Omarsun taking 2nd in Working Group Wine Country K.C., April 1984. Owned by Jim and Sharon Hurst, Auburn, California.

to enter their pointed dogs in it, under the false impression that by doing so they assure themselves of greater attention from the judges. This really is not so, and some people feel that to enter in one of the less competitive classes, with a better chance of winning it and thus earning a second opportunity of gaining the judge's approval by returning to the ring in the Winners Class, can often be a more effective strategy.

One does not enter the **Winners Class.** One earns the right to compete in it by winning first prize in Puppy, Novice, Bred-by-Exhibitor, American-bred, or Open. No dog who has been defeated on the same day in one of these classes is eligible to compete for Winners, and every dog who has been a blue-ribbon winner in one of them and not defeated in another, should he have been entered in more than one class (as occasionally happens), *must* do so. Following the selection of the Winners Dog or the Winners Bitch, the dog or bitch receiving that award leaves the ring. Then the dog or bitch who placed second in that class, unless previously beaten by another dog or bitch in another class at the same show, re-enters the ring to compete against the remaining first-prize winners for Reserve. The latter award indicates that the dog or bitch selected for it is standing "in reserve" should the one who received Winners be disqualified or declared ineligible through any technicality when the awards are checked at the American Kennel Club. In that case, the one who placed Reserve is moved up to Winners, at the same time receiving the appropriate championship points.

Winners Dog and Winners Bitch are the awards which carry points toward championship with them. The points are based on the number of dogs or bitches actually in competition, and the points are scaled one through five, the latter being the greatest number available to any one dog or bitch at any one show. Three-, four-, or five-point wins are considered majors. In order to become a champion, a dog or bitch must have won two majors under two different judges, plus at least one point from a third judge, and the additional points necessary to bring the total to fifteen. When your dog has gained fifteen points as described above, a championship certificate will be issued to you, and your dog's name will be published in the champions of record list in the records, have completed the requirements for a championship after the closing of entries for the show (but whose championships are unconfirmed) may be transferred from one of the regular classes to the Best of Breed competition, provided this transfer is made by the show superintendent or show secretary *prior to the start of any judging at the show.*

This has proved an extremely popular new rule, as under it a dog can finish on Saturday and then be transferred and compete as a Special on Sunday. It must be emphasized that *the change must be made prior to the start of any part of the day's judging, not for just your individual breed.*

In the United States, Best of Breed winners are entitled to compete in the Variety Group which includes them. This is not mandatory; it is a privilege which exhibitors value. (In Canada, Best of Breed winners *must* compete in the Variety Group or they lose any points already won.) The dogs winning *first* in each of the seven Variety Groups *must* compete for Best in Show. Missing the opportunity of taking your dog in for competition in its Group is foolish, as it is there where the general public is most likely to notice your breed and become interested in learning about it.

Non-regular classes are sometimes included at the all-breed shows, and they are almost invariably included at Specialty shows. These include Stud Dog Class and Brood Bitch Class, which are judged on the basis of the quality of the two offspring accompanying the sire or dam. The quality of the latter two is beside the point and should not be considered by the judge; it is the youngsters who count, and the quality of *both* are to be averaged to decide which sire or dam is the best and most consistent producer. Then there is the Brace Class (which, at all-breed shows, moves up to Best Brace in each Variety Group and then Best Brace in Show) which is judged on the similarity and evenness of appearance of the two brace members. In other words, the two dogs should look like identical twins in size, color, and conformation and should move together almost as a single dog, one person handling with precision and ease. The same applies to the Team Class competition, except that four dogs are involved and, if necessary, two handlers.

The Veterans Class is for the older dog, the minimum age of whom is seven years. This class is judged on the quality of the dogs, as the winner competes in Best of Breed competition and has, on a respectable number of occasions, been known to take that top award. So the point is *not* to pick out the oldest dog, as some judges seem to believe, but the best specimen of the breed, exactly as in the regular classes.

Then there are Sweepstakes and Futurity Stakes sponsored by many Specialty clubs, sometimes as part of their regular Specialty shows and sometimes as separate events on an entirely different occasion. The difference between the two stakes is that Sweepstakes entries usually include dogs from six to eighteen months of age with entries made at the same time as the others for the show, while for a Futurity the entries are bitches nominated when bred and the individual puppies entered at or shortly following their birth.

JUNIOR SHOWMANSHIP COMPETITION

If there is a youngster in your family between the ages of ten and sixteen, there is no better or more rewarding hobby than becoming an active participant in Junior Showmanship. This is a marvelous activity for young people. It teaches responsibility, good sportsmanship, the fun of competition where one's own skills are the deciding factor of success, proper care of a pet, and how to socialize with other young folks. Any youngster may experience the thrill of emerging from the ring a winner and the satisfaction of a good job well done.

Entry in Junior Showmanship Classes is open to any boy or girl who is at least ten years old and under seventeen years old on the day of the show. The Novice Junior Showmanship Class is open to youngsters who have not already won, at the time the entries close, three firsts in this class. Youngsters who have won three firsts in Novice may compete in the Open Junior Showmanship Class. Any junior handler who wins his third first-place award in Novice may participate in the Open Class at the same show, provided that the Open Class has at least one other junior handler entered and competing in it that day. The Novice and Open Classes may be divided into Junior and Senior Classes. Youngsters between the ages of ten and twelve, inclusively, are eligible for the Junior division; and youngsters between thirteen and seventeen, inclusively, are eligible for the Senior division.

Any of the foregoing classes may be separated into individual classes for boys and for girls. If such a division is made, it must be so indicated on the premium list. The premium list also indicates the prize for Best Junior Handler, if such a prize is being offered at the show. Any youngster who wins a first in any of the regular classes may enter the competition for this prize, provided the youngster has been undefeated in any other Junior Showmanship Class at that show.

Junior Showmanship Classes, unlike regular conformation classes in which the quality of the dog is judged, are judged solely on the skill and ability of the junior handling the dog. Which dog is best is not the point—it is which youngster does the best job with the dog that is under consideration. Eligibility requirements for the dog being shown in Junior Showmanship, and other detailed information, can be found in *Regulations for Junior Showmanship*, available from the American Kennel Club.

A junior who has a dog that he or she can enter in both Junior Showmanship and conformation classes has twice the opportunity for success and twice the opportunity to get into the ring and work with the dog, a combination which can lead to not only awards for expert handling, but also, if the dog is of sufficient quality, for making a conformation champion.

PRE-SHOW PREPARATIONS

Preparation of the items you will need as a dog show exhibitor should not be left until the last moment. They should be planned and arranged several days in advance of the show in order for you to remain calm and relaxed as the countdown starts.

The importance of the crate has already been mentioned and should already be part of your equipment. Of equal importance is the grooming table, which very likely you have also already acquired for use at home. You should take it along with you to the shows, as your dog will need last minute touches before entering the ring. Should you have not yet made this purchase, folding tables with rubber tops are made specifically for this purpose and can be purchased at most dog shows, where concession booths with marvelous assortments of "doggy" necessities are to be found, or at your pet supplier. You will also need a sturdy tack box (also available at the dog show concessions) in which to carry your grooming tools and equipment. The latter should include:

brushes; combs; scissors; nail clippers; whatever you use for last minute clean-up jobs; cotton swabs; first-aid equipment; and anything you are in the habit of using on the dog, including a leash or two of the type you prefer, some well-cooked and dried-out liver or any of the small packaged "dog treats" for use as bait in the ring, an atomizer in case you wish to dampen your dog's coat when you are preparing him for the ring, and so on. A large turkish towel to spread under the dog on the grooming table is also useful.

Take a large thermos or cooler of ice, the biggest one you can accommodate in your vehicle, for use by "man and beast." Take a jug of water (there are lightweight, inexpensive ones available at all sporting goods shops) and a water dish. If you plan to feed the dog at the show, or if you and the dog will be away from home more than one day, bring food for him from home so that he will have the type to which he is accustomed.

You may or may not have an exercise pen. While the shows do provide areas for exercise of the dogs, these are among the most likely places to have your dog come in contact with any illnesses which may be going around, and having a pen of your own for your dog's use is excellent protection. Such a pen comes in handy while you're travelling; since it is roomier than a crate, it becomes a comfortable place for your dog to relax and move around in, especially when you're at motels or rest stops. These pens are available at the show concession stands and come in a variety of heights and sizes. A set of "pooper scoopers" should also be part of your equipment, along with a package of plastic bags for cleaning up after your dog.

Bring along folding chairs for the members of your party, unless all of you are fond of standing, as these are almost never provided by the clubs. Have your name stamped on the chairs so that there will be no doubt as to whom the chairs belong. Bring whatever you and your family enjoy for drinks or snacks in a picnic basket or cooler, as show food, in general, is expensive and usually not great. You should always have a pair of boots, a raincoat, and a rain hat with you (they should remain permanently in your vehicle if you plan to attend shows regularly), as well as a sweater, a warm coat, and a change of shoes. A smock or big cover-up apron will

256

Ch. Beau Brummel of Caribou, by Ch. Bauzuhl of Caribou ex Tsiuhkagta's Tano of Chielee, owned by Joe and Mable Dyer and Bruce Holland. Photo from Mt. Ogden K.C. in 1968.

Ch. Ku Techi, C.D., by Suruka Orr's Toomthon ex Snow Cloud II, bred by John Konecny, owned and handled by Don and Dot Hodges (Kipperic Kennel). He completed title and placed in the Top Ten Winning Samoyeds 1969. Had about 50 Bests of Breed when retired.

assure that you remain tidy as you prepare the dog for the ring. Your overnight case should include a small sewing kit for emergency repairs, bandaids, headache and indigestion remedies, and any personal products or medications you normally use.

In your car, you should always carry maps of the area where you are headed and an assortment of motel directories. Generally speaking, Holiday Inns have been found to be the nicest about taking dogs. Ramadas and Howard Johnsons generally do so cheerfully (with a few exceptions). Best Western generally frowns on pets (not always, but often enough to make it necessary to find out which do). Some of the smaller chains welcome pets; the majority of privately-owned motels do not.

Have everything prepared the night before the show to expedite your departure. Be sure that the dog's identification and your judging program and other show information are in your purse or briefcase. If you are taking sandwiches, have them ready. Anything that goes into the car the night before the show will be one thing less to remember in the morning. Decide upon what you will wear and have it out and ready. If there is any question in your mind about what to wear, try on the possibilities before the day of the show; don't risk feeling you may want to change when you see yourself dressed a few moments prior to departure time!

In planning your outfit, make it something simple that will not detract from your dog. Remember that a dark dog silhouettes attractively against a light background and vice-versa. Sport clothes always seem to look best at dog shows, preferably conservative in type and not overly "loud" as you do not want to detract from your dog, who should be the focus of interest at this point. What you wear on your feet is important. Many types of flooring can be hazardously slippery, as can wet grass. Make it a habit to wear rubber soles and low or flat heels in the ring for your own safety, especially if you are showing a dog that likes to move out smartly.

Your final step in pre-show preparation is to leave yourself plenty of time to reach the show that morning. Traffic can get amazingly heavy as one nears the immediate area of the show, finding a parking place can be difficult, and other delays may occur. You'll be in better humor to enjoy the day if your trip to the show is not fraught with panic over fear of not arriving in time!

258

ENJOYING THE DOG SHOW

From the moment of your arrival at the show until after your dog has been judged, keep foremost in your mind the fact that he is your reason for being there and that he should therefore be the center of your attention. Arrive early enough to have time for those last-minute touches that can make a great difference when he enters the ring. Be sure that he has ample time to exercise and that he attends to personal matters. A dog arriving in the ring and immediately using it as an exercise pen hardly makes a favorable impression on the judge.

When you reach ringside, ask the steward for your arm-card and anchor it firmly into place on your arm. Make sure that you are where you should be when your class is called. The fact that you have picked up your arm-card does not guarantee, as some seem to think, that the judge will wait for you. The judge has a full schedule which he wishes to complete on time. Even though you may be nervous, assume an air of calm self-confidence. Remember that this is a hobby to be enjoyed, so approach it in that state of mind. The dog will do better, too, as he will be quick to reflect your attitude.

Always show your dog with an air of pride. If you make mistakes in presenting him, don't worry about it. Next time you will do better. Do not permit the presence of more experienced exhibitors to intimidate you. After all, they, too, were once newcomers.

The judging routine usually starts when the judge asks that the dogs be gaited in a circle around the ring. During this period the judge is watching each dog as it moves, noting style, topline, reach and drive, head and tail carriage, and general balance. Keep your mind and your eye on your dog, moving him at his most becoming gait and keeping your place in line without coming too close to the exhibitor ahead of you. Always keep your dog on the inside of the circle, between yourself and the judge, so that the judge's view of the dog is unobstructed.

Calmly pose the dog when requested to set up for examination. If you are at the head of the line and many dogs are in the class, go all the way to the end of the ring before starting to stack the dog, leaving sufficient space for those behind you to line theirs up as well, as requested by the judge. If you are not at the head of the line but between other exhibitors, leave sufficient space ahead of your dog for the judge to examine him. The dogs should be spaced so that the judge is able to move among them to see them from all angles. In practicing to "set up" or "stack" your dog for the judge's examination, bear in mind the importance of doing so quickly and with dexterity. The judge has a schedule to meet and only a few moments in which to evaluate each dog. You will immeasurably help yours to make a favorable impression if you are able to "get it all together" in a minimum amount of time. Practice at home before a mirror can be a great help toward bringing this about, facing the dog so that you see him from the same side that the judge will and working to make him look right in the shortest length of time.

Listen carefully as the judge describes the manner in which the dog is to be gaited, whether it is straight down and straight back; down the ring, across, and back; or in a triangle. The latter has become the most popular pattern with the majority of judges. "In a triangle" means the dog should move down the outer side of the ring to the first corner, across that end of the ring to the second corner, and then back to the judge from the second corner, using the center of the ring in a diagonal line. Please learn to do this pattern without breaking at each corner to twirl the dog around you, a senseless maneuver that has been noticed on occasion. Judges like to see the dog in an uninterrupted triangle, as they are thus able to get a better idea of the dog's gait.

It is impossible to overemphasize that the gait at which you move your dog is tremendously important and considerable study and thought should be given to the matter. At home, have someone move the dog for you at different speeds so that you can tell which shows him off to best advantage. The most becoming action almost invariably is seen at a moderate gait, head up and topline holding. Do not gallop your dog around the ring or hurry him into a speed atypical of his breed. Nothing being rushed appears at its best; give your dog a chance to move along at his (and the breed's) natural gait. For a dog's action to be judged accurately, that dog should move with strength and power, but not excessive speed, holding a straight line as he goes to and from the judge.

As you bring the dog back to the judge, stop him a few feet away and be sure that he is standing in a becoming position. Bait him to show the judge an alert expression, using whatever tasty

Ch. Blue Sky's Honey Bun has multiple Group placements to her credit and is dam of a Best in Show and of three Group-placing winners. Another splendid Samoyed owned by the Hooymans, Blue Sky Samoyeds, Pine, Colorado.

morsel he has been trained to expect for this purpose or, if that works better for you, use a small squeak-toy in your hand. A reminder, please, to those using liver or treats: take them with you when you leave the ring. Do not just drop them on the ground where they will be found by another dog.

When the awards have been made, accept yours graciously, no matter how you actually may feel about it. What's done is done, and arguing with a judge or stomping out of the ring is useless and a reflection on your sportsmanship. Be courteous, congratulate the winner if your dog was defeated, and try not to show your disappointment. By the same token, please be a gracious winner; this, surprisingly, sometimes seems to be still more difficult.

Chapter 14

Grooming Your Samoyed
by Joyce Johnson

Whether grooming the Samoyed for show or as a pet, the basics are the same. Having the proper grooming tools is the first essential. These are as follows:

    1) large pin brush
    2) slicker brush
    3) greyhound comb
    4) single-edge thinning shears
    5) nail clipper
    6) pet rake

BRUSHING

This is the most important part of grooming. Once a week brush out the coat with the pin brush. Check to see if the nails need cutting, and if the hair needs to be trimmed on the bottoms of the feet. Pay special attention to the soft, silky hair around the dog's ears, as this is a spot that mats easily.

Never bathe a dog who has not been thoroughly brushed, as the latter removes dirt or mud. If the dog is shedding, it is an absolute *must* to have as much loose hair as possible removed before bathing. For this use the slicker brush and the rake. Short, quick strokes loosen and remove the hair fastest without "brush burning" the dog.

The easiest method of brushing is to start at the hocks or above the elbows and line brush. Do not take too much hair into your

Facing page:
Headstudy of Ch. Celestial's Optical Illusion, C.D., owned by Arlene Heffler, Crystal Lake, Illinois.

line or you will be unable to brush down to the skin correctly. Brush towards you and work up to the back and head of the dog. Lay the dog on his side and start in the middle of the tummy, working to the middle of the back. Roll over and repeat. Use a pin brush on the tail, as a stiffer brush can break the hair here, which takes such a long time to grow back to its former beauty once destroyed.

Whether your Samoyed is a pet or a show dog, we suggest the purchase of a rubber-topped grooming table equipped with an arm and noose for holding the dog securely in place. This will add immeasurably to the ease and comfort of grooming sessions, and the table folds flat to be easily stored when not in use.

BATHING

Warm water is the best, followed at the end (when all the soap is out) with a cool rinse to bring out the silver tips when the coat dries.

Check with the pet supply shops in your area to see what shampoo works the best over white dogs. We use the every-day shop shampoo with about one tablespoonful of bluing added to each gallon of shampoo. We have also found that something in the bluing, when added to the shampoo, will kill fleas if the infestation is a light rather than a heavy one.

We also like to use plain *bar* Ivory soap. This does a good job of cleaning (even stains from choke chain collars disappear) and is very mild and gentle.

Blow-drying the dog really helps the coat fluff up nicely. Also it gives you the opportunity to check the skin, seeing if there are any fleas or ticks or dead skin that may indicate a health problem. Using a dryer with a hose attachment also gets out any remaining dead hair, and this helps guard against matting, which will occur if the dead hair remains.

If the dog is not shedding, after you have drawn a lot of the excess water off, you can complete the drying in a crate with a stand dryer set on cold. *Never* put the dryer on high or on hot directed on a dog in a crate, and be sure to keep the dryer directed *away* from the eyes. We use a 500 size crate with a grate in the bottom.

After the dog is dry, return him to the grooming table and brush through the coat, using the pin brush or rake to make sure that all knots and mats are gone. Trim any excess hair from the pads of the feet and hocks.

A bath every three to four months, with weekly brushings, should keep the pets and retired show dogs in good shape and condition.

SHOW TIPS

Invest in a good blow dryer and use it at least twice weekly or more frequently to keep the coat in condition. This gets rid of old, dead hair and dirt and promotes new growth. Never brush a dry coat. Mist with water to prevent hair breakage.

When the dog is "blowing coat" (full shedding) and turning yellow in places, you can put a final rinse on the coat when bathing, consisting of one cup white vinegar in a gallon of water. Let the coat dry with this remaining on. Do not use this method frequently, as it does tend to dry the coat.

Instead of chalk or powder, we use a combination of cornmeal and corn starch. It brushes out more easily. We've also found that Bio-groom White Magic Spray works best. I use it on elbows and on hocks when needed for quick clean-ups.

Trimming of the feet and hocks is a matter of personal preference. Some like round feet while others prefer to see each toe defined. Hocks should be straight to the floor, so as not to appear cow-hocked. Feet should be cleared on the bottom (trimmed) in order for the judge to see the pads as the dog moves away. This trimming is always trial and error at first, but watching others do the job helps, and a good pair of thinning scissors can cover up mistakes.

Do not use a lot of sprays on the coat. These will yellow and dry it. Do not use "people products" to remove yellow or stains. I've seen too many purple dogs, including one of my own several years ago. (We all learn the hard way.) Small stain areas can be treated with a paste of boric acid and hydrogen peroxide. Put it on and let it dry until it falls off. It's not perfect but it helps. And finally, remember that you should be able to get a comb through the dog's coat before the bath and before he goes into the ring.

Chapter 15

On Spinning Samoyed Hair

To many Samoyed owners, spinning the combings from their Samoyeds is an added and special bonus of owning this breed. For truly, spinning is something of which dreams have been made to come true through the years, since pioneer ladies spent hours at their wheels to supply their families with fiber for clothing. Thus a beautiful art is also practical.

Eleanor (Tommie) Lohmiller, who lives at Grand Junction, Colorado, and owns the Sunset Samoyeds, is not a pioneer, but a modern lady who appreciates the wonders a spinning wheel can provide. We are grateful to her for discussing the subject with us, and for explaining to our readers who may feel disposed to try exactly how it is done.

Eleanor Lohmiller explains that the wheels with which most of us are familiar from stories and pictures are the Great wheel, Castle wheel, and Saxony wheel. There are others, too, nowadays—even including electric wheels.

"Would you believe, this is *dog* fur?" That is the usual comment of a person seeing the results for the first time. As their eyes grow larger, they reach out to touch a shawl. Then before you know it, people are gathering around to ask further questions and learn more. Thus the wearer again finds herself explaining the process

Facing page:
Eleanor Lohmiller wearing an exquisite shawl of scalloped hairpin lace made from fur donated by the Samoyed Trailblazer's Star at Sunset, C.D. On her lap is the famed Ch. Trailblazer's Yukon Sunset, U.D. Photo by Curtis Photography, Grand Junction, Colorado.

of spinning dog fur from the beautiful Samoyed standing at the end of her leash in order to create the stunning shawl she is so proudly wearing.

If the art of spinning interests you, it is a good idea to learn how before embarking on a project of so doing. Spinning teachers can usually be found by contacting shops selling and stocking handspun; or perhaps your local weaver's guild can be of help. It is also a good idea to try more than one kind of wheel prior to investing, for another person's preference may not be yours.

Tommie Lohmiller learned spinning on dog fur, so it is not impossible although she would not recommend it. If you do learn with dog fur, card in some guard hair or wool to help with your first attempts.

Spinning is a hands-on experience, and this chapter is intended to just give the reader a general idea of what is involved. With this in mind, let's follow the Samoyed fur from the dog all the way to the finished article.

Original Fiber: There being astounding differences in shades and texture from dog to dog, it is a good idea to plan a project around the fur from one dog. Biscuit is beautiful if you know it's there. Save only the undercoat, discarding short leg fur, and put it in a brown paper bag as you comb it out, labeling the bag with the name of the dog, saving it until the bag is full or until the dog has finished that shedding. Put a moth ball or two in the bag, tape it closed, and keep for future use.

If you spin fur from other people, ascertain that their dogs are healthy and well groomed. Also tell the person how you want the fur handled. When you are lucky enough to discover a dog that has just the type of undercoat you want, tell the owner how pleased you are, and ask them to save that particular dog's sheddings for you. Tommie Lohmiller's own "spinning dream" belongs to Betty Moody, she notes, and her name is Novaskaya Tsarina Lafay, or "Butchie." When her fur comes to Tommie, she knows it will be perfect for special projects, such as hairpin lace or delicate crochet patterns. The owners are usually happy to do this for you, but do craft something nice for them by way of saying "thank you," for after all, they are doing you a huge favor.

Preparation and Carding: Of course, any dirt and mats are discarded. This is the time to pick out guard hair that has slipped past in grooming. It is easy to spot as you put the fur on the card-

Shawl, done in Queen's Crown crochet pattern, created by Eleanor Lohmiller, Grand Junction, Colorado, from fur donated by Holly.

Close-up of Queen's Crown crochet pattern from Eleanor Lohmiller's shawl created from Samoyed fur.

ers. When you finish carding each handful of fur, roll it into what is called a rolag. Then put each of these into a paper bag with the dog's name. Fill the bag, or sometimes two, and you are ready to spin.

Spinning: Have your wheel well oiled and near a window for the best light. Lay a dark cloth in your lap so that the fibers are easier to see, and tie a strand of yarn the size you want to spin to the wheel for quick reference. It is easy to get thicker or thinner as you spin. Fine singles make nicer yarn than a single that is thick spun. Of course this depends on what use you are planning for it. Thick spun has a tendency to fuzz; but if you need a heavier yarn for knitting, it is not difficult to just ply two or three strands together, which will provide you with the bulk needed. Do remember that Samoyed fur is known for its insulating qualities and can become very hot. It is also known for its lack of odor and for wonderful softness.

Plying: If you want a two ply yarn, spin two bobbins of singles. As you take each bobbin from the wheel, transfer it to your Lazy Kate. With your two bobbins of singles on the Lazy Kate, take the fiber and from each bobbin reverse the direction of the wheel and spin them again. Plying makes yarn stronger and is very important because uneven plying can ruin an otherwise lovely yarn. When you have one bobbin plied on the wheel, it is time to wind the fiber from the wheel bobbin to the Niddy Noddy. Half the fun of learning to spin is using equipment with such wonderful old-fashioned names.

Washing: When the plied skeins are removed from the Niddy Noddy, tie them with a bit of spun dog fur in four places, then soak in warm water and a mild soap. Rinse thoroughly, and do not wring or scrub.

Stretching: Put the washed fiber up on a hook and stretch a bit with light weights. This allows the fibers to set more smoothly and to dry. Leave it at least overnight before you again take the skein and wind it on a swift for final drying. This usually takes a day or two. There is no hurry, as spinning should be done slowly, quietly, and with pleasure.

Skeining: Now we are on the home stretch. All you do is take the yarn off the swift and make skeins. Put a tag with the dog's name and weight of the skein, and it is ready to store. "I sprinkle a bit of dried lavender on my finished skeins," Tommie notes. You

Hat and neck warmer created by Eleanor Lohmiller from Samoyed and Old English Sheepdog fur, one of her favorite combinations.

may choose to wind the skein from the swift directly on the ball winder for immediate use.

Crafting: Hats, scarves, purses, shawls, or whatever—let your imagination, and good directions, be your guide.

This brings us all the way from combing the dog to the finished article. When you make an item for someone other than yourself (or even for yourself), if possible include a picture of the dog who donated the fur and a note telling about the dog. We think you will enjoy having skeins of yarn you can call by name, and will find that it is great fun to create something beautiful and practical. A combination much like Sams themselves!

Chapter 16

The Samoyed in Obedience
by Barbara Cole

Often people have said to me, "I hear Samoyeds are dumb, and hard to train." Nothing could be farther from the truth. When you approach training a Samoyed, you must keep in mind their heritage and what they were bred for. They were bred to be *with* people, to do things *for* people, and to use their own ingenuity when it was necessary; which is precisely how they approach obedience. Three things are necessary in training a Samoyed: patience, praise, and consistency.

I prefer to train Sams in 'house manners' from the time they are very young; things such as coming when called, not jumping on people, lying down and being quiet when told, etc. If the puppy has a bad habit you think is cute when it is young, that same habit is not going to be nearly as amusing when the dog is full grown. Many clubs and schools have "Puppy Socialization" or "Puppy Kindergarten" classes that tell you how to teach your pup good manners in a very gentle way. I highly recommend these classes.

Samoyeds love to please people, and every Sam loves a ham, so if you really act it up, and sound really mad, using your lowest gruffest voice when puppy is bad, and your highest, happiest voice when he's good, the results can be phenomenal. You can

Facing page:

Top: Tundra Baer, U.D., is a movie star. She has appeared in 22 movies and TV shows, and won the PATSY Award (Performing Animal Top Star of the Year) for 1983. Tundra understands 200 word commands and over 70 hand signals. She started in obedience in Colorado and later moved to Hollywood, California, where she resides with owners Ted and Lynette Baer. *Bottom*: The Samoyeds owned by Jack and Amelia Price at Commack, Long Island, have distinguished themselves in obedience, conformation show and sled work. Here is Bubbling Oaks Rue The Day, C.D.X., showing his skill and grace in the obedience ring. Bred by the Prices and owned by Harriet Manko.

train a Samoyed with voice inflections almost as much as with a training collar!

Most Samoyeds are not ready to comprehend structured obedience until they are 8 or 9 months old. Those put in at the standard 6 months do not usually do as well, and don't seem to totally understand what is expected of them.

Obedience classes are to train the handlers more than the dogs. I recommend obedience for everyone owning a Sam, because it teaches you to relate to your dog and how to tell him how to do what *you* want, so he can understand and please you, as that is what he wants the most—to please you, his owner. If you do not work the dog at home between classes, during the time it is most essential to learning, you can't expect him to retain the lessons of the week. Many owners don't realize that it is very hard for a pup to concentrate, much less learn, in a class situation, with all the excitement and dogs. It does help somewhat if you arrive early each week to let your pup get wound down and a little used to the thrill of it all.

Obedience time should be quality learning time, and the dog should have short, pleasant lessons. Do not ask him to do something when you cannot enforce it, or when you know he will find it nearly impossible to do what you say, (i.e. telling him to sit when he has no lead on, and beloved Grandma has just walked through the door). When you tell the dog something, *tell* him, with a firm authoritative voice, and do not "ask" him with a pleading tone. Never try to train when you do not have control, or your dog is without a lead and collar. Tell the dog to do what you want only *once*, then make him do it. Be consistent, and always enforce this. Avoid becoming a "3 sit" owner, or the dog will soon push you to tell him "sit" four times, and then five, and soon after he will be doing whatever he pleases whenever he wants.

You should not be too harsh on the dog if he doesn't understand. You must use patience, as you would with a baby. Sams *do* have a way of having convenient "memory lapses" after they have learned something, and if you're absolutely sure they know what you're asking and how to do it, you must be firm, and very disapproving. However, you must also continue to stimulate their interest by allowing them to have the option to do well or fail, winning your hearty approval when they live up to your expectations.

Each dog is an individual, and there is no one method that

works for every dog. Any dog can be trained with force, but there are alternatives that preserve the dogs' love and respect for you, without resorting to harsh techniques. Sams resent "force" techniques such as ear pinch, pinch collars, shock and noise collars, and stringing up, and will rebel in their own way sooner or later. With a little time, patience, and understanding, without using force, you can accomplish your objectives and more, while having a happy dog that likes obedience because it is a fun, rewarding experience that makes his master happy.

You must work (practice) the dog every day, and be very consistent. Behavior that is not acceptable at certain times should never be allowed at *any* time. Lessons should never be done if you are in a bad mood. They should be kept short and pleasant so the dog can't wait for more, instead of thinking, "Oh, no, not again." It is also good to have a phrase associated with practice, such as, "Want to go work?" said in a very up and happy tone while getting out the lead and collar.

Some people use food as an incentive in obedience. I look upon this as an unnecessary intermediate step that only needs elimination later. If the dog is to work for your love and approval, he should always do so. If you train with food, your Samoyed is very likely to say, "Phooey," if you turn up without it one day. A treat or special playtime after the lesson is a good idea, to reward him for a good session.

If you only want a well mannered dog, you should work toward that, and not go overboard in obedience, trying to impress your friends at the dog's expense, or expect the dog to retain things if you don't practice. Practice must be fun; try not to take it too seriously, and know what you want out of it before you start. Learn how to become your dog's best friend, and he'll do anything for you.

One problem to beware of in practice is where the trainer gets so involved watching the dog do well, and waiting for a mistake, or with how to coordinate as a team, that he forgets to praise the dog when it is doing well during the exercise. Remember, in practice, it is acceptable and very preferable to talk to your pal. The dog needs the reassurance when he is doing things right, to recognize the difference when he does things wrong! Dogs do not think in shades of gray; they think in black and white, right and wrong.

Consistency is also important in that you must give equal praise with equal correction. If you give too much praise, and not equal correction, the dog still does not learn right from wrong, as he thinks everything he does is right. This 50:50 praise/correction ratio is very important to the learning process.

The dog should always have the same trainer for lessons, as each person has different innuendos, gestures, and expectations. It will only result in confusing the dog and lessen the effectiveness of his training if he has more than one trainer, whose desires he needs to interpret.

The method of correction is essential to getting good results. The training collar should be put on correctly (if it is not, it will not release), and the corrections should be one or several short jerk-and-release corrections. It is very important for the jerk to be quick and short, and released immediately. The correction should make a "zip, zip" sound, the sound in later training being almost as important as the correction itself, and it *must* be released. If the collar is tight all the time, without the release, the dog will not benefit from the 50:50 praise/correction ratio, and will not learn as easily.

Do not nag your dog with the collar. It is very common for people who are nervous to jerk, jerk, jerk, while standing still. This decreases the effectiveness of the correction when it *does* come, as well as making the dog neurotic because he is always getting corrections, even when he is not doing anything wrong. The same case for ineffective corrections can be made for the person who drags the dog around, instead of giving the proper jerk and release corrections, followed by praise. This dog will not become neurotic, but by the same means, will learn nothing. Likewise, if you take the dog for walks on a training collar, as opposed to a nylon buckle collar, and the collar is always tight, he will develop a "tough neck," and the corrections during training will not mean as much. This is still not a case for a pinch collar; if something doesn't work in obedience, you should never try a short cut, but instead, go back to basics, start again, and work towards your goal.

Train your dog, at first, in an area with very few distractions, and once he knows the exercises, graduate to a spot with a few more distractions, progressing to many distractions, such as class. You should not work the dog in the area in which he plays, such as his back yard. A good place to start is a side yard, or the front yard, followed by a quiet parking lot, a quiet place in a park, near a school yard, and finally in a class or near other dogs. If you feel like you have two left feet, try practicing without the dog. If the neighbors think you are crazy, don't worry; most people with Sams find their neighbors eventually think they're crazy anyway.

Do not ever send your Sam off for someone else to train. Spending the large amount of money to do this is no substitute for your communication and affection for your pet. If you don't have the time to spend or relate to him, then you should consider placing the dog in another home.

For obedience training to be successful, it is very important that the dog get regular exercise. If obedience lessons are the only exercise the dog gets, you can hardly expect him to give it his full attention, or to be very controllable. Unless the dog is getting an adequate amount of additional exercise, such as run or play, training is mostly futile, for both the dog and owner.

Walks should not be used to control the dog, although he shouldn't jerk you off your feet, either. If the walk is all the outside exercise the dog gets in a day, it is cruel to expect him to heel the whole time he is out. A long line or retractible leash with a nylon buckle collar would be good, if the walk is not on a busy street. However, if the dog has plenty of other exercise, walking at heel down the block is good practice for him, and teaches him to be a good neighbor. (If you have a leash law, but there are still stray, unfriendly dogs, you should carry a can of dog repellent.)

Never strike your dog. If he is so bad that you are tempted, either force his head and upper body to the ground with you over him, making him assume a submissive position, or take him by the hair on the *sides* of his neck (never the back of the neck) and lift his forefeet off the ground, look him right in the eye, and tell him who's the boss. Don't forgive too quickly, or he won't take you seriously. A half hour is a good time, or less, depending on how bad he was, and let *him* come to you. Your spouse should also support you, as the pup should not be able to run to Dad for "protection" if Mother has reprimanded him, and vice versa.

There are many good books on obedience that encourage "praise training." Some of the authors I recommend are Pearsall, Strickland, Saunders, and Benjamin. I also highly recommend an excellent paperback book on behavior by Michael Fox, titled *Understanding Your Dog*. Understanding your dog is the key to obedience, which should be something you both like that brings you closer to each other, and helps you to enjoy each other's company even more.

There is a controversy over whether obedience ruins a conformation dog. I do think that a dog should have a firm foundation in conformation first, but I feel obedience enhances conformation performance. I do not recommend training in *both* at the same time, as this seems to confuse the dog. Most of the people who disdain training in both obedience and conformation have never done obedience. They are of the misconception that the dogs sit when you stop, and generally do obedience things when you don't want them do. Samoyeds are *smart,* sometimes too smart, and they can tell the difference in obedience and conformation as clearly as you or I. You use different leads and collars, as well as have the dog working for food in conformation, and your approval and praise in obedience. When you stop in obedience you are facing forward, and in conformation you swing around to the side or front of your dog.

Some plusses for obedience dogs in conformation are that they know what you expect of them, so are able to deliver with more clarity, they stay by your side when you are gaiting, and you can tell them *stand* and *stay,* and they do! Variety is the spice of life, and Sams, being the intelligent dogs they are, seem to like the challenge of obedience after they have been in conformation for awhile, while Sams who have only done obedience are thrilled with the prospect of doing conformation, where they get treats for standing and looking pretty!

One thing conformation people *should* be concerned about is that the best training collar to use for obedience will cut the neck hair off to about ½ inch, if it is not protected. The alternatives are to use a less effective training collar, or devise a neck protector, which I have diagrammed. The problem with using a less effective training collar is that the "zip" sound that comes with the proper short-jerk correction, and which is so important to the dog's learning and response, is not as audible; but with the neck protector, you can use the best training collar, and still preserve the dog's coat.

While most people want to attend an obedience class for the purpose of learning how to have their dog be a more pleasant housemate, some will find that they want to continue into formal

278

Barbara's neck protector: turtleneck dickey with extended neck, band around bottom, and Velcro® attachments on each side.

Am. and Can. Ch. Silvermist's Winter Blizzard, Am. and Can. C.D.X., doing the jumps with ease. Owned by Arlene and Dan Heffler, Illusion Samoyeds, Crystal Lake, Illinois.

279

obedience competition, at shows and trials licensed by the American Kennel Club.

You do not need to put your Samoyed into formal obedience competition to have him be just as loved and special a family member, but competition does provide a nice hobby with others who have a similar interest, and who are as eager to see you win and qualify as you are. This camaraderie is due to the fact you do not compete against each other, but against a score, 170 points out of a possible 200 being qualifying. To qualify, you must also get half the points available in each exercise, and qualify at 3 trials, under 3 different judges, to get your title.

Licensed trials consist of several classes which relate to the level of accomplishment you and your dog have achieved. You must start at the beginning, and cannot skip levels. These levels basically relate to the human equivalent of Elementary School, High School, and College, with a "Masters" also being available, but only to a special few. Titles are awarded for each level, and these become part of your dog's name, after he has acquired them.

The first is C.D., which stands for Companion Dog; the next C.D.X., which stands for Companion Dog Excellent; and the final title is U.D., which stands for Utility Dog. The "Masters" title is the ultimate, and is the O.T.Ch., Obedience Trial Champion.

For the C.D., called the Novice class, the exercises are the heel on lead, heel free, figure 8, stand for examination, recall, and the group sit and down. For the C.D.X. title, called the Open class, the dog must do the heel free and figure 8, the drop on recall, the retrieve on the flat, the retrieve over the high jump, and the broad jump, as well as the group sit and down with the handler out of sight. To achieve the Utility title, from the class of the same name, the dog must do the signal exercises (heeling, drop, sit, and recall with hand signals only), two scent discrimination exercises (where the dog finds his owner's scent on a specific dumbbell in a group), the directed retrieve, and the directed jumping, both of which rely on the dog correctly reading your hand signals. He must also do the group stand for examination.

The Obedience Trial Championship can only be attempted after the U.D. title has been completed, and it is acquired by getting first and second places in the Open B and Utility classes, with a specific number of firsts in each class. The dog must also accrue 100 points, which are based on the number of dogs defeated. Un-

280

like conformation, dogs which have the O.T.Ch. title can and do continue to compete, winning even more O.T.Ch. points, making the acquisition of this title even more difficult, as the points are not passed on to dogs that do not have the title yet. AKC has designed this relatively new title so that, theoretically, it will be awarded to only 6 dogs, all breeds, per year, though recently there have been more.

Another title that dogs can achieve is the Tracking title, which is for "tracking" the scent on the ground left by a person. Tracking is less restrictive than obedience, and Samoyeds seem to really enjoy it. There are several good books on this subject, as well as regional clubs and private instructors. Tracking is best done when the dog is young (but can be done anytime), and before he starts formal obedience. In tracking the dog uses his own senses, and learns to stay out in front of you. He wears a harness and 40 foot lead, as opposed to a 6 foot lead and collar for obedience. Tracking gives the dog confidence in his own abilities, and still provides you with an activity that you and he can relate to, increasing your bond, and making him a better dog to live with. The American Kennel Club holds licensed Tracking trials, and the dog must be certified by a licensed Tracking judge before you can enter him in one. The Tracking test is pass or fail, and the dog only needs to pass one test to be able to add the letters T.D. after his name, which proclaims that he is a Tracking Dog. There is also the relatively new T.D.X. test, which stands for Tracking Dog Excellent, and is considerably more difficult to pass, as there are many more turns, more lengths (or legs), more difficult terrain, and much older tracks with other scents across them. In Tracking, the owner must rely on the dog to follow the track, as the handler is given no hint of where it is, and he must not direct the dog to follow it, if he can see where it goes. The handler can only tell the dog to "track," and the dog must indicate the glove or item when he comes upon it.

A different aspect of tracking is the Search and Rescue dog, who uses air scenting, as well as ground scenting, to find people lost in avalanches, earthquakes, or lost in the woods for a very long time, sometimes a matter of days. They find the person, dead or alive, return to the handler, indicating the find, and lead the handler to the find. The American Kennel Club does not recognize service oriented organizations like this, but they provide a valuable public need. To my knowledge, there are only two Samoyeds that have been involved in rescue organizations. They are Kendara's Tops of White Thunder, C.D., T.D., who is a member of the Illini Search and Rescue, and O.T.Ch. Barron's White Lightnin', who was formerly a member of CARDA, California Rescue Dog Association.

Another valuable public service that many Samoyeds are becoming involved with is Therapy Dogs International. These dogs are certified to go into hospitals and homes for the aged, underprivileged, or mentally disturbed, and bring cheer and hope by communication in their special way with those who sometimes find it hard to communicate with other people, or who have no people to come and visit them, and show that someone *does* care. Sams, with their love of people, are an ideal breed for this, and the many TDI dogs are happy ambassadors for our breed.

OUTSTANDING OBEDIENCE SAMOYEDS

Mrs. Bernice Ashdown had many firsts in Samoyeds in the 1940's and 50's. Her Wychwood Kennels boasts the first Champion C.D., C.D.X., U.D., and U.D.T., Ch. Rimsky of Norka, U.D.T. She also had the first female C.D. and C.D.X., who was also the first Champion female C.D. and C.D.X., Ch. Marina of Wychwood, C.D.X. Marina's grandsire, Ch. Anastasia's Rukavitza, C.D., was the first male C.D. Samoyed (he attained his Ch. after Ch. Rimsky attained his C.D.), as well as the first Samoyed in AKC history to attain a C.D. He was owned by Anastasia McBain, and all the Wychwood dogs were trained by Charles Rollins.

Don and Dorothy Hodges' Am. Can. Ch. Kipperic Kandu of Suruka Orr, C.D. was an all-breed and National Specialty Best in Show winner, and Bob and Wanda Krauss' Ch. K-Way's Omen of Destiny, C.D.X. is a top producer, and runs on their sled team, as does Larry and Ginny Corcoran's Sukhona's Arrogance, U.D.

Debbie and John Orr's Am. Can. Ch. Dajmozek Am. U.D.T.X., Can. U.D.T., is the most titled Samoyed in history, and their Am. Can. Ch. Dajmozek's Taveresh O' Kendara, U.D. has produced a record number of obedience titlists in only two litters.

Tasha Byrd, as she was called, proved herself and her get in the conformation ring as well as the obedience ring. Many people put titles on dogs that are of inferior quality. Often it is the handler's

Am. and Can. Ch. Dajmozek, Am. U.D.T.X., Can. U.D.T., is a multi-titled Samoyed, has weight pulling wins, and also works in harness on John and Debbie Orr's Illinois sled team. Debbie (who died in 1982), was, along with Zeke, an inspiration to many in obedience today.

Foge's Snow Job, C.D.,T.D., and owner Frances Roe of California are a team to inspire those who say, "I can't do it," or "My dog can't do it." Frances is confined to crutches, yet she and Snow still managed to get her T.D.

expertise, patience, and communication that make him a good obedience dog. Just because a dog does well in obedience is not a recommendation to breed him. Many obedience dogs should *not* be bred, and those that should be should also prove themselves to be an asset to the breed, by competing and winning in the conformation ring as well, before breeding should even be considered. Your dog will be a better house pet and family dog if he or she is spayed or neutered, and the various Samoyed Rescues attest to the overpopulation problem, so think before you breed.

Mary Bradley is the proud owner and trainer of Hazel and Ken's White Shadow, U.D.T.X., the first Samoyed Tracking Dog Excellent, a title which she achieved at the age of 13 years. In Hollywood, California, the Samoyed has made an impression on the world of television and movies, with Ted Baer's Tundra Baer, U.D., who received the Patsy Award (the animal equivalent of the Academy Award) for 1983. Tundra knows 200 word commands and 70 hand signals.

Barbara and Dan Cole own the first Obedience Trial Champion Samoyed, O.T.Ch. Barron's White Lightnin', who has been a Search and Rescue dog with CARDA, and also possesses his TDI certification. He is also the only 3-time recipient of the Samoyed Club of America Top Obedience Samoyed Award, in 1979, 80, and 83. His roommate, Am. Can. Ch. Nordika's Polar Barron, C.D., is a top 10 conformation dog, Best in Specialty, Group, and Merit Award winner, as well as possessing his T.T. (for Temperament Test, sponsored by the American Temperament Test Association, not recognized by AKC), TDI, and producing other Champions as well as obedience titlists. Both boys have also run on a competitive sled team in California.

Bill Lee has owned two female Samoyeds that have received the SCA Top Obedience Award, also having the distinction of being mother and daughter. Winterway's Owenover Mistaya won top honors in 1978, and her daughter, Stasia's Tad of Winterway was SCA Top Obedience Samoyed in 1982 and 1984, as well as being the first female Obedience Trial Champion Samoyed.

The first Samoyed to receive the Goodrich Award for Top Obedience Samoyed, given by the Samoyed Club of America, was Ch. Snowline's Joli Shashan C.D.X., who won the award the year of its inception in 1979, owned by Tom and Mary Mayfield.

Winners of the Samoyed Club of America
Top Obedience Samoyed

1969	Ch. Snowline's Joli Shashan C.D.X.	(Mayfield)
1970	Ell-Thee's Square Do Tasha	(Gormley)
1971	Snowman of Whitehall U.D.	(Smith)
1972	Snowman of Whitehall U.D.	(Smith)
1973	Silver Charm of Starfire U.D.	(Decker)
1974	Ch. Tsarovich of Kobray U.D.	(Ruby)
1975	White Glamour of Starfire	(Decker)
1976	Shebaska Sulaykha Pakova	(Gruber)
1977	Am. Can. Ch. Dajmozek Am. U.D.T. Can. C.D.X.	(Orr)
1978	Winterways Owenover Mistaya	(Lee)
1979	Barron's White Lightnin' C.D.X.	(Horne/Cole)
1980	Barron's White Lightnin' U.D.	(Horne/Cole)
1981	Stasia's Tad of Winterway C.D.	(Lee)
1982	Darshan's Honey Bear C.D.	(Schiddell)
1983	O.T.Ch. Barron's White Lightnin'	(Cole)
1984	O.T.Ch. Stasia's Tad of Winterway	(Lee)

Several obedience-titled dogs have also gone on to win Best of Breed honors at the Samoyed Club of America National Specialties. They are:

1941	Ch. Anastasia's Rukavitza C.D.	(McBain)
1965	Ch. Kenny's Blazer Boy of Caribou C.D.X.	(Yocum)
1966	Ch. Park-Cliffe Snowpack Sanorka C.D.	(McGoldrich)
1971	Ch. Elrond, Czar of Rivendell C.D.	(Gaffney)
1973	Ch. Kipperic Kandu of Suruka Orr C.D.	(Hodges)

Chapter 17

Sledding with Samoyeds
by Brenda E. Abbott

Samoyeds and snow just naturally seem to go together, but snow is not an absolute necessity for sledding with your dogs. Many areas of the country have races without snow. These latter races are run using three or four wheeled carts often used primarily for training by those drivers lucky enough to have snow. As long as you and your Samoyeds enjoy working together, you can enjoy the sport of sledding.

Many drivers begin their involvement at local races by competing in the weight pulling contest, which is often held the first afternoon of a two-day race. The natural step to take next is into the 3-dog race class, which requires a minimum of two dogs. There are relatively few Samoyed teams competing in organized races today compared to mixed-breed and Siberian Husky teams. But there are many Samoyed fanciers who sled with their dogs, doing so purely for the pleasure and not attending organized races due to personal, financial, or geographical reasons. These people do, nonetheless, receive the side benefits of their dogs being better conditioned, healthier pets and show dogs. The companionship derived is also a real plus.

Facing page:
Top: Don Hodges (Kipperic Samoyeds) and Harry and Joyce Emerson (Nordkap Samoyeds) enjoy a romp on the sled with their Samoyeds, joined by a friend's Siberian Husky. Photo courtesy of Mr. and Mrs. Donald Hodges, Poynette, Wisconsin. *Bottom*: Geoff Abbott, Donna Dannen and Leslie Fields with their Samoyed weight pullers at the Colorado State Championship Weight Pull, Fairplay, Colorado. Kriskella's Andy Isaboy (*right*), 60–80 pound class. Ch. Wind River Talkeetna, C.D., (*center*) and Kriskella's Kris Kringle, both under 60-pound class.

Samoyed teams at races have been making quite respectable showings in recent years. Several all-Samoyed teams have received ISDRA (International Sled Dog Racing Association) ranking points and competition for the honor of OWS (Organization for the Working Samoyed) Top Team each year is becoming quite keen. Samoyed teams are rarely last in a given race heat, and just as rarely are first; but given the ideal weather conditions which make the most of the breed assets of steadiness and endurance, being first is not impossible! As a rule Samoyeds, both individually and as a team, present fewer discipline problems on the trail then do the more high strung, typical sled dog types. Some areas of the country (Colorado, the Midwest, and the East Coast) do have a higher concentration of 1) sled races; 2) Samoyeds; and 3) northern breed dogs in general.

The Samoyed Club of America is now recognizing this aspect of the breed's ability to work by offering both a Sled Dog Class for dogs and bitches, and a Samoyed Club of America Annual Award for the Top Placing Team driven by an S.C.A. member. The sled class was first held in 1982 in Seattle, Washington, and the award was initiated in 1983.

The Samoyed standard states that the breed "should give the appearance of being capable of great endurance," and where would this be required except in a working capacity? Not all Samoyed drivers like sprint racing (usually a mile or two distance *per number of dogs* on the team, i.e., five-dog teams run five to ten miles in a one day heat). Distance racing is gaining popularity within the breed fancy because it does, obviously, require less speed and more endurance.

These distance races may be 20 or more miles long per day; again in two heats per weekend. A true working dog will run with his head and tail level with his back or lower. Any dog, regardless of breed, who runs with head up and tail flying isn't "working."

The conformation faults of a dog do play some part in his working efficiency. However, any dog with the right attitude and a desire to run can make a good sled dog.

A dog who is close in the rear will lack some power. A short upper arm will result in a shorter, less efficient stride, and a dog who is either too wide or too close in front will tire sooner than one with the proper rib-spring and chest depth. A Samoyed foot should have thick, cushioned pads to absorb shock and a tight paw to eliminate snow binding up between the toes. Any dog who is too old, too fat, or too lazy will not be a willing, competent sled dog.

A dog with hip dysplasia can be worked, but moderation and common sense are the key words. At any sign of lameness or stress, a dog should be removed from the harness immediately.

Above all, a dog's attitude toward his driver and his job is the most important factor in a good sled dog. Use patience and understanding while training your Samoyeds and you will be rewarded with steadier, more dependable dogs.

The sex of a working dog seems to make no difference in ability if the female is not in season. In the latter case, either males or females may cause problems. Likewise, size makes no difference in endurance if a dog is properly trained and conditioned for the length of the race and the prevailing weather and snow conditions.

The muscles developed by sledding and those developed by weight pulling seem to differ. Conformation faults in the rear, such as cowhocks, may even be accentuated by the frequent weight pulling of a dog in heavy training and competition. On the other hand, regular sledding will develop the chest and rib cage, so beware of this if a dog has a tendency towards an overdeveloped front. Conformation faults are *not* created by working a dog; faults which *already* exist may be emphasized by certain forms of exercise.

EQUIPMENT

Improper equipment can be both dangerous and time consuming. When racing the clock at an organized event, a broken snap or frayed gangline could mean the difference between first and fifth place. The first piece of equipment that is usually purchased is the dog's harness. When measuring a Samoyed for a sledding or weight pulling harness, be sure to measure the dog and not the hair. A harness must fit properly or a dog cannnot work to his full potential. Wearing an ill-fitting harness would be like making the driver wear ill-fitting boots. Homemade harnesses work quite well if fitted properly, but they are time consuming to make and usually wear out faster than those made by a professional outfitter. A professionally made racing harness costs less than $20, will last for years, and usually looks much nicer than homemade. The strongest ones are reinforced with leather at the stress points, and should be well padded at the chest and around the neck.

Never exercise a sled dog on a chain or choke collar. This is dangerous and could become the cause of a dog's death in just a matter of seconds. Most drivers use a semi-slip collar which, when pulled tight, still leaves a two-inch play, and cannot be pulled tight enough to choke a dog. We do make our own collars out of tubular nylon (mountaineering strap) and two 1½ inch steel rings. Other acceptable collars include a buckle collar in a specific size, or one that buckles and is adjustable. The semi-slip collar with rings has the advantage of having no sharp edges or points. Any collar should fit snugly enough that a dog cannot back out of it.

The gangline is made of small diameter nylon rope. Each dog is attached to the gangline by a tugline which snaps into a loop on his harness at the base of the dog's tail. Each team dog is also attached by his collar to a neckline which is in turn snapped to the gangline. The leaders (if there are two) are snapped to each other's collars by a separate neckline, and their tuglines form the front section of the gangline.

Snaps are the smallest piece of equipment but the wrong ones can really cause some big problems. Flimsy, lightweight snaps can break easily, have sharp edges, and have small openings when the clip is pulled. The very best type of snap to use is made of *brass*, because it will only freeze at much lower temperatures than steel.

The pivot post should be solid; hollow ones are more common and easier to find, but they will break more easily. There should be a widemouth opening and large pull-clip for ease of snapping with gloves on. All snaps should be checked for sharp edges which might cut a dog or driver.

In order to begin roadwork and conditioning exercises in the fall months when there is no snow, some type of wheeled training rig is needed. Some drivers use a bicycle, but this method is *not* recommended for more than one dog, and then only a well behaved one. Many drivers make their first training cart, but find that one built by a professional outfitter will save time and money in the long run. A training cart must have brakes, wheels, and something by which to steer. A locking emergency brake will hold the team when the driver must get off. The weight of a training cart depends on the size of the team to be run; 75 pounds to 125 pounds is about right for a three to five dog team.

Winter 1986. The Bubbling Oaks Long Distance Sled Team on a training run of 20 miles. Owned by Jack and Amelia Price, Bubbling Oaks Samoyeds, Commack, Long Island.

Heather and Paul, children of Paul and Katherine Kochever, take part in Estes Park's Cleanup Week by hitching Spinner to a wagon to collect litter in the Devon Hills area. Spinner belongs to neighbors Kent and Donna Dannen.

The most expensive piece of equipment is probably the sled. These range from $200 to $500, or about as much as one is willing to spend. They come in all styles, sizes, weights, and flexibility. The height of the driving bow should be customized for the primary driver to prevent back strain. When choosing a sled, consider the size of the driver, size of the team to be run, and the type of trail most common in the area. Lashed sleds are more flexible and more expensive than ones which are bolted together. A rigid, bolted sled with long runners would be very stable and fine for straight, flat trails. In mountains, or heavily treed areas, one would need a flexible lashed sled with shorter runners for mamaneuverability. A freight sled is longer, heavier, and is used to pull loads, not run sprints.

When a team is stopped on snow, there are two acceptable methods for making it secure. One is the snubline, which is a long piece of rope or nylon cord by which the sled can be tied to a nearby tree. In areas where a tree may not be so handy, drivers use a snow hook. This is a two-pronged anchor with a bar across the top to enable the driver to kick it solidly into the snow at an angle. Both the snow hook and the snubline should be attached to the sled under the basket at the same point as the gangline. Do not connect any "braking system" such as this to a wooden stanchion or slat as it will break. If you use the snubline method, learn to tie a knot which can be quickly released with one good pull.

Transporting a large number of dogs is best done by mounting wooden boxes on the bed of a pick-up truck or into a panel van. Some boxes are made of fiberglass, all have shavings or hay in them to provide warmth. Boxes should be large enough for a dog to turn around in, but *not* large enough to permit the dog to *stand* comfortably. Injuries are more likely to occur in a sudden stop if a dog is standing. The boxes should be ventilated from all four sides if possible. Each dog should have his own box.

There are several suppliers of sledding equipment throughout the United States. Harnesses and ganglines will not vary in price much from one to another. Sled and training carts will vary widely in quality, style and price. Many suppliers will give discounts on large orders from groups of interested mushers. Also available from these outlets are a large number of books and pamphlets on every phase of sled dog racing.

292

TRAINING

Training begins in the fall as the weather begins to cool down. There is seldom any snow this time of year so training carts or "rigs" are used in order to get the dogs accustomed to running the required distance. Start short, a mile or so, and work up to several miles longer than the dogs would be asked to go in a race. Cool, dry conditions are ideal, but be careful *not* to run young Samoyeds when the humidity is high.

Any overweight dogs should go on a diet before attempting harness work, and all harnesses should be checked for accurate fit several times during training and racing. Pay special attention to the condition of the dogs in general, and feet in particular. If a dog changes rhythm while running, stop immediately and check for rocks or glass. Boots or commercial pad tougheners are useful if a dog has thin pads. Do not train on asphalt or cement; *run only on dirt, snow, or grass.*

If a dog has never been in harness, introduce him to it with patience. Snap a line onto his tug and encourage him to pull as you walk along behind him. Put a little drag on the line, and ask him to pick up speed. There are several complete books which have been written on training sled dogs, which are worth purchasing if you are in an area with no other fanciers to guide you. If anyway possible, it is best to train with another team. Dogs can be taught to wait until given the command to "go," and they can be taught to pass and be passed when another team is involved in the training sessions.

Many sled drivers use a double lead. This relieves one dog of the complete responsibility, which is important as leaders do feel stress. The wheel position (just in front of the sled) is also very important as these dogs must take the shock of turns and the majority of the strain of getting the sled up a hill. Avoid putting very young dogs at lead or wheel on a competitive team if possible. We repeat, leaders feel mental stress and very young wheelers may fear the noise of the cart or sled just behind them.

Training should be a time of experimentation. Don't be afraid to re-position dogs on a team or go from single to double lead if circumstances indicate such a change is needed.

Competitive racing is organized by class, depending on the number of dogs on a team. At this time, ISDRA recognizes classes

293

for 3, 6, 8 and unlimited dog teams. A well-conditioned team of Samoyeds should always be able to go the required distance in any race. An advantage to running in an ISDRA sanctioned race should be that the trail will be safe and laid according to certain guidelines. "Out and back" trails require head-on passing and are dangerous and unpopular. "Loops" are acceptable; they require teams to run some part of the trail twice in order to meet the necessary mileage.

Anyone who races in organized events should know and follow the rules of the International Sled Dog Racing Association. Remember, the rules were written to insure the safety of dogs and drivers. Both individual and club memberships are available, and one big advantage of a club membership is the group insurance coverage for racing events.

Dogs running in ISDRA races are marked with spray paint on the hips or shoulders before each race. Samoyeds begin to look quite colorful towards the end of a racing season. If you show your dogs, most of these markings can be removed with careful combing and the use of a very fine tooth comb (flea comb). If you cannot remove all of the color, many judges do know what it is and

Lead dog Ch. Wind River Talkeetna Karibou sports medal he helped win, along with a bottle of champagne, for driver Donna Dannen. Left wheel dog Snowflower Spun Sugar added much to the effort at the Steamboat Springs, Colorado, 24-mile race.

The *first* Sled Dog Class ever held at the National Samoyed Club of America, 1982. First prize winner, Kriskella's Adam Up Again, C.D., bred and owned by Brenda and Geoffrey Abbott, Kriskella Samoyeds, Pine, Colorado.

if one does not, tell him. ISDRA markings should be the proud badge of a working sled dog. The markings are used to designate team dogs in each class (i.e., red for three dog, blue for six dog, etc.) This rule prevents an unscrupulous driver from running a good dog in more than one heat per day, and also from replacing weaker dogs on the second day of a race.

The Organization for the Working Samoyed (OWS) offers several year-end awards in different categories including obedience, sledding, and weight pulling. Twenty-two Samoyeds have to date received the OWS 1000 Point Working Certificate, which recognizes excellent, consistent performances. Seventeen drivers submitted team points in 1984, and the numbers continue to grow in all aspects of working Samoyeds.

Chapter 18

Breeding Your Samoyed

The first responsibility of any person breeding dogs is to do so with care, forethought, and deliberation. It is inexcusable to breed more litters than you need to carry on your show program or to perpetuate your bloodlines. A responsible breeder should not cause a litter to be born without definite plans for the safe and happy disposition of the puppies.

A responsible dog breeder makes absolutely certain, so far as is humanly possible, that the home to which one of his puppies will go is a good home, one that offers proper care and an enthusiastic owner. To be admired are those breeders who insist on visiting (although doing so is not always feasible) the prospective owners of their puppies to see if they have suitable facilities for keeping a dog, to find out if they understand the responsibility involved, and to make certain if all members of the household are in accord regarding the desirability of owning one. All breeders should carefully check out the credentials of prospective purchasers to be sure that the puppy is being placed in responsible hands.

No breeder ever wants a puppy or grown dog he has raised to wind up in an animal shelter, in an experimental laboratory, or as a victim of a speeding car. While complete control of such a situation may be impossible, it is important to make every effort to turn over dogs to responsible people. When selling a puppy, it is a good idea to do so with the understanding that should it become necessary to place the dog in other hands, the purchaser will first contact you, the breeder. You may want to help in some way, possibly by buying or taking back the dog or placing it elsewhere. It is not fair to sell puppies and then never again give a thought to their welfare. Family problems arise, people may be forced to move where dogs are prohibited, or people just grow bored with a dog and its care. Thus the dog becomes a victim. You, as the dog's breeder, should concern yourself with the welfare of each of your dogs and see to it that the dog remains in good hands.

The final obligation every dog owner shares, be there just one dog or an entire kennel involved, is that of making detailed, explicit plans for the future of these dearly loved animals in the event of the owner's death. Far too many people are apt to procrastinate and leave this very important matter unattended to, feeling that everything will work out or that "someone will see to them." Neither is too likely, at least not to the benefit of the dogs, unless you have done some advance planning which will assure their future well-being.

Life is filled with the unexpected, and even the youngest, healthiest, most robust of us may be the victim of a fatal accident or sudden illness. The fate of your dogs, so entirely in your hands, should never be left to chance. If you have not already done so, please get together with your lawyer and set up a clause in your will specifying what you want done with each of your dogs, to whom they will be entrusted (after first making absolutely certain that the person selected is willing and able to assume the responsibility), and telling the locations of all registration papers, pedigrees, and kennel records. Just think of the possibilities which might happen otherwise! If there is another family member who shares your love of the dogs, that is good and you have less to worry about. But if your heirs are not dog-oriented, they will hardly know how to proceed or how to cope with the dogs themselves, and they may wind up disposing of or caring for your dogs in a manner that would break your heart were you around to know about it.

It is advisable to have in your will specific instructions concerning each of your dogs. A friend, also a dog person who regards his or her own dogs with the same concern and esteem as you do, may agree to take over their care until they can be placed accordingly and will make certain that all will work out as you have planned. This person's name and phone number can be prominently displayed in your van or car and in your wallet. Your lawyer can be made aware of this fact. This can be spelled out in your will. The friend can have a signed check of yours to be used in case of an emergency or accident when you are traveling with the dogs; this check can be used to cover his or her expense to come and take over the care of your dogs should anything happen to make it impossible for you to do so. This is the least any dog owner should do in preparation for the time their dogs suddenly find themselves alone. There have been so many sad cases of dogs unprovided for by their loving owners, left to heirs who couldn't care less and who disposed of them in any way at all to get rid of them, or left to heirs who kept and neglected them under the misguided idea that they were providing them "a fine home with lots of freedom." These misfortunes must be prevented from befalling your own dogs who have meant so much you!

Conscientious breeders feel quite strongly that the only possible reason for producing puppies is the ambition to improve and uphold quality and temperament within the breed—definitely *not* because one hopes to make a quick cash profit on a mediocre litter, which never seems to work out that way in the long run and which accomplishes little beyond perhaps adding to the nation's heartbreaking number of unwanted canines. The only reason ever for breeding a litter is, with conscientious people, a desire to improve the quality of dogs in their own kennel or, as pet owners, to add to the number of dogs they themselves own with a puppy or two from their present favorites. In either case, breeding should not take place unless one definitely has prospective owners for as many puppies as the litter may contain, lest you find yourself with several fast-growing young dogs and no homes in which to place them.

THE BROOD BITCH

Bitches should not be mated earlier than their second season, by which time they should be from fifteen to eighteen months old. Many breeders prefer to wait and finish the championships of their show bitches before breeding them, as pregnancy can be a disaster to a show coat and getting the bitch back in shape again takes time. When you have decided what will be the proper time, start watching at least several months ahead for what you feel would be the perfect mate to best complement your bitch's quality and bloodlines. Subscribe to the magazines which feature your breed exclusively and to some which cover all breeds in order to familiarize yourself with outstanding stud dogs in areas other than your own, for there is no necessity nowadays to limit your choice to a local dog unless you truly like him and feel that he is the most suitable. It is quite usual to ship a bitch to a stud dog a distance away, and this generally works out with no ill effects. The important thing is that you need a stud dog strong in those features where your bitch is weak, a dog whose bloodlines are compatible with hers. Compare the background of both your bitch and the stud dog under consideration, paying particular attention to the quality of the puppies from bitches with backgrounds similar to your bitch's. If the puppies have been of the type and quality you admire, then this dog would seem a sensible choice for yours, too.

Stud fees may be a few hundred dollars, sometimes even more under special situations for a particularly successful sire. It is money well spent, however. *Do not* ever breed to a dog because he is less expensive than the others unless you honestly believe that he can sire the kind of puppies who will be a credit to your kennel and your breed.

Contacting the owners of the stud dogs you find interesting will bring you pedigrees and pictures which you can then study in relation to your bitch's pedigree and conformation. Discuss your plans with other breeders who are knowledgeable (including the one who bred your own bitch). You may not always receive an entirely unbiased opinion (particularly if the person giving it also has an available stud dog), but one learns by discussion so listen to what they say, consider their opinions, and then you may be better qualified to form your own opinion.

As soon as you have made a choice, phone the owner of the stud dog you wish to use to find out if this will be agreeable. You will be asked about the bitch's health, soundness, temperament, and freedom from serious faults. A copy of her pedigree may be requested, as might a picture of her. A discussion of her background over the telephone may be sufficient to assure the stud's owner that she is suitable for the stud dog and that she is of type, breeding, and quality herself, capable of producing the kind of puppies for which the stud is noted. The owner of a top-quality stud is often extremely selective in the bitches permitted to be bred to his dog, in an effort to keep the standard of his puppies high. The owner of a stud dog may require that the bitch be tested for brucellosis, which should be attended to not more than a month previous to the breeding.

Check out which airport will be most convenient for the person meeting and returning the bitch, if she is to be shipped, and also what airlines use that airport. You will find that the airlines are also apt to have special requirements concerning acceptance of animals for shipping. These include weather limitations and types of crates which are acceptable. The weather limits have to do with extreme heat and extreme cold at the point of destination, as some airlines will not fly dogs into temperatures above or below certain levels, fearing for their safety. The crate problem is a simple one, since, if your own crate is not suitable, most of the airlines have specially designed crates available for purchase at a fair and moderate price. It is a good plan to purchase one of these if you intend to be shipping dogs with any sort of frequency. They are made of fiberglass and are the safest type to use for shipping.

Normally you must notify the airline several days in advance to make a reservation, as they are able to accommodate only a certain number of dogs on each flight. Plan on shipping the bitch on about her eighth or ninth day of season, but be careful to avoid shipping her on a weekend when schedules often vary and freight offices are apt to be closed. Whenever you can, ship your bitch on a direct flight. Changing planes always carries a certain amount of risk of a dog being overlooked or wrongly routed at the middle stop, so avoid this danger if at all possible. The bitch must be accompanied by a health certificate which you must obtain from your veterinarian before taking her to the airport. Usually it will be necessary to have the bitch at the airport about two hours prior to flight time. Before finalizing arrangements, find out from the stud's owner at what time of day it will be most convenient to have the bitch picked up promptly upon arrival.

It is simpler if you can bring the bitch to the stud dog yourself. Some people feel that the trauma of the flight may cause the bitch to not conceive; and, of course, undeniably there is a slight risk in shipping which can be avoided if you are able to drive the bitch to her destination. Be sure to leave yourself sufficient time to assure your arrival at the right time for her for breeding (normally the tenth to fourteenth day following the first signs of color); and remember that if you want the bitch bred twice, you should allow a day to elapse between the two matings. Do not expect the stud's owner to house you while you are there. Locate a nearby motel that takes dogs and make that your headquarters.

Just prior to the time your bitch is due in season, you should take her to visit your veterinarian. She should be checked for worms and should receive all the booster shots for which she is due plus one for parvovirus, unless she has had the latter shot fairly recently. The brucellosis test can also be done then, and the health certificate can be obtained for shipping if she is to travel by air. Should the bitch be at all overweight, now is the time to get the surplus off. She should be in good condition, neither underweight nor overweight, at the time of breeding.

The moment you notice the swelling of the vulva, for which you should be checking daily as the time for her season approaches, and the appearance of color, immediately contact the stud's owner and settle on the day for shipping or make the appointment for your arrival with the bitch for breeding. If you are shipping the bitch, the stud fee check should be mailed immediately, leaving ample time for it to have been received when the bitch arrives and the mating takes place. Be sure to call the airline, making her reservation at that time, too.

Do not feed the bitch within a few hours before shipping her. Be certain that she has had a drink of water and been well exercised before closing her in the crate. Several layers of newspapers, topped with some shredded newspaper, make a good bed and can be discarded when she arrives at her destination; these can be replaced with fresh newspapers for her return home. Remember that the bitch should be brought to the airport about two hours before flight time, as sometimes the airlines refuse to accept late arrivals.

If you are taking your bitch by car, be certain that you will arrive at a reasonable time of day. Do not appear late in the evening. If your arrival in town is not until late, get a good night's sleep at your motel and contact the stud's owner first thing in the morning. If possible, leave children and relatives at home, as they will only be in the way and perhaps unwelcome by the stud's owner. Most stud dog owners prefer not to have any unnecessary people on hand during the actual mating.

After the breeding has taken place, if you wish to sit and visit for awhile and the stud's owner has the time, return the bitch to her crate in your car (first ascertaining, of course, that the temperature is comfortable for her and that there is proper ventilation). She should not be permitted to urinate for at least one hour following the breeding. This is the time when you attend to the business part of the transaction. Pay the stud fee, upon which you should receive your breeding certificate and, if you do not already have it, a copy of the stud dog's pedigree. The owner of the stud dog does not sign or furnish a litter registration application until the puppies have been born.

Upon your return home, you can settle down and plan in happy anticipation a wonderful litter of puppies. A word of caution! Remember that although she has been bred, your bitch is still an interesting target for all male dogs, so guard her carefully for the next week or until you are absolutely certain that her season has entirely ended. This would be no time to have any unfortunate incident with another dog.

THE STUD DOG

Choosing the best stud dog to complement your bitch is often very difficult. The two principal factors to be considered should be the stud's conformation and his pedigree. Conformation is fairly obvious; you want a dog that is typical of the breed in the words of the Standard of perfection. Understanding pedigrees is a bit more subtle since the pedigree lists the ancestry of the dog and involves individuals and bloodlines with which you may not be entirely familiar.

To a novice in the breed, the correct interpretation of a pedigree may at first be difficult to grasp. Study the pictures and text of this book and you will find many names of important bloodlines and members of the breed. Also make an effort to discuss the various dogs behind the proposed stud with some of the more experienced breeders, starting with the breeder of your own bitch. Frequently these folks will be familiar with many of the dogs in question, will be able to offer opinions of them, and may have access to additional pictures which you would benefit by seeing. It is very important that the stud's pedigree be harmonious with that of the bitch you plan on breeding to him. Do not rush out and breed to the latest winner with no thought of whether or not he can produce true quality. By no means are all great show dogs great producers. It is the producing record of the dog in question, and the dogs and bitches from which he has come, that should be the basis on which you make your choice.

Breeding dogs is never a money-making operation. By the time you pay a stud fee, care for the bitch during pregnancy, whelp the litter, and rear the puppies through their early shots, worming, and so on, you will be fortunate to break even financially once the puppies have been sold. Your chances of doing this are greater if you are breeding for a show-quality litter which will bring you higher prices, as the pups are sold as show prospects. Therefore, your wisest investment is to use the best dog available for your bitch regardless of the cost; then you should wind up with more valuable puppies. Remember that it is equally costly to raise mediocre puppies as it is top ones, and your chances of financial return are better on the latter. Breeding to the most excellent, most suitable stud dog you can find is the only sensible thing to do, and it is poor economy to quibble over the amount you are paying in a stud fee.

It will be your decision as to which course you follow when you breed your bitch, as there are three options: linebreeding, inbreeding, and outcrossing. Each of these methods has its supporters and its detractors! Linebreeding is breeding a bitch to a dog belonging originally to the same canine family, being descended from the same ancestors, such as half brother to half sister, grandsire to granddaughter, niece to uncle (and vice-versa) or cousin to cousin. Inbreeding is breeding father to daughter, mother to son, or full brother to sister. Outcross breeding is breeding a dog and a bitch with no or only a few mutual ancestors.

Linebreeding is probably the safest course, and the one most likely to bring results, for the novice breeder. The more sophisticated inbreeding should be left to the experienced, longtime breeders who throroughly know and understand the risks and the possibilities involved with a particular line. It is usually done in an effort to intensify some ideal feature in that strain. Outcrossing is the reverse of inbreeding, an effort to introduce improvement in a specific feature needing correction, such as a shorter back, better movement, more correct head or coat, and so on.

It is the serious breeder's ambition to develop a strain or bloodline of their own, one strong in qualities for which their dogs will become distinguished. However, it must be realized that this will involve time, patience, and at least several generations before the achievement can be claimed. The safest way to embark on this plan, as previously mentioned, is by the selection and breeding of one or two bitches, the best you can buy and from top-producing kennels. In the beginning you do *not* really have to own a stud dog. In the long run it is less expensive and sounder judgement to pay a stud fee when you are ready to breed a bitch than to purchase a stud dog and feed him all year; a stud dog does not win any popularity contests with owners of bitches to be bred until he becomes a champion, has been successfully Specialed for a while, and has been at least moderately advertised, all of which adds up to quite a healthy expenditure.

The wisest course for the inexperienced breeder just starting out in dogs is to keep the best bitch puppy from the first several litters. After that you may wish to consider keeping your own stud dog, if there has been a particularly handsome male in one of your litters that you feel has great potential or if you know where there is one available that you are interested in, with the feeling that he would work in nicely with the breeding program on which you have embarked. By this time, with several litters already born, your eye should have developed to a point enabling you to make a wise choice, either from one of your own litters or from among dogs you have seen that appear suitable.

The greatest care should be taken in the selection of your own stud dog. He must be of true type and highest quality as he may be responsible for siring many puppies each year, and he should come from a line of excellent dogs on both sides of his pedigree which themselves are, and which are descended from, successful producers. This dog should have no glaring faults in conformation; he should be of such quality that he can hold his own in keenest competition within his breed. He should be in good health, be virile and be a keen stud dog, a proven sire able to transmit his correct qualities to his puppies. Need one say that such a dog will be enormously expensive unless you have the good fortune to produce him in one of your own litters? To buy and use a lesser stud dog, however, is downgrading your breeding program unnecessarily since there are so many dogs fitting the description of a fine stud whose services can be used on payment of a stud fee.

You should *never* breed to an unsound dog or one with any serious disqualifying faults according to the breed's standard. Not all champions by any means pass along their best features; and by the same token, occasionally you will find a great one who can pass along his best features but never gained his championship title due to some unusual circumstances. The information you need about a stud dog is what type of puppies he has produced, and with what bloodlines, and whether or not he possesses the bloodlines and attributes considered characteristic of the best in your breed.

If you go out to buy a stud dog, obviously he will not be a puppy, but rather a fully mature and proven male with as many of the best attributes as possible. True, he will be an expensive investment, but if you choose and make his selection with care and forethought, he may well prove to be one of the best investments you have ever made.

Of course, the most exciting of all is when a young male you have decided to keep from one of your litters, due to his tremendous show potential, turns out to be a stud dog such as we have described. In this case he should be managed with care, for he is a valuable property that can contribute inestimably to this breed as a whole and to your own kennel specifically.

Do not permit your stud dog to be used until he is about a year old, and even then he should be bred to a mature, proven matron accustomed to breeding who will make his first experience pleasant and easy. A young dog can be put off forever by a maiden bitch who fights and resists his advances. Never allow this to happen. Always start a stud dog out with a bitch who is mature, has been bred previously, and is of even temperament. The first breeding should be performed in quiet surroundings with only you and one other person to hold the bitch. Do not make it a circus, as the experience will determine the dog's outlook about future stud work. If he does not enjoy the first experience or associates it with any unpleasantness, you may well have a problem in the future.

Your young stud must permit help with the breeding, as later there will be bitches who will not be cooperative. If right from the beginning you are there helping him and praising him, whether or not your assistance is actually needed, he will expect and accept this as a matter of course when a difficult bitch comes along.

Things to have handy before introducing your dog and the bitch are K-Y jelly (the only lubricant which should be used) and a length of gauze with which to muzzle the bitch should it be necessary to keep her from biting you or the dog. Some bitches put up a fight; others are calm. It is best to be prepared.

At the time of the breeding, the stud fee comes due, and it is expected that it will be paid promptly. Normally a return service is offered in case the bitch misses or fails to produce one live puppy. Conditions of the service are what the stud dog's owner makes them, and there are no standard rules covering this. The stud fee is paid for the act, not the result. If the bitch fails to conceive, it is customary for the owner to offer a free return service; but this is a courtesy and not to be considered a right, particularly in the case of a proven stud who is siring consistently and whose fault the failure obviously is *not*. Stud dog owners are always anxious to see their clients get good value and to have, in the ring, winning young stock by their dog; therefore, very few refuse to mate the second time. It is wise, however, for both parties to have the terms of the transaction clearly understood at the time of the breeding.

If the return service has been provided and the bitch has missed a second time, that is considered to be the end of the matter and the owner would be expected to pay a further fee if it is felt that the bitch should be given a third chance with the stud dog. The management of a stud dog and his visiting bitches is quite a task, and a stud fee has usually been well earned when one service has been achieved, let alone by repeated visits from the same bitch.

The accepted litter is one live puppy. It is wise to have printed a breeding certificate which the owner of the stud dog and the owner of the bitch both sign. This should list in detail the conditions of the breeding as well as the dates of the mating.

Upon occasion, arrangements other than a stud fee in cash are made for a breeding, such as the owner of the stud taking a pick-of-the-litter puppy in lieu of money. This should be clearly specified on the breeding certificate along with the terms of the age at which the stud's owner will select the puppy, whether it is to be a specific sex, or whether it is to be the pick of the entire litter.

The price of a stud fee varies according to circumstances. Usually, to prove a young stud dog, his owner will allow the first breeding to be quite inexpensive. Then, once a bitch has become pregnant by him, he becomes a "proven stud" and the fee rises accordingly for bitches that follow. The sire of championship quality puppies will bring a stud fee of at least the purchase price of one show puppy as the accepted "rule-of-thumb." Until at least one champion by your stud dog has finished, the fee will remain equal to the price of one pet puppy. When his list of champions starts to grow, so does the amount of the stud fee. For a top-producing sire of champions, the stud fee will rise accordingly.

Almost invariably it is the bitch who comes to the stud dog for the breeding. Immediately upon having selected the stud dog you wish to use, discuss the possibility with the owner of that dog. It is the stud dog owner's prerogative to refuse to breed any bitch deemed unsuitable for this dog. Stud fee and method of payment should be stated at this time and a decision reached on whether it is to be a full cash transaction at the time of the mating or a pick-of-the-litter puppy, usually at eight weeks of age.

If the owner of the stud dog must travel to an airport to meet the bitch and ship her for the flight home, an additional charge will be made for time, tolls, and gasoline based on the stud owner's proximity to the airport. The stud fee includes board for the day on the bitch's arrival through two days for breeding, with a day in between. If it is necessary that the bitch remain longer, it is very likely that additional board will be charged at the normal per-day rate for the breed.

Be sure to advise the stud's owner as soon as you know that your bitch is in season so that the stud dog will be available. This is especially important because if he is a dog being shown, he and his owner may be unavailable, owing to the dog's absence from home.

Ch. Suzuki's Final Edition started her show career winning the Junior Puppy Working Group at Sussex Hills Puppy Match, June 1976. By Am. and Can. Ch. Kristik's English Autumn ex Windom's Suzuki Snowstorm. Owned by Patricia Kirms, Suzuki Samoyeds, Farmingdale, New Jersey.

Pretty 8-week-old puppies: Heritage Tricks Are For Kids and Heritage Jenny Kissed Me. Owned by Phoebe Castle Faulmann, Heritage Samoyeds, Gainesville, Florida.

As the owner of a stud dog being offered to the public, it is essential that you have proper facilities for the care of visiting bitches. Nothing can be worse than a bitch being insecurely housed and slipping out to become lost or bred by the wrong dog. If you are taking people's valued bitches into your kennel or home, it is imperative that you provide them with comfortable, secure housing and good care while they are your responsibility.

There is no dog more valuable than the proven sire of champions, Group winners, and Best in Show dogs. Once you have such an animal, guard his reputation well and do *not* permit him to be bred to just any bitch that comes along. It takes two to make the puppies; even the most dominant stud cannot do it all himself, so never permit him to breed a bitch you consider unworthy. Remember that when the puppies arrive, it will be your stud dog who will be blamed for any lack of quality, while the bitch's shortcomings will be quickly and conveniently overlooked.

Going into the actual management of the mating is a bit superfluous here. If you have had previous experience in breeding a dog and bitch, you will know how the mating is done. If you do not have such experience, you should not attempt to follow directions given in a book but should have a veterinarian, breeder friend, or handler there to help you with the first few times. You do not turn the dog and bitch loose together and await developments, as too many things can go wrong and you may altogether miss getting the bitch bred. Someone should hold the dog and the bitch (one person each) until the "tie" is made and these two people should stay with them during the entire act.

If you get a complete tie, probably only the one mating is absolutely necessary. However, especially with a maiden bitch or one that has come a long distance for this breeding, a follow-up with a second breeding is preferred, leaving one day in between the two matings. In this way there will be little or no chance of the bitch missing.

Once the tie has been completed and the dogs release, be certain that the male's penis goes completely back within its sheath. He should be allowed a drink of water and a short walk, and then he should be put into his crate or somewhere alone where he can settle down. Do not allow him to be with other dogs for a while as they will notice the odor of the bitch on him, and, particularly with other males present, he may become involved in a fight.

PREGNANCY, WHELPING, AND THE LITTER

Once the bitch has been bred and is back at home, remember to keep an ever watchful eye that no other males get to her until at least the twenty-second day of her season has passed. Until then, it will still be possible for an unwanted breeding to take place, which at this point would be catastrophic. Remember that she actually can have two separate litters by two different dogs, so take care.

In other ways, she should be treated normally. Controlled exercise is good and necessary for the bitch throughout her pregnancy, tapering it off to just several short walks daily, preferably on lead, as she reaches her seventh week. As her time grows close, be careful about her jumping or playing too roughly.

The theory that a bitch should be overstuffed with food when pregnant is a poor one. A fat bitch is never an easy whelper, so the overfeeding you consider good for her may well turn out to be a hindrance later on. During the first few weeks of pregnancy, your bitch should be fed her normal diet. At four to five weeks along, calcium should be added to her food. At seven weeks her food may be increased if she seems to crave more than she is getting, and a meal of canned milk (mixed with an equal amount of water) should be introduced. If she is fed just once a day, add another meal rather than overload her with too much at one time. If twice a day is her schedule, then a bit more food can be added to each feeding.

A week before the pups are due, your bitch should be introduced to her whelping box so that she will be accustomed to it and feel at home there when the puppies arrive. She should be encouraged to sleep there but permitted to come and go as she wishes. The box should be roomy enough for her to lie down and stretch out in but not too large, lest the pups have more room than is needed in which to roam and possibly get chilled by going too far away from their mother. Be sure that the box has a "pig rail"; this will prevent the puppies from being crushed against the sides. The room in which the box is placed, either in your home or in the kennel, should be kept at about 70 degrees Fahrenheit. In winter it may be necessary to have an infrared lamp over the whelping box, in which case be careful not to place it too low or close to the puppies.

Newspapers will become a very important commodity, so start collecting them well in advance to have a big pile handy for the whelping box. With a litter of puppies, one never seems to have papers enough, so the higher pile to start with, the better off you will be. Other necessities for whelping time are clean, soft turkish towels, scissors, and a bottle of alcohol.

You will know that her time is very near when your bitch becomes restless, wandering in and out of her box and out of the room. She may refuse food, and at that point her temperature will start to drop. She will dig at and tear up the newspapers in her box, shiver, and generally look uncomfortable. Only you should be with your bitch at this time. She does not need spectators; and several people hanging over her, even though they may be family members whom she knows, may upset her to the point where she may harm the puppies. You should remain nearby, quietly watching, not fussing or hovering; speak calmly and frequently to her to instill confidence. Eventually she will settle down in her box and begin panting; contractions will follow. Soon thereafter a puppy will start to emerge, sliding out with the contractions. The mother immediately should open the sac, sever the cord with her teeth, and then clean up the puppy. She will also eat the placenta, which you should permit. Once the puppy is cleaned, it should be placed next to the bitch unless she is showing signs of having the next one immediately. Almost at once the puppy will start looking for a nipple on which to nurse, and you should ascertain that it is able to latch on successfully.

If the puppy is a breech (*i.e.*, born feet first), you must watch carefully for it to be completely delivered as quickly as possible and for the sac to be removed quickly so that the puppy does not drown. Sometimes even a normally positioned birth will seem extremely slow in coming. Should this occur, you might take a clean towel, and as the bitch contracts, pull the puppy out, doing so gently and with utmost care. If, once the puppy is delivered, it shows little signs of life, take a rough turkish towel and massage the puppy's chest by rubbing quite briskly back and forth. Continue this for about fifteen minutes, and be sure that the mouth is free of liquid. It may be necessary to try mouth-to-mouth breath-

Litter of ten puppies by Ch. Kondako's Sun Dancer ex Kobe Jubilee of Encino, bred by Carol and Andy Hjort. This was the foundation breeding for Jubillie Samoyeds.

Windigo's Ring Master, 1985 Northern California Samoyed Fanciers Specialty Best Puppy in Show, is by Ch. Sansaska's Mark of Evenstar ex Ch. West Free's Bet on a Star. Bred by Pat Krief and Sue Templar. Owned by Sue Templar and Marilyn Gitelson.

ing, which is begun by pressing the puppy's jaws open and, using a finger, depressing the tongue which may be stuck to the roof of the mouth. Then place your mouth against the puppy's and blow hard down the puppy's throat. Rub the puppy's chest with the towel again and try artificial respiration, pressing the sides of the chest together slowly and rhythmically—in and out, in and out. Keep trying one method or the other for at least twenty minutes before giving up. You may be rewarded with a live puppy who otherwise would not have made it.

If you are successful in bringing the puppy around, do not immediately put it back with the mother as it should be kept extra warm. Put it in a cardboard box on an electric heating pad or, if it is the time of year when your heat is running, near a radiator or near the fireplace or stove. As soon as the rest of the litter has been born, it then can join the others.

An hour or more may elapse between puppies, which is fine so long as the bitch seems comfortable and is neither straining nor contracting. She should not be permitted to remain unassisted for more than an hour if she does continue to contract. This is when you should get her to your veterinarian, whom you should already have alerted to the possibility of a problem existing. He should examine her and perhaps give her a shot of Pituitrin. In some cases the veterinarian may find that a Caesarean section is necessary due to a puppy being lodged in a manner making normal delivery impossible. Sometimes this is caused by an abnormally large puppy, or it may just be that the puppy is simply turned in the wrong position. If the bitch does require a Caesarean section, the puppies already born must be kept warm in their cardboard box with a heating pad under the box.

Once the section is done, get the bitch and the puppies home. Do not attempt to put the puppies in with the bitch until she has regained consciousness, as she may unknowingly hurt them. But do get them back to her as soon as possible for them to start nursing.

Should the mother lack milk at this time, the puppies must be fed by hand, kept very warm, and held onto the mother's teats several times a day in order to stimulate and encourage the secretion of milk, which should start shortly.

314

Assuming that there has been no problem and that the bitch has whelped naturally, you should insist that she go out to exercise, staying just long enough to make herself comfortable. She can be offered a bowl of milk and a biscuit, but then she should settle down with her family. Freshen the whelping box for her with newspapers while she is taking this respite so that she and the puppies will have a clean bed.

Unless some problem arises, there is little you must do for the puppies until they become three to four weeks old. Keep the box clean and supplied with fresh newspapers the first few days, but then turkish towels should be tacked down to the bottom of the box so that the puppies will have traction as they move about.

If the bitch has difficulties with her milk supply, or if you should be so unfortunate as to lose her, then you must be prepared to either hand-feed or tube-feed the puppies if they are to survive. Tube-feeding is so much faster and easier. If the bitch is available, it is best that she continues to clean and care for the puppies in the normal manner, excepting for the food supplements you will provide. If it is impossible for her to do this, then after every feeding you must gently rub each puppy's abdomen with wet cotton to make it urinate, and the rectum should be gently rubbed to open the bowels.

Newborn puppies must be fed every three to four hours around the clock. The puppies must be kept warm during this time. Have your veterinarian teach you how to tube-feed. You will find that it is really quite simple.

After a normal whelping, the bitch will require additional food to enable her to produce sufficient milk. In addition to being fed twice daily, she should be given some canned milk several times each day.

When the puppies are two weeks old, their nails should be clipped, as they are needle sharp at this age and can hurt or damage the mother's teats and stomach as the pups hold on to nurse.

Between three and four weeks of age, the puppies should begin to be weaned. Scraped beef (prepared by scraping it off slices of beef with a spoon so that none of the gristle is included) may be offered in very small quantities a couple of times daily for the first few days. Then by the third day you can mix puppy chow with warm water as directed on the package, offering it four times daily. By now the mother should be kept away from the puppies and out of the box for several hours at a time so that when they have reached five weeks of age she is left in with them only overnight. By the time the puppies are six weeks old, they should be entirely weaned and receiving only occasional visits from their mother.

Most veterinarians recommend a temporary DHL (distemper, hepatitis, leptospirosis) shot when the puppies are six weeks of age. This remains effective for about two weeks. Then at eight weeks of age, the puppies should receive the series of permanent shots for DHL protection. It is also a good idea to discuss with your vet the advisability of having your puppies inoculated against the dreaded parvovirus at the same time. Each time the pups go to the vet for shots, you should bring stool samples so that they can be examined for worms. Worms go through various stages of development and may be present in a stool sample even though the sample does not test positive in every checkup. So do not neglect to keep careful watch on this.

The puppies should be fed four times daily until they are three months old. Then you can cut back to three feedings daily. By the time the puppies are six months of age, two meals daily are sufficient. Some people feed their dogs twice daily throughout their lifetime; others go to one meal daily when the puppy becomes one year of age.

The ideal age for puppies to go to their new homes is between eight and twelve weeks, although some puppies successfully adjust to a new home when they are six weeks old. Be sure that they go to their new owners accompanied by a description of the diet you've been feeding them and a schedule of the shots they have already received and those they still need. These should be included with the registration application and a copy of the pedigree.

Index

318

320